The Black Book
of the American Left

The Black Book of the American Left

The Collected Conservative Writings of David Horowitz

Volume VIII
The Left in the University

Second Thoughts Books
Los Angeles

First American edition published in 2017 by Second Thoughts Books.

Manufactured in the United States and printed on acid-free paper. The paper used in this publication meets the minimum requirements of ANSI/NISO Z39.48 1992 (R 1997) *(Permanence of Paper).*

Book design and production by Catherine Campaigne; copy-edited by David Landau; research provided by Mike Bauer.

FIRST AMERICAN EDITION

LIBRARY OF CONGRESS CATALOGING-IN-PUBLICATION DATA

Horowitz, David, 1939–
    The black book of the American left : the collected conservative
  writings of David Horowitz / by David Horowitz.
    volumes   cm.
    Includes bibliographical references and index.
    ISBN 978-1-941262-04-7 (hardback)
    1. Social movements—United States—History. 2. Radicalism—
  United States. 3. Anti-Americanism—United States. 4. Horowitz,
  David, 1939– Political and social views. I. Title.
  HX86.H788 2013
    335.00973   2013000496

10   9   8   7   6   5   4   3   2   1

Contents

Introduction to
The Left in the University

This is the eighth themed volume in the series of my writings collected under the general title, *The Black Book of the American Left*. Like the previous installments, it has been edited to stand on its own, in this case as a book about one of the underappreciated tragedies of our times: the successful campaign of the left to subvert the curricula of collegiate institutions and transform entire academic departments and schools—including Schools of Education—into doctrinal training centers for their social and political causes. This transformation of the educational system in turn has underpinned the steady dismantling of America's social contract, which has been the ongoing project of the left since the 1960s.

The present volume is actually the sixth book I have written on the subject of the transformation and its destructive consequences.[1] In addition to whatever analytic contributions are made in these pages, they provide a compendium of anecdotal evidence about the manner in which progressive activists have taken control of liberal arts curricula and reverted them to their 19th-century origins as instruments of religious indoctrination. The new doctrines differ from their 19th-century predecessors in that they are political and secular, having been shaped by Marxism and its

---

[1]The five previous books are: *Uncivil Wars: The Controversy Over Reparations For Slavery*, 2001; *The Professors*, 2005; *Indoctrination U.*, 2008; *One-Party Classroom* (with Jacob Laksin), 2009; and *Reforming Our Universities: The Story of the Campaign for an Academic Bill of Rights*, 2010

derivatives. These "progressive" doctrines, however, share with traditional religions the same impulse to redeem a fallen world and to suppress what they regard as hostile—therefore heretical—ideas in the name of human progress.[2]

One can measure the current corruption of the academic profession through a summary observation about the views of academic historians that was published in the peer-reviewed *Journal of the Historical Society*. The summary appears in an article written by Jennifer Delton, a tenured history professor at Skidmore College—a top-tier liberal arts school. It describes a purported orthodoxy in historians' views of Cold War anti-communism. According to Delton, this historical consensus regards Cold War anti-communism as an irrational phenomenon and a species of political persecution. Equally as striking as this problematic characterization is Delton's assumption that an orthodoxy about so controversial an issue can and should be a normal condition of academic scholarship. Here are her words: "However fiercely historians disagree about the merits of American communism [sic!], they almost universally agree that the post-World War II red scare signaled a rightward turn in American politics. The consensus is that an exaggerated, irrational fear of communism, bolstered by a few spectacular spy cases, created an atmosphere of persecution and hysteria that was exploited and fanned by conservative opportunists such as Richard Nixon and Joseph McCarthy.... We may add detail and nuance to this story, but *this, basically, is what we tell our students about post-World II anti-communism, also known as McCarthyism.*"[3] (emphasis added)

In other words, it is the professional opinion of this tenured professor, the editors of the *Journal of the Historical Society* and, apparently, academic historians generally that concern about a

---

[2]"Progressivism" is a doctrine analyzed in Volume 2 of this series: Horowitz, *Progressives*, 2014

[3]Jennifer Delton, "Rethinking Post-World War II Anticommunism," *Journal of the Historical Society*, Volume 10, Issue 1, pages 1–41, March 2010. Delton is a Professor of History at Skidmore College.

domestic communist threat during the Cold War was equivalent to "McCarthyism"—a witch-hunting mania about imaginary demons.[4] This, according to Delton, is what academic historians "tell our students," and not as mere opinion but as a historical consensus, and thus an academic fact. This consensus exists, apparently, in the face of easily established, indisputable facts that refute it: the fact that McCarthy was censured by an anti-communist Senate, including senators who sat on his committee; the fact that he was opposed by an anti-communist president, Dwight Eisenhower, and by anti-communist liberals such as Arthur Schlesinger, Jr., who wrote one of the seminal anti-communist books of the period, *The Vital Center*; or the proven fact that the federal government had been penetrated by communist agents at the time, and at the highest levels.

It goes without saying that no conservative scholar could agree with the conclusion of Professor Delton and her colleagues, and thus no conservative scholar could be readily regarded by the consensus she describes as a reasonable member of her profession.

To ideologues like Delton, the contents of this volume will seem an extreme view of what has taken place in American liberal arts colleges and graduate institutions. But to recognize the intellectual corruption of the contemporary academy is hardly what is extreme; what is extreme is the politicized state of academic discourse, the confusion of scholarship with propaganda, and therefore the widespread debasement of the academic enterprise. What is extreme is the general comfort level of the academic community with this travesty of scholarship and, worse, with the practice of indoctrinating students in the classroom.

The ramifications of this reversion to doctrinal instruction and pre-scientific standards of scholarship have been destructive not only to higher education but to society at large. Since collegiate

---

[4]For a book-length study of this academic consensus, see Harvey Klehr and John Earl Haynes, *In Denial: Historians, Communism and Espionage*, 2003

institutions are the training grounds for all professions, this corruption has adversely affected a widespread array of policies, both foreign and domestic; it has warped cultural attitudes towards race and gender (see volumes 5 and 6 in this series); and it has intruded political biases into such civically crucial professions as the law, journalism and secondary school education.

The contents of this volume were immediately inspired by a campaign I conducted to counter these trends and promote a restoration of the academic values associated with the modern research university, in particular the identification of scientific standards of inquiry with academic professionalism.[5] The goal of the campaign, which lasted for roughly seven years and ultimately failed, could also be viewed as an attempt to restore a professional standard appropriate to education in a democratic society—that teachers should teach students how to think and not tell them what to think. This standard was established in a famous "Declaration on the Principles of Academic Tenure and Academic Freedom" issued by the American Association of University Professors (AAUP) in 1915, and until recently verbally embraced by all reputable academic institutions.

The campaign I organized to defend those principles was ferociously opposed by the tenured left, most strikingly by the very organization that had devised the original standard: the American Association of University Professors, whose governance had fallen into radical hands. Although my campaign failed, it revealed the extent of the AAUP's defection from its original purposes and its determination to protect a new professorial "right"—the "right" of faculty to indoctrinate their students. This was made indisputably clear in the AAUP's opposition to a crucial passage of the Declaration that I regularly cited in my campaign, and which had been adopted verbatim by Penn State University as its academic freedom policy. There can be no better introduction to the present

---

[5]Even the concept of "professionalism" is under assault by leftist faculty, who are now regularly represented by trade unions such as the United Auto Workers.

volume than to recount the fate of this policy at the hands of the AAUP and its academic agents.

Known as HR 64, the Penn State policy read: "It is not the function of a faculty member in a democracy to indoctrinate his/her students with ready-made conclusions on controversial subjects. The faculty member is expected to train students to think for themselves, and to provide them access to those materials, which they need if they are to think intelligently. Hence, in giving instruction upon controversial matters the faculty member is expected be of a fair and judicial mind, and to set forth justly, without supersession or innuendo, the divergent opinions of other investigators."[6]

The AAUP's attack on this specific policy was launched in the winter of 2010, just after events in Pennsylvania convinced me of the futility of my reform efforts. Legislative hearings to inquire into the state of academic freedom in Pennsylvania—hearings in which I played a seminal role—were effectively subverted by the AAUP and the teacher unions, while the Republican Party and conservative groups that should have supported the reform effort sat on the sidelines.[7] Without their active involvement there was little more that I could do.

The AAUP's attack was led by its leftist president, Cary Nelson, whose book *No University Is an Island*, was published that December. In his book Nelson assaulted me personally and followed his assault with an attack on the Penn State policy I had championed. Nelson described the Penn State policy on academic freedom as an attempt to restrict faculty speech and curtail academic freedom. This was the same Orwellian position the AAUP

---

[6]http://www.nas.org/articles/Free_to_Indoctrinate_The_AAUP_Applauds_Penn_States_Retreat_from_Academic_Fr

[7]See the account of these hearings in David Horowitz, *Reforming Our Universities: The Campaign for an Academic Bill of Rights*, 2010 Chapter 9: The Pennsylvania Hearings. Cf. also, Part IV, chapters 10 and 11 in this volume: "The Professor Unions' Battle" and "What We're Up Against."

had advanced throughout the controversy; but it was the first time anyone had made that argument specifically against the Penn State policy I had praised. Nelson and I had debated each other on several occasions, so he was thoroughly familiar with my campaign and the fact that I had made HR 64 and the 1915 Declaration its cornerstones. His attack also targeted the "Academic Bill of Rights" I had attempted to persuade universities to adopt, which was an attempt to codify the principles of the 1915 Declaration. Nelson did not merely criticize the Penn State policy but condemned it as "especially bad" and an example of "McCarthy era rhetoric." His objection to the policy was that it denied professors the right to advance their political agendas in the classroom. According to Nelson: "Like Horowitz, Penn State failed at the time to conceptualize the sense in which all teaching and research is fundamentally and deeply political."[8] This was a candid admission of the anti-academic agendas of both Nelson and the AAUP. To them, "academic freedom" meant a license for professors to use their classrooms as political platforms to indoctrinate their students.

Political agendas aside, Nelson's smear of the Penn State academic freedom policy and my efforts made no logical sense. Far from seeking to suppress dissenting ideas, the 1915 Declaration, the Penn State policy and my Academic Bill of Rights stipulated that faculty were obligated to present *conflicting* opinions on controversial matters in a fair-minded manner. In other words, they were statements *in behalf* of intellectual diversity. Neither document denied professors the right to express their views, or to freely draw conclusions from their research. They did require them to observe a professional standard in the classroom; in particular, to be mindful that students were in the process of forming their opinions and should be allowed to do so. It was only in this sense that it restricted professors' "freedom of speech"—specifically the

---

[8]Cary Nelson, *No University Is An Island: Saving Academic Freedom,* NYU Press, 2010, p. 189

"right" to use their classrooms for political attitudinizing. But this was no more restrictive than the codes governing doctors or lawyers in their professional settings. And it was in accord with the views of the leading academic authority on academic freedom: Robert C. Post, dean of the Yale Law School.[9]

In dismissing Penn State's policy, Nelson suggested that the AAUP had "more nuanced" methods of determining such matters than the Penn State officials, and that "what Penn State ended up with is nothing less than thought control." The absurdity of this was transparent. To require professors to present divergent views to their students, and to do so in a fair-minded manner, was hardly "thought control."

Shortly after Nelson's book appeared, the Faculty Senate at Penn State went into action to implement his agenda, voting to formally eviscerate policy HR 64 and rewrite it to permit the abuses it was designed to prevent. Specifically, the Penn State Faculty Senate removed the following sentence: "It is not the function of a faculty member in a democracy to indoctrinate his/her students with ready-made conclusions on controversial subjects." The Senate then rewrote the policy, restricting professorial fairness to those controversial viewpoints that were part of the discourse of the academic professions—professions that had effectively purged themselves of non-leftist viewpoints. The revised version read: "Faculty members are expected to present information fairly, and to set forth justly, divergent opinions *that arise out of scholarly methodology and professionalism.*" (emphasis added) In other words, practically speaking, only the divergent opinions of left-wing academics need be presented fairly and justly. Other opinions—notably conservative opinions—which were not part of existing "scholarly methodology and professionalism,"

---

[9]Robert Finkin and Robert C. Post, *For the Common Good: Principles of Academic Freedom,* 2009. See also my discussion of Post's views in *Indoctrination U.,* pp. 15–16 Post, however, played a dubious role as a member of the AAUP's academic freedom committee by turning a blind eye to the way the AAUP subverted the very policy he espoused.

would not be covered by this fairness requirement. The instigator of these changes, Cary Nelson, applauded the revision in a statement that made no sense at all: "Penn State had one of the most restrictive and troubling policies limiting intellectual freedom in the classroom that I know of. It undermined the normal human capacity to make comparisons and contrasts between different fields and between different cultures and historical periods."[10] Incoherent as this explanation was, Nelson had successfully engineered a policy that formally permitted professors to indoctrinate their students. This remains the policy of the AAUP and faculty throughout the liberal arts academy today. In short, I had to face the reality that my seven year campaign to restore the concept of academic freedom as defined by the AAUP in its 1915 Declaration had led to the formal repudiation of its principles by the same organization.

Part I of the present volume is an essay selected because it frames the subject, a practice I have adopted in previous volumes. It is an edited version of the introduction to *The Professors*, a book I wrote in 2005 about the unprofessional classroom attitudes of over 100 prominent professors. In the controversy generated by the book, the substance of this introduction was completely ignored. Not a single response from my academic opponents addressed the substantive critiques contained in its text.

Part II recounts my experiences on college campuses in the five years preceding the creation of the Academic Bill of Rights, along with my observations regarding the decline of academic discourse under pressures from the academic left.

Part III describes my campaign for an Academic Bill of Rights. This document was a codification of the principles set forth in the 1915 Declaration. It was inspired by the idea that if professors have an obligation to act professionally in the classroom, then stu-

---

[10]Ashley Thorne and Steve Balch, "Free to Indoctrinate: The AAUP Applauds Penn State's Retreat from Academic Freedom," December 14, 2010, http://www.nas.org/articles/Free_to_Indoctrinate_The_ AAUP_ Applauds_Penn_States_Retreat_from_Academic_Fr

dents have a right to expect a professional instruction; in particular, to hear fair-minded presentations of divergent views on controversial issues, along with the freedom to draw their own conclusions.

Part IV continues the account of the campaign for an Academic Bill of Rights and describes the attacks against it by the American Association of University Professors, the American Federation of Teachers, and faculty senates like the one at Penn State.

Part V recounts the controversies surrounding two of the books I wrote, *The Professors* and *Indoctrination U.*, and more of my failed attempts to persuade the academic community of their obligation to present contested issues as controversial and to observe a professional decorum in the classroom.

I have concluded the text with an epilogue containing a proposal for reforming universities and re-establishing standards of instruction in the classroom. I wrote this proposal in 2010, before the AAUP eviscerated the Penn State academic freedom policy. I did not publish it then because I knew that any proposal associated with me would be dead in the water because of the war the AAUP had declared on all my efforts, however modest and reasonable. I publish it now because I have given up any hope that universities can institute such a reform. The faculty opposition is too devious and too strong; and even more importantly there is no conservative will to see such reforms enacted. Therefore there seems to be no harm in publishing the document now, and it does serve to clarify my goals in undertaking my campaign.

As in all these volumes, the texts have been edited for clarity and readability, and are printed—with the exception of the opening essay—in chronological order, so as to provide insight into the progress of the campaign.

PART I

Trials of the Intellect

The Post-Modern Academy

In January 2005, Professor Ward Churchill became a figure of national revulsion when his impending visit to Hamilton College was linked to an article claiming that the victims of 9/11 were "little Eichmanns" who deserved their fate. Churchill's article produced an outcry of such force that it led to the removal of the faculty head of the host committee at Hamilton, as well as the resignation of the president of the University of Colorado where Churchill was professor of Ethnic Studies and department chair. As a result of the uproar, Churchill himself was removed as head of the Ethnic Studies Department, and university authorities began an investigation into how he had acquired his faculty position in the first place.

Far from being a marginal crank, Ward Churchill was a prominent personage at the University of Colorado and in the academic world at large. He was a leading figure in his field of Ethnic Studies, and widely published. His appearance at Hamilton would have marked the 40th campus that had invited him to speak in the three years since his Eichmann article.[1] The opinions expressed in it were themselves far from obscure to his academic colleagues.[2]

This essay is the introduction to my book, *The Professors* (2005), re-edited for the present edition.

[1] Scott Smallwood, "Inside A Free Speech Firestorm: How A Professor's 3-year-old Essay Sparked A National Controversy," *Chronicle of Higher Education,* February 18, 2005, http://chronicle.com/article/Inside-a-Free-Speech-Firestorm/8488

[2] Ward Churchill, "Some People Push Back: On The Justice of Roosting Chickens," *Pockets of Resistance #11,* September 2001, http://www.kersplebedeb.com/mystuff/s11/churchill.html.

They reflected views comparing America to Nazi Germany that were part of the intellectual core of his academic work, familiar both to university authorities in Colorado and to his faculty hosts at Hamilton. These facts made the scandal an event whose significances extended far beyond the fate of one individual to implicate the academic culture itself.

The series of incidents that led to the Churchill scandal began in the fall of 2004, when a convicted terrorist named Susan Rosenberg was invited to join the faculty at Hamilton College as a visiting professor to teach a course on "Resistance Memoirs." As the course title suggested, far from repudiating her political past, Rosenberg embraced it.[3] She was, in fact, an active member of a network of veteran radicals, many still in jail, who remained loyal to the violent causes they had served. Rosenberg had been apprehended in 1984 as she was moving more than 600 pounds of explosives into a Cherry Hill, New Jersey warehouse. She had been sentenced to 58 years in prison for her crime, but was released as one of President Clinton's last-minute pardons after serving only fourteen years of her term.

Rosenberg had been hired to the Hamilton faculty by Nancy Rabinowitz, a professor of Comparative Literature and head of the Kirkland Project on Gender, Society and Culture at the school. The Kirkland Project was a self-described "social justice organization" run by faculty and funded by a university endowment. Although the nation at large was engaged in a "War on Terror" in Iraq and only three years earlier had been the target of the 9/11 attack, Professor Rabinowitz was oblivious to the public reaction her decision might provoke. The behavior of Rabinowitz and her faculty colleagues reflected the insularity of an academic environment in which virtually every inhabitant was politically on the left and which, consequently, had become an echo chamber for ever more radical attitudes and ideas. It was this environment that

---

[3]I have written about Rosenberg and her book about her prison experiences, in *Radicals: Portraits of a Destructive Passion*, Regnery, 2012.

prevented the directors of the Kirkland Project from perceiving any impropriety in conferring academic legitimacy on an individual who had been sentenced to prison for terrorist acts.

Even when the outcries caused Rosenberg to withdraw, Rabinowitz remained adamant. Apparently unconscious of the damage she was about to inflict on herself, on two schools and on the university culture, Rabinowitz followed her first false step with a second when she decided, only a month after the Rosenberg controversy, to honor a previous invitation for Churchill to speak at Hamilton.

Hamilton College, named for the conservative American Founder, is a small liberal arts school set in a rural landscape in upstate New York. Its colonial architecture and sylvan views provide a setting suited to the contemplative life. Along with sister schools like Williams and Colgate, Hamilton aspires to be a second-tier Ivy institution. Generations of graduates have sent their children there to carry on a family legacy and reap the intellectual benefits of the school they remember. It is this loyalty to a remembered tradition that maintains the flow of donations to Hamilton and attracts students, who pay a yearly tuition of $30,000 to attend. Along with other American universities, however, Hamilton has undergone a sea change over the last several decades. Significant departments of the school have ceased to be part of the ivory tower that its alumni recall. Many of its faculty members are no longer devoted to pursuits that are purely "academic," and the curriculum has been expanded to include agendas about "social change" that are overtly political; thus, an invitation to a convicted terrorist could seem appropriate rather than merely appalling.

This transformation has been the work of an academic generation that came of age as anti-war radicals in the Vietnam era. Many of these activists stayed in school to avoid the military draft and earn Ph.D.s; when they became professors they took their political activism with them. They were determined to do away with the "ivory tower" conception of the university they had protested during their student days. Entering tenure tracks in the 1970s, they scorned the contemplative life that liberal arts colleges like Hamilton sought to institutionalize. They rejected the idea of the university as a temple of the intellect in which the term "academic" described a curriculum insulated from the political passions of the times. Instead, they were intent on making the university "relevant" to current problems and events and to their own partisan agendas. Accordingly, they set about re-shaping the university curriculum to support their political interests, which appeared grandiosely in their own minds as crusades for "social justice."

To accomplish these ends, they created new institutional frameworks and new fields of study, casting old standards and disciplines aside. The new departments that began to appear had objectives that were frankly political and maintained no pretense of including intellectually diverse viewpoints or pursuing academic inquiries unconnected to the conclusions they might reach. The new departments were given names like Black Studies and Women's Studies but their political subtexts were really black nationalism, radical feminism and similarly ideological programs. They were often created through political protests. One of the first Black Studies programs was established at Cornell University as a concession to black radicals who had occupied the administration building with loaded shotguns and refused to leave until their demands were met. Among the demands the university administration agreed to was the "right" of the radicals to appoint their own professors.

The new departments were presented at first as part of a broader social movement to "serve" minority groups previously "under-served," or neglected. But as the cohort of activists on academic faculties grew, even the new disciplines proved insufficient to encompass the social and intellectual agendas the radicals favored. Thus were born Cultural Studies, Peace Studies, Whiteness Studies, Post-Colonial Studies, Global Studies and even Social Justice Studies—interdisciplinary fields shaped by narrowly one-sided political agendas. Some of these programs attacked American foreign policy and the American military, others America's self-image and national identity. Collectively they marked a dramatic departure from the academic interests of the past, providing institutional settings for political indoctrination: the exposition and development of radical theory, the education and training of radical cadre and the recruitment of students to radical causes.

Because the new activist departments were "interdisciplinary," they were able to spread their influence through the traditional fields until virtually every English Department, History Department and Law School, for example, now draws on Women's Studies and African American Studies departments for courses and faculty. The political movement thus created has been so powerful in shaping the university curriculum that it has affected the educational philosophy of the institutions themselves. Previously, modern research universities defined their purposes in official templates as being "dedicated to the disinterested pursuit of knowledge."[4] Under the new dispensation, they have embraced the mission brought to them by the radical generation and now often refer to themselves as institutions dedicated to "social change."[5]

Nancy Rabinowitz was one of the tenured radicals who had come to Hamilton to promote the new dispensation. Though formally a professor of Comparative Literature, she was unable to leave her activist passions at the campus gates and thus became the guiding influence and head of Hamilton's Kirkland Project for Gender, Society and Culture, where she implemented her extra-academic agendas by inviting radicals like Susan Rosenberg to teach.

---

[4]When I was at Columbia in the fifties, it was the academic custom not to deal with subjects more recent than 25 years in the past in order to avoid "present-mindedness" in scholarly discourses.

[5]These templates can be found in university catalogues. When I visited with the president of Brandeis College, Yehuda Reinharz, he had throw pillows on his office sofa inscribed with the words, "Peace" and "Social Justice."

Professor Rabinowitz's connection to Rosenberg was also something more than academic. Rabinowitz had married into a famous radical family which was linked to Rosenberg through her most infamous crime. Rabinowitz's father-in-law was the celebrated Communist lawyer Victor Rabinowitz whose clients included Fidel Castro and other violent radicals, including the political terrorists of the Puerto Rican FALN. Victor Rabinowitz's lifelong friend and law partner was Leonard Boudin, also a Communist, and the father of Kathy Boudin, one of the leaders of the Weather Underground, a terrorist cult that had declared a formal "war" on "Amerikkka' in the 1970s and carried out bombings of the Pentagon, the U.S. Capitol and other official buildings. The principal leaders of the Weather Underground subsequently surfaced and became professors themselves. When the Weather Underground dissolved in 1976, Kathy Boudin joined the "May 19 Communist Movement." which in 1981 robbed a Brinks armored car in Nyack, New York, murdering two guards and a policemen, and leaving nine children fatherless. Susan Rosenberg was herself part of the Weather Underground network and was indicted for the Nyack crime.

Kathy Boudin was convicted for her role in the Nyack robbery-murders, but Rosenberg, though indicted, was never tried. This was because prosecutors in the Nyack case saw no reason to pursue her after she had received her 58-year sentence for other crimes. This was the sentence from which President Clinton— petitioned by New York Democratic congressman Jerrold Nadler—finally released her.

Susan Rosenberg was, in fact, only one of several Weather Underground terrorists who had recently surfaced and begun touring college campuses. Still committed radicals, they had formed a "political prisoners" network[6] and were looking to rehabilitate themselves and their political agendas. Uncontrite about the

---

[6]David Horowitz, "Prisoners of War," *FrontPageMag.com*, September 5, 2001, http://archive.frontpagemag.com/readArticle.aspx?ARTID=24443

revolutionary politics that had led to their crimes, they made appearances at colleges across the country, where they were invited to lecture by radical professors who presented them to students as advocates for "social justice." When convicted bomber and Weather Underground member Laura Whitehorn was invited as an official guest of the African American Studies Department at Duke University, for example, she was presented as a "human rights activist" by Duke faculty. It was left to conservative Duke students to research her history on the Internet and reveal her terrorist past and criminal conviction, and to protest the faculty deception.[7] The professors running the Kirkland Project at Hamilton had presented Susan Rosenberg in equally misleading terms as "an award-winning writer, an activist, and a teacher who offers a unique perspective as a writer." She was further described as a victim of government persecution, imprisoned because of her "political activities" with the Black Liberation Army. No mention was made of her crimes or theirs, which included several murders.

While some Hamilton faculty voiced moral outrage at the Rabinowitz invitation, the concerns of those involved were mainly focused on the possibility of public reaction. This did not mean that the faculty sympathized with the public concern. On the contrary, most faculty tended to feel themselves superior to the public and would regard any negative response to the Rosenberg invitation as a reflection of ignorance, and attitudes that were "reactionary." In their minds, the problem raised by the hiring of a convicted terrorist was whether the free-speech rights of the terrorist could be protected, not the implications of such an appointment for academic values.

While members of the Hamilton community worried the issue, a Hamilton sophomore, named Ian Mandel, stepped forward to spark the outrage that would eventually thwart Professor Rabinowitz's political agendas. As Jacob Laksin reported for

---

[7]James Taranto, "A Terrorist at Duke," *OpinionJournal*, January 16, 2003, http://www.wsj.com/news/articles/SB1043372708226532464; http://www.voy.com/53203/123.html

Frontpagemag.com, "Ian Mandel had personal reasons to oppose Rosenberg's appointment. A Nyack native, he grew up with the names Waverly Brown and Edward O'Grady etched into his mind. They were the two Nyack police officers killed in the 1981 robbery [for which Rosenberg was indicted]. 'Every day of my life until I left for Hamilton, I drove by the memorial to officers Brown and O'Grady located about one mile from my house,' he recalled. Mandel explained that Nyack's tight-knit community was profoundly shaped by the murders of the two officers. 'To this day it is a tough subject for many to speak about,' he wrote. It was a measure of the anger and disgust he felt about Rosenberg's hiring that Mandel, a member of the Hamilton College Democrats, agreed to speak about it. Like many Nyack residents, Mandel had thoroughly researched the robbery. He concluded that Rosenberg was indeed involved. 'To me, and I'd assume to most members of the Nyack community and of the larger law-enforcement community, that makes Susan Rosenberg a cop-killer,' he said. Haunted by Rosenberg's grim legacy at Nyack, Mandel was determined not to let it follow him to Hamilton. 'I think that bringing Susan Rosenberg to teach a class at Hamilton is a disgrace and a black-eye to the college,' he said."[8]

The Hamilton student was quickly invited to appear on TV and radio talk shows. Simultaneously, police officers staged a demonstration to protest the Rosenberg outrage at a New York fundraiser for Hamilton. This, in turn, led to an alumni revolt. As the media events unfolded, donors began to withdraw their pledges from the college while irate phone calls from alumni and citizens flooded the president's office. This public pressure eventually overwhelmed the institution's resistance and led to a resolution of the crisis with Rosenberg's withdrawal from the program. The faculty radicals led by Professor Rabinowitz remained defiant, however, referring to the events as a witch-hunt. It was this defiance

---

[8]Jacob Laksin, "Terrorist Teacher," *FrontPageMag.com*, December 2, 2004, http://archive.frontpagemag.com/readArticle.aspx?ARTID=10443

that led directly to the second incident, whose ramifications were to prove even greater than the first. Well before the Rosenberg fiasco, the Kirkland program had scheduled a speaking engagement for Colorado Ethnic Studies professor Ward Churchill. Despite the damage they had already inflicted on their college, the Kirkland directors made no move to reconsider or postpone the Churchill appearance.

Like Rosenberg, Churchill's link to Rabinowitz was political rather than academic. One of the items he made public was that, during the 1970s, he had trained members of the Weather Underground in the use of weapons and explosives. Churchill was already well known in academic circles for his views that America was a genocidal nation and that its leaders were international criminals—views shared by the Weather Underground terrorist cult and many radical professors. This was one of the reasons that Rabinowitz and the faculty advisors to the Kirkland project had decided to invite him in the first place, and they did not want to cancel the invitation now. Going ahead with his scheduled appearance as planned would be an "in-your-face" gesture to a public that, in their eyes, had persecuted Susan Rosenberg for her political views and to an administration that had failed to defend her.

During the crisis, several moderate faculty voices surfaced to challenge this view. "If the administration cannot see the contradiction between this hire and the clearly stated mission of the college to foster scholarship and academic excellence, then God help us all," commented Robert Paquette, one of Hamilton's handful of conservative professors.[9] Economics professor James Bradfield was similarly disturbed that the Hamilton administration had adopted the radicals' view of the issue as Rosenberg's free speech. "I disagree with the administration's presenting this as a matter of free speech, which it is not," he said. "It is a matter of standards.... Even if Susan Rosenberg possessed the intellect or had achieved

---

[9]Ibid.

the scholarly or artistic preeminence of people such as Albert Einstein, Milton Friedman, Lionel Trilling, or Leonard Bernstein, I would argue that her character, as manifestly demonstrated by the choices that she made as an adult over a sustained period of years, would preclude her appointment to the faculty of Hamilton College."[10]

Although several faculty members were visibly troubled by the Rosenberg invitation, opposition to the faculty radicals was confined to a minority bold enough to express an opinion publicly. The hand of this minority had been greatly strengthened by the damage the Rosenberg debacle had already inflicted on the college. The revenue loss from withdrawn donations had already prompted a rumor that there might be no faculty salary increases in the coming year.[11] Consequently, Rabinowitz's determination to use the college as a platform for her political agendas in the face of these problems became a practical matter as well.

When the spring schedule of events for the Kirkland Project was published, a government professor named Theodore Eismeier noticed Ward Churchill's name among the invited speakers. Eismeier immediately logged on to the Internet and came up with an article Churchill had written three years before, which in his eyes was a smoking gun for rejecting him as a Kirkland speaker. Written just after the attacks of 9/11, Churchill's article was called, "Some People Push Back: On the Justice of Roosting Chickens."

Churchill's imperfect sense of English syntax made his title more obscure than its inflammatory message warranted. What he meant was that the heinous terrorist attacks of 9/11 were a *case* of the chickens coming home to roost; that the horrors of 9/11 were in fact, Americans' just deserts. "Let's get a grip here, shall we?" Churchill wrote. "True enough, [the victims of 9/11] were civilians of a sort. But innocent? Give me a break. If there was a better, more effective, or in fact any other way of visiting some penalty

---

[10]Ibid.
[11]Confidential faculty source

befitting their participation upon the little Eichmanns inhabiting the sterile sanctuary of the twin towers, I'd really be interested in hearing about it."

In this mangled prose, Churchill was merely articulating the theme of his entire academic career: America was like Hitler Germany, a nation dedicated to the extermination of minorities; its capitalist economic machine was starving poor people all over the world, all the time. Therefore, the "civilians" who comprised what Churchill referred to as its "technical core"—the inhabitants of the World Trade Center—were in fact little Eichmanns, cogs in a machine that churned out mass murder. In Churchill's view, there was no "better way of visiting some penalty befitting their participation" in the workings of America's global economy (and thus global genocide) than incinerating Americans in their place of work.

That such views could earn an individual like Churchill a full professorship at a major state university, let alone the responsibility and power of a department chair, spoke volumes about the corruption of the academic enterprise—not only in Colorado but throughout the Ethnic Studies field. That Churchill was a sought-after speaker by university faculties across the country was a chilling indictment of an entire system.

Theodore Eismeier was convinced that the invitation to Churchill spelled disaster for his college. He sent the essay, along with "other troubling writings" of Churchill's, to the school's administrators.[12] The result was a series of meetings with Rabinowitz and the executive committee of the Kirkland Project. According to Rabinowitz's account of these meetings, there was dissension among the Kirkland board of advisors. The administration thought the event "was going to be as bad as Susan Rosenberg" and wanted the Kirkland board to defuse it by converting Churchill's speech into a panel, which would include anti-Churchill faculty like government professor (now Dean of Students) Phil Klinkner.

---

[12]Smallwood, "Inside A Free Speech Firestorm," op. cit.

Rabinowitz protested: "Let's take a strong stand for freedom of speech," she said.[13]

The Kirkland Project was paying Churchill $3,500 plus expenses to come to Hamilton, which was probably twice what it would have cost to bring a nationally renowned scholar in the humanities or social sciences. Rabinowitz and the directors of the Kirkland Project hadn't offered Churchill this kind of money to provide students with an example of free speech. They had invited him because, like Rabinowitz, they shared his extreme views and found them academically reasonable. Promoting views like Churchill's was in fact the purpose of the Kirkland Project. *This* was their standard, and this standard—not free speech—was the issue that their decision posed.

As the date of Churchill's visit approached, the Syracuse *Post-Standard* published a report on the event that included interviews with the growing campus opposition. Professor Eismeier was quoted as saying that the proposed panel was "akin to inviting a representative of the KKK to speak and then asking a member of the NAACP to respond." Other media began to report the controversy. Through Internet postings, talk-radio chatter and further press coverage, the controversy picked up momentum until a Hamilton student appeared on Fox News Channel's *O'Reilly Factor* and blew the affair wide open.

Like Ian Mandel before him, Matthew Coppo was a sophomore at Hamilton, but his relationship to the political events that provided a subtext for the occasion was more intimate. Matthew's father had been killed in the World Trade Center on 9/11 and was thus one of the innocent victims Ward Churchill had described as "little Eichmanns" who deserved to die. Matthew Coppo appeared on two consecutive segments of *The O'Reilly Factor*, the first with his mother. In the show's opening editorial segment, O'Reilly declared that Hamilton was morally wrong to have provided

---

[13]Ibid.

Churchill with an academic template and said that his hateful comments "should not be rewarded by any sane person," which was a perfectly reasonable view. As a result of the broadcast, an avalanche of angry emails (more than 8,000, according to college officials) descended on Hamilton president Joan Hinde Stewart, leading her to cancel the event.

In explaining the cancellation, Stewart insisted on presenting herself and Hamilton not as the embarrassed authors of bad decisions and abysmal standards but as the failed defenders of free speech. She thus accepted, for a second time, the self-serving view of Hamilton's faculty radicals that the real problem was not the behavior of the faculty left but the public's reaction. To this claim, she added an administrative concern for campus security: "We have done our best to protect what we hold most dear—the right to speak, think and study freely—but there is a higher responsibility that this institution carries, and that is the safety of our students." Stewart alleged that threats of violence had been made, and that these had prompted her decision to cancel the event.

Such threats probably were made (though it is also possible that Churchill and others exaggerated them). However, threats of violence in fact occur quite regularly in regard to campus speeches and they are normally dealt with by ample campus security, including armed guards and an occasional German shepherd.[14] Significantly, Stewart made no attempt to address the issue of academic standards as they pertained to extending an official university invitation to someone with Churchill's views.

Because of the embarrassment to the college, and the considerable costs it incurred, Nancy Rabinowitz was forced to resign as

---

[14]At a speech at the University of Michigan, which I gave in the spring of 2002, university officials provided twelve armed guards and a German shepherd. The previous spring, during a controversy over my opposition to slave reparations paid to living Americans who had never been slaves, the University of California, Berkeley assigned 30 armed guards to maintain security at a speech I gave there. See my *Uncivil Wars: The Controversy Over Reparations for Slavery*, Encounter, 2001.

chair of the Kirkland Project and a faculty committee was appointed to conduct an inquiry and offer recommendations for reform. When the inquiry was completed, President Stewart announced that the Kirkland budget would be significantly cut and its missions and programs reviewed. In future, all campus speakers would be paid for in part through a central fund to be reported to the administration, thus giving her office control over the decisions that her professors had abused.

Immediately, one of the members of the committee stepped forward to make it known that Stewart's solution was not one the faculty committee had recommended. Margaret Thickstun, a professor of English and the chair of Hamilton's faculty, told reporters that the President's decision was "more restrictive" than what the committee had recommended. This was because the Hamilton faculty, in Professor Thickstun's view, didn't think there was anything wrong with the invitations to Rosenberg and Churchill or with Kirkland Project standards. "I think that the faculty as a whole felt that the Kirkland project wasn't the issue," she said; "the media coverage was the issue."[15]

On Churchill's home campus at the University of Colorado, an even larger drama was unfolding. Churchill's extreme views had been known to University of Colorado authorities for a long time, but they had done nothing about them. Since Churchill was a full professor and chairman of his academic department, there was nothing they really could do. He was protected by tenure rules and academic-freedom considerations that left university officials few options. Once Churchill had attained tenured rank, he was for all intents and purposes untouchable.

The University of Colorado did have a tenure review process which was supposed to be administered annually. But the policy had not been observed in years.[16] Nor was it conceivable, even if

[15]Scott Jaschik, "Fallout at Hamilton," *Inside Higher Ed News*, July 5, 2005, https://www.insidehighered.com/news/2005/07/05/hamilton
[16]Interview with Colorado University regent Tom Lucero.

the procedures were observed, that Churchill's tenure would be put in jeopardy simply because he had abhorrent views. A celebrated attempt by the City University of New York to fire Leonard Jeffries, a racist professor of Black Studies, for making a flagrantly anti-Semitic speech had failed in the courts, some years earlier, because it was based on his public speech, not his classroom performance. His racism in the classroom, which was indisputable, was not considered by the university to be possible grounds for his dismissal. The tenure protections of professors were that strong.[17]

The national publicity generated by the Hamilton crisis dramatically altered this situation by bringing Churchill's views to the attention of the public at large, which regarded them as the incomprehensible ravings of a fringe radical. The fact that the nation was at war with a ruthless enemy, with whom Churchill clearly identified, caused an uproar in the Colorado media and led the Republican governor of the state and other officials to demand that he be fired.

In the weeks that followed, several facts about Churchill's academic career were brought to light to provide other grounds for questioning his university position. Although Churchill was a department head who received an annual salary of $120,000, he had no doctorate, which was a standard requirement for tenured positions, not to mention chairs. Moreover, his academic training had been in communications as a graphic artist, not in an academic field related to Ethnic Studies. The master's degree he held was from a third-rate experimental college which did not even give grades in the 1970s when he attended, and which no longer existed. He had lied to qualify for his affirmative-action hire when he claimed on his application that he was a member of the Keetoowah Band of the Cherokee tribe. In fact his ancestors were Anglo-Saxon,

---

[17]I, myself, filed an amicus brief in behalf of Jeffries, precisely because it was a free speech issue. I also wrote an op-ed column for the *Denver Rocky Mountain News* defending Ward Churchill's free speech rights, which were separate from the question of whether he had the qualifications to be a tenured professor, which he did not.

and the Keetoowah Band had publicly rejected him. An investigative series by the *Rocky Mountain News* also maintained that he had plagiarized other professors' academic work and had made demonstrably false claims about American history in his own writing, literally making up American atrocities that never happened.[18]

Despite these revelations, hundreds of professors and thousands of students across the country sprang to Churchill's defense, signing petitions in his behalf and protesting the "witch-hunt" against academic "liberals."[19] At the Indiana University Law School, Professor Florence Roisman took around a petition in Churchill's behalf. When law professor William Bradford, a Chiricahua Apache with a stellar academic resume, refused to sign the petition, Professor Roisman retorted, "What kind of a Native American are you?" and launched a campaign to have Bradford fired.[20] The American Association of University Professors ignored the Bradford case but issued an official declaration of support for Churchill, invoking "the right to free speech and the nationally recognized standard of academic freedom in support of quality instruction and scholarship."[21] Churchill made a public appearance in his own defense to

---

[18]"And the Verdict: He's Got to Go," *RockyMountainNews.com*, June 10, 2005, http://www.freerepublic.com/focus/f-news/1421108/posts; "Rocky Mountain News Earns Reader Respect," *Discarded Lies*, June 22, 2005, http://discardedlies.com/entry/?3883_rocky-mountain-news-earns-reader-respect; Berny Morson, "The Charge: Mischaracterization," *RockyMountainNews.com*, June 8, 2005, http://www. freerepublic. com/focus/ f-news/1418662/posts.

[19]Rafael Renteria, "Petition on Ward Churchill and Academic Freedom," *University of Dayton*, February 2005, http://academic.udayton.edu/ race/miscell/WardChurchill.htm; Jacob Laksin, "Churchill's Champions," *FrontPageMag.com*, February 28, 2005, http://archive.frontpagemag. com/readArticle.aspx?ARTID=9423; Elizabeth Mattern Clark, "Ad Demands Halt to Review," *dailycamera.com buffzone*, February 26, 2005, http://www.timescall.com/ci_1305645.

[20]FrontPage Magazine, "Indian Hunt in Indiana," *FrontPageMag.com*, August 10, 2005, http://www.frontpagemag.com/Articles/ReadArticle. asp?ID=19081

[21]"Faculty Action In the Ward Churchill Case," *American Association of University Professors*, (Updated) March 2005, http://www.aaup.org/ newsroom/Newsitems/Faculty&churchill.htm.

a cheering University of Colorado audience of 1,500, and went on to tour other campuses, where he received a similar hero's welcome from large university crowds.[22] These events further revealed the extent to which a radical philosophy at the very edges of the American political spectrum had established a central place in the curriculum of American universities.

How could the university have hired and then raised to such heights an individual of such questionable character and preposterous views as Ward Churchill? How many professors with similar resumes had managed to acquire tenured positions at Colorado University and at other institutions of higher learning? How pervasive was the conflation of political interests and academic pursuits on university campuses or in college classrooms? Why were the administrations seemingly unable to assert and enforce standards of academic excellence? Such were the issues the Churchill scandal raised.

The Changed University

In fact, the influence of radical attitudes is not confined to the radical community on an academic faculty, but has a tendency to spread throughout an institution. Robert Reich, a former cabinet secretary in the Clinton administration and now a professor of Economics and Social Policy at Brandeis University, is not a political radical in the Churchill mode. But he is a leftist with a political rather than an academic agenda. Reich is a member of the faculty committee of the "Social Justice and Social Policy Program" in the undergraduate division. The Social Justice and Social Policy

---

[22]Dan Werner, "200 Teachers Sign Ad Asking That Churchill Inquiry Be Dropped," *9News.com*, February 26, 2005 (Updated March 3, 2005), http://www.freerepublic.com/focus/f-news/1352596/posts; Charlie Brennan, "Churchill Throws Down Gauntlet at Speech in Boulder," *RockyMountainNews.com*, February 9, 2005, http://www.siliconinvestor.com/ readreplies.aspx?msgid=21035531; Craig Gima, "Churchill Attacks Essay's Critics," *(Honolulu) Starbulletin.com*, February 23, 2005, http://www.siliconinvestor.com/readreplies.aspx?msgid= 21035531.

Program, as the name implies, is a training course for students to become advocates for expanding the welfare state and generally expanding the power of the state in the name of the greater good. In other words, it is a program of indoctrination in the strictest sense—"to imbue with a partisan or ideological point of view"—an inappropriate agenda for an academic curriculum. The proper setting for such a course would be a training institute maintained by the Democratic Party and other organizations of the left.

A former SDS radical, now a professor of Journalism at Columbia University, explained the achievements of his faculty allies in an essay that appeared in 2004. After the Sixties, wrote Todd Gitlin, "all that was left to the Left was to unearth righteous traditions and cultivate them in universities. The much-mocked 'political correctness' of the next academic generations was a consolation prize. We lost—we squandered the politics—but won the textbooks."[23]

Professor Richard Rorty, a renowned professor of philosophy and ardent left-winger, described this development with equally refreshing candor: "The power base of the left in America is now in the universities, since the trade unions have largely been killed off. The universities have done a lot of good work by setting up, for example, African-American Studies programs, Women's Studies programs, Gay and Lesbian Studies programs. They have created power bases for these movements."[24] That a distinguished philosopher like Rorty would find in this political debasement of the university a development to praise, speaks volumes about the changes that have taken place in academic culture since the war in Vietnam.

Because activists ensconced in programmatic fields like Black Studies and Women's Studies also teach in traditional departments like History and English, and influence them as well, the

---

[23]Todd Gitlin, "Varieties of Patriotic Experience" in George Packer, ed. *The Fight Is for Democracy: Winning the War of Ideas in America and the World*, Perennial Books, 2003.

[24]Collier and Horowitz, eds., *Surviving the PC University*, Center for the Study of Popular Culture, 1996

statements by Rorty and Gitlin actually understate the ways in which a radical left has colonized a significant part of the university system and transformed it to serve its political ends. In September 2005, the American Political Science Association's annual meeting, for example, featured a panel devoted to the question, "Is It Time to Call It Fascism?"—meaning the administration of George W. Bush. Given the vibrant reality of American democracy in the year 2005, this was obviously a political rather than a scholarly agenda.[25] The faculty members of the Ethnic Studies Department that Ward Churchill chairs shared views similar to Churchill's, and declared their solidarity with him throughout the crisis.

Professors have a right to express their opinions, but they also have a professional obligation as teachers not to impose their biases on their students or present them as though they were scientific facts. In a democracy, the task of professors is to teach students how to think, not to tell them what to think. In short, it is the responsibility of professors to be professional—and therefore "academic"—in their classrooms. This includes the duty not to present their opinions and prejudices as fact, and not to require students to agree with them on matters that are controversial.

---

[25]An email from the panel Chair, Professor Dvora Yanow of California State, Hayward, described the proposed session in these words: "The panel, which is co-sponsored by the Conference Group on Theory, Policy, & Society, the Latino Caucus, New Political Science, and the Women's Caucus, emerged from a question that [Professor] Kathy Ferguson started asking last winter-spring (at ISA and WPSA) to focus on both substantive aspects and strategic/tactical ones: Is there theoretical-definitional grounding to make a claim for the present US administration as fascist, and is it useful, critically, to use that language at this point in time? One of the original intentions was also to create a teaching tool out of this discussion—a handout that presents these questions and offers relevant information to students to think about it for themselves." The panel included professors from the Universities of Hawaii, California and Colorado, among other schools, and the suggestion that the "questions" should be handed to students—undigested—indicated an intention to disseminate their views of the Bush Administrations to undergraduates, again for obvious political reasons. The email was relayed to the author by political scientist John Earl Haynes.

The privileges of tenure and academic freedom are specifically granted in exchange for this professionalism. Society does not provide tenure to politicians—and for good reason. To merit their tenure privileges, professors are expected to adhere to professional standards and avoid political attitudinizing. As professionals, their interpretations should be tempered by the understanding that all human knowledge is uncertain and only imperfectly grasped; that such knowledge must be based on the collection of evidence, evaluated according to professionally agreed-on methodologies and standards. As teachers they are expected to make their students aware of the controversies surrounding the evidence, including the significant challenges to their own interpretations. Hired as experts in scholarly disciplines and fields of knowledge, professors are granted tenure in order to protect the integrity of their academic inquiry, not their right to leak into the classroom their uninformed prejudices on subjects that are outside their fields of expertise.

Therefore, professors must be careful to distinguish between matters of opinion and matters of fact; between a subjective reading of the data and the data itself. Professors have a classroom responsibility to respect both the standards of research and inquiry of their profession and the still-unformed intellects of their students, who are their charges. Their teaching must not seek the arbitrary imposition of personal opinions and prejudices on students, enforced through the power of the grading process and the authority of the institution they represent.

It is a reasonable assumption that many university professors remain professionals and are devoted to traditional academic methods and pursuits. But these scholars are often intimidated from expressing their views on subjects like the Susan Rosenberg and Ward Churchill affairs because of their concern not to be labeled "racist" or "sexist" or "reactionary" by their more aggressive radical peers. They are not always so intimidated, and can sometimes be seen standing up to defend academic standards under assault. At the University of Colorado, for example, Paul

Campos, a liberal member of the University of Colorado law faculty and a columnist for the Denver *Rocky Mountain News*, issued one of the strongest statements on Churchill's tenured position: "To compare the victims of the 9/11 massacre to one of the chief architects of the Holocaust is both intellectually bankrupt and morally depraved. To do so in a published essay, and to repeat this opinion to the media, after being asked whether he wishes to consider it, calls into question the author's fitness to continue as a member of this university's faculty. Members of our faculty should keep in mind that a grant of tenure is not a guarantee of perpetual employment. Tenure protects against dismissal without cause; but professional incompetence and moral depravity are both sufficient grounds for firing tenured faculty."[26]

Two years earlier, a prominent member of the academic left and a distinguished Milton scholar, Stanley Fish, wrote an article in *The Chronicle of Higher Education* in which he stressed the importance of the drawing the line between political attitudinizing and scholarly discourse. His article was titled, "Save the World on Your Own Time," and cautioned academics about getting involved *as academics* in moral and political issues such as the War on Terror. In a paradoxical summary statement, he warned: "It is immoral for academics or academic institutions to proclaim moral views."[27] The reason, according to Fish, was provided long ago in a faculty report to the president of the University of Chicago. "The report declares that the university exists 'only for the limited ... purposes of teaching and research,'" Fish wrote. "Since the university is a community only for those limited and

---

[26]Paul Campos, "Finding Responsive, Responsible Leadership at CU is Just a Dream," *Denver Rocky Mountain News*, January 29, 2005, http://www.highbeam.com/doc/1G1-127933293.html.

[27]Stanley Fish, "Save The World On Your Own Time," *The Chronicle of Higher Education*, Jan. 23, 2003, http://chronicle.com/article/Save-the-World-on-Your-Own/45335/; Fish has written two books on the same subject, *Professional Correctness*, Oxford University Press, 1995, and *Save the World on Your Own Time*, Oxford University Press, 2008.

distinctive purposes, it is a community which cannot take collective action on the issues of the day without endangering the conditions for its existence and effectiveness."

The conclusion Professor Fish drew was straightforward: "Teachers should teach their subjects. They should not teach peace or war or freedom or diversity or uniformity or nationalism or anti-nationalism or any other agenda that might properly be taught by a political leader or a talk-show host. Of course they should teach *about* such subjects, *something very different from urging them as commitments*—when they are part of the history or philosophy or literature or sociology that is being studied. The only advocacy that should go on in the classroom is the advocacy of what James Murphy has identified as the intellectual virtues, 'thoroughness, perseverance, intellectual honesty,' all components of the cardinal academic virtue of being 'conscientious in the pursuit of truth.'" (emphasis added)

This was once the prevailing view among academic professionals. But now it is under significant challenge by radicals firmly entrenched in departments in the liberal arts fields. Organizations like "Historians Against the War" or the "Radical Philosophical Association" directly challenge the idea of academic neutrality on controversial political issues. In 2002, Columbia University hosted a conference of academic radicals called, "Taking Back the Academy: History of Activism, History as Activism."[28] The published text of the conference papers was provided with a foreword by Professor Eric Foner, who is a past president of both the Organization of American Historians and the American Historical Association, and a leading academic figure. Far from sharing Professor Fish's view that a sharp distinction should be drawn between political advocacy and the scholarly disciplines, Professor Foner expressed the position that political activism is *essential* to the academic mission: "The chapters in this excellent volume," wrote

---

[28]Jim Downs and Jennifer Manion, eds., *Taking Back The Academy!: History of Activism, History as Activism*, Routledge Books, 2004

Foner, "derive from a path-breaking conference held at Columbia University in 2002 to explore the links between historical scholarship and political activism.... As the chapters that follow demonstrate, scholarship and activism are not mutually exclusive pursuits, but are, at their best, symbiotically related."[29]

The implications of this symbiosis were drawn by the conference panels, which are listed in the table of contents as follows: "Student Movements," "Student Unions," "Historians for Social Justice," and "Bridging the Gap Between Academia and Activism." In other words, the symbiosis of activism and scholarship reflected a self-conception in which radical professors would function as the mentors and protectors of student activists, deploying their intellectual skills in behalf of "progressive" political causes. History professor Jesse Lemisch, a founding member of "Historians Against The War," began his presentation with these words: "As historians, teachers and scholars, we oppose the expansion of American empire...." Speaking on the final conference panel, Professor Lemisch spelled out the connection that academic radicals like himself made between their roles as scholars and their political goals: "Being an activist is a necessary prerequisite for historians who want to see through the reigning lies, and I take it as a given that we *must* be activists. Writing history is about challenging received authority. Activist experience gives the historian experiential understanding of the power of the state, repression, social change ... the depth of commitment of those with power to maintaining the standing order through their journalists, historians, police and law firms.... You can't *begin* to understand how history happens unless you have this basic training as a historian/activist. A good dose of tear gas makes us think more clearly as historians."[30]

Far from being marginal, Lemisch's endorsement of activist scholarship is shared by leaders of the academic profession. Jacquelyn Hall

---

[29]Ibid. p. xi
[30]Ibid. p. 188 (emphasis in original)

is a professor of History at the University of North Carolina and, like Eric Foner, a former president of the Organization of American Historians. Like Foner and Lemisch, she is also a member of Historians Against the War and had this to say about *Taking Back the Academy:* "In considering the broad social and political responsibilities of intellectuals in society, this book calls for a revitalized definition of what it means to be a scholar-citizen in the twenty-first century. For scholars in the humanities, that call could not be more timely. Alternatively maligned as politically irrelevant or dangerously subversive, historians and other stewards of society's subjective truths increasingly must be prepared to articulate—and defend—their function in today's marketplace of ideas and corporatized universities."[31] These are the words of an activist rather than a scholar. But at the Columbia University conference the distinction was no longer recognized.

The Law of Group Polarization

Critics of the university have long complained that the system of tenure, which provides lifetime job security, also serves to protect mediocrity and encourage incompetence. The efforts to politicize the curriculum over the last three decades have predictably created new opportunities for both tendencies to flourish. As already noted, an important factor contributing to the debasement of intellectual standards in the university is its politicized environment. It is relatively easy for politically like-minded individuals to mistake adherence to partisan formulas for substantive thought and even intellectual achievement. Some years ago, the power of this phenomenon was demonstrated to devastating effect by a physicist named Alan Sokal.[32]

Sokal was himself a political leftist but concerned about the debasement of intellectual standards by his political allies in the university. In a famous thought experiment, Sokal submitted a

---

[31]Ibid.
[32]Sokal was himself a leftist, disturbed over what he (correctly) saw as the corruption of "progressive" thought.

paper to *Social Text*—a "peer-reviewed" academic journal, whose articles were viewed by many as on the "cutting edge of radical theory." By design, the substance of the paper Sokal wrote and submitted was pure nonsense, but its content—also by design— was "politically correct." "To test prevailing intellectual standards," Sokal explained, "I decided to try a modest (though admittedly uncontrolled) experiment: Would a leading North American journal of Cultural Studies—whose editorial collective includes such luminaries as [Duke professor] Fredric Jameson and [Princeton professor] Andrew Ross—publish an article liberally salted with nonsense if (a) it sounded good and (b) it flattered the editors' ideological preconceptions."[33]

The article Sokal submitted to *Social Text* was called, "Transgressing the Boundaries: Towards a Transformative Hermeneutics of Quantum Gravity." Its thesis was that gravity was merely a social construct, an instrument of phallocentric hegemony. "In the second paragraph I declare, without the slightest evidence or argument, that 'physical "reality" [note the scare quotes] ... is at bottom a social and linguistic construct.' Not our *theories* of physical reality, mind you, but the reality itself. Fair enough: anyone who believes that the laws of physics are mere social conventions is invited to try transgressing those conventions from the windows of my apartment. (I live on the 23rd floor.)"

Social Text published the article, only to be embarrassed nationally when Sokal revealed the hoax. "The editors of *Social Text* liked my article," he explained afterwards, "because they liked its *conclusion:* that 'the content and methodology of postmodern science provide powerful intellectual support for the progressive political project.'" This is as a clear an example as one might wish of why initiating inquiries with the politically correct conclusions already in

---

[33]Alan D. Sokal, "A Physicist Experiments With Cultural Studies," *New York University*, June 5, 1996, http://www.physics.nyu.edu/faculty/ sokal/lingua_franca_v4/lingua_franca_v4.html. For a book on the controversy, see Alan Sokal and Jean Bricmont, *Fashionable Nonsense: Post-Modern Intellectuals' Abuse of Science*, Picador Books, 1998.

hand is antithetical to the intellectual enterprise; and why activism in the university is in its essence an anti-intellectual project, even though entire academic departments in the liberal arts divisions are now organized on these bases. Conformity to the parameters of the "progressive political project" is a widespread standard of academic judgment in the liberal arts, not only for the selection and design of its curricula but for the hiring and promotion of faculty as well. While mediocrity and incompetence have always had a place in the academic world, it is also the case that never before in the history of the modern research university have entire departments and fields been devoted to purely ideological pursuits. Nor has overt propagandizing had such a respected and prominent place in university classrooms. Even more disturbingly, the last few decades mark the first time in their history that America's institutions of higher learning have become a haven for political extremists.

A primary cause of this development is a well-known principle of group dynamics called the "law of group polarization," which holds that if a room is filled with like-minded people, the center of the room will move towards the extreme. This is because the room has become an echo chamber of approbation, while the natural clamor for attention among individual egos provides an incentive to push the envelope of approved opinions to their natural limit.[34] In many fields the academic community has become such an echo chamber. Numerous surveys of political attitudes among university professors have established that the ratio of faculty members holding views to the left of the political spectrum, over those holding conservative views ranges, from 5–1 to 9–1 and is steadily increasing.[35] At Ward

---

[34]Cass Sunstein, "The Law of Group Polarization," *Social Science Research Network—University of Chicago Law School*, December 1999, http://papers.ssrn.com/sol3/papers.cfm?abstract_id=199668.

[35]Daniel Klein and Charlotta Stern, "Surveys on Political Diversity in American Higher Education," *Students For Academic Freedom*, December 31, 2002, http://www.studentsforacademicfreedom.org/reports/Surveys.html; Daniel Klein and Charlotta Stern, "How Politically Diverse Are The Social Sciences and Humanities?," *Social*
continued

Churchill's university in Boulder, the figure is 30–1.[36] This, in fact, reflects the academic future at schools as disparate as Stanford and Berkeley, where a 30–1 ratio already exists among junior faculty (assistant and associate professors).[37] The atmosphere created by such a one-sided dialogue is what makes possible support for an intellectual rogue like Ward Churchill by academic organizations like the Kirkland project, the American Association of University Professors and thousands of professors nationwide.

Some academics like Paul Krugman have challenged this claim to argue that the vast disparity in the representation of different intellectual perspectives is a matter of self-selection: "It's a fact, documented by two recent studies, that registered Republicans and self-proclaimed conservatives make up only a small minority of professors at elite universities. But what should we conclude from that? One answer is self-selection—the same sort of self-selection that leads Republicans to outnumber Democrats four to one in the military. The sort of person who prefers an academic career to the private sector is likely to be somewhat more liberal than average, even in engineering."[38]

Science Research Network, February 9, 2005, http://papers.ssrn.com/sol3/Delivery.cfm/SSRN_ID664042_code278705.pdf?abstractid=664042&mirid=1.

[36]Vincent Carroll, "Republican Professors? Sure, There's One," *Wall Street Journal*, May 11, 1998, http://www.wsj.com/articles/SB89483361874856500; Rob Natelson, "Academia Locks Out Conservative Professors," *The Billings Outpost*, February 17, 2005, http://www.belgrade-news.com/opinion/article_bd26b3ff-2de4-5767-b760-fed9193739e3.html; David Horowitz and Eli Lehrer, "Political Bias in the Administrations and Faculties of 32 Elite Colleges and Universities," *Students For Academic Freedom*, August 28, 2003, http://www.studentsforacademicfreedom.org/news/1898/lackdiversity.html.

[37]Daniel Klein and Charlotta Stern, "Surveys on Political Diversity in American Higher Education," op. cit. They conducted a separate study of junior faculty at both schools reflecting this disparity.

[38]Paul Krugman, "An Academic Question," *New York Times*, April 5, 2005, http://www.nytimes.com/2005/04/05/opinion/05krugman.html?_r=0.

Professor Krugman's argument about self-selection could easily have been used to explain the absence of women or African Americans on university faculties forty years ago, when they were as rare as Republicans are today. Would Professor Krugman's attitude be the same if he were called on to explain *those* disparities? It is not obvious that the military and the academy can be compared in the way that Professor Krugman proposes. There is no intellectual apprenticeship required for inclusion in the military, and its recruitment process hardly entails the kind of pervasive inquiry into a candidate's opinions and judgments as does an academic hire. There are many Republican lawyers, to pick only one obvious profession that has an academic analogue; but the percentage of Republican law professors at academic institutions is no greater than the percentage of Republicans on other faculties.[39]

As a political columnist, Krugman must also be aware that not all Republicans—not even most Republicans—are businessmen, or employed in business professions. The Republican Party is competitive with Democrats in virtually all social sectors; while a reliable indicator of a Democratic vote is proximity to and length of membership in academic communities where there is a restricted marketplace of ideas. Moreover, as a professor at Princeton, which is governed by the trustees of the "Princeton Corporation," Krugman must be aware that a significant segment of the university community is actually part of the private sector, and a lucrative part at that for academic entrepreneurs like himself. If Republicans are motivated by a desire to succeed in the private sector, why would they deny themselves the opportunities provided by private corporations like Princeton and Harvard?

Krugman's self-selection hypothesis also cannot explain the results of the study by Professor Daniel Klein and Andrew Western, showing that the ratio of Republicans to Democrats among

---

[39]David Horowitz and Joseph Light, "Representation of Ideological Perspectives," *Students For Academic Freedom*, November 21, 2005, http://www.studentsforacademicfreedom.org/news/1135/LawJournalism StudyRevisedFinal112205.htm.

junior faculty at Berkeley and Stanford is a third of what it is among senior faculty.[40] In other words, the exclusion of Republicans is increasing over time. Nor can it explain why the percentage of faculty conservatives should have dramatically declined in the last twenty years, as a recent study by Rothman, Nevitte and Lichter shows.[41] In a survey of 1643 faculty members drawn from 183 colleges and universities, the authors concluded that over the course of 15 years, self-described liberals grew from a slight plurality to a 5 to 1 majority on college faculties, while the ratio of liberals to conservatives in the general population remained relatively constant.[42] These statistics, on the other hand, are perfectly compatible with the view that the exclusion of conservatives began roughly thirty years ago when a generation of political activists started to acquire power over faculty hiring and promotion committees. The political activists who flooded university faculties in the early Seventies were encouraged by their own theories to regard the university as an instrument for social change, whose levers of power it was important for "progressives" to manipulate and control.

Academic radicals self-consciously drew their strategies from the writings of the Italian Communist Antonio Gramsci, around whom an academic cult formed in the 1970s, just as they were ascending the tenure ladder. Gramsci was an innovator in Marxist theory whose ideas focused on the importance of acquiring cultural "hegemony" as the fulcrum of revolutionary change. Gramsci explicitly urged radicals to gain control of the "means of cultural production" to further their ends. Foremost among these

---

[40]Daniel Klein and Andrew Western, "How Many Democrats per Republican at UC Berkeley and Stanford?," "Surveys on Political Diversity in American Higher Education," *Students For Academic Freedom*, December 31, 2002, http://www.studentsforacademicfreedom.org/news/1909/Surveys.html

[41]Stanley Rothman, S. Robert Lichter, Neil Nevitte, "Politics and Professional Advancement Among College Faculty," *The Forum*, Vol. 3, Iss. 1, Art. 2, 2005, http://www.cwu.edu/~manwellerm/academic%20bias.pdf

[42]Rothman, Lichter, Nevitte, op. cit.

means were the universities and the media. The considerations that led Gramsci to these conclusions encouraged faculty activists to seek institutional power within the university by acquiring control of its hiring and tenure committees.[43]

Herbert Marcuse, a professor at Brandeis and a veteran of the famed "Frankfurt School" of European Marxism, was another figure whose writings flourished with the new radical presence on university faculties. His notorious essay "Repressive Tolerance," written in 1965, is a justification for the suppression of conservative speech and conservative access to cultural platforms on grounds that the views of right-wing intellectuals reflect the rule of an oppressive and dominant social class.[44] In Orwellian fashion, Marcuse identified "revolutionary tolerance" as "tolerance that enlarged the range and content of freedom." Revolutionary tolerance, he argued, could not be neutral towards rival viewpoints but had to be "partisan" in behalf of the radical cause. In other words, it had to be "intolerant towards the protagonists of the repressive *status quo*." In short, revolutionary tolerance requires the suppression of conservative voices. This was a transparent prescription for not hiring academic candidates with conservative views. Blacklists were instruments of "liberation."

Whatever the cause, senior conservative professors (and most conservative professors are now senior) find themselves regularly excluded from search and hiring committees, and a dwindling presence on university faculties. A typical case was reported to a visitor to the University of Delaware in November 2001, who asked a senior member of the history department and its lone conservative how the system that had made him such a solitary figure worked. The professor answered, "Well, they haven't allowed me to sit on a Search Committee since 1985. In that year I was its

---

[43]On the importance and functioning process of these committees, see David Horowitz, *The Professors*, Chapter 3: "The Representative Nature of the Professors Profiled in this Volume," Regnery, 2006.

[44] Herbert Marcuse, "Repressive Tolerance," 1965. http://la.utexas.edu/ users/hcleaver/330T/350kPEEMarcuseToleranceTable.pdf

chair and we hired a Marxist. This year [2001] we had an opening for a scholar of Asian history. We had several candidates among whom the best qualified was from Stanford. Yet he didn't get the job. So I went to the chair of the Search Committee and asked him what had happened. 'Oh,' he said, 'you're absolutely right. He was far and away the most qualified candidate and we had a terrific interview about his area of expertise. But then we went to lunch and he let out that he was for school vouchers. And that killed it."[45] Apparently, a politically incorrect view on K-12 school voucher proposals implied incorrect views about the Ming Dynasty or the Meiji Restoration, disqualifying the bearer for academic employment.

The intolerant attitude of the current academic culture towards conservatives is inevitably a factor in the blacklisting process. In the spring of 2005, *The Skidmore News* published an article called, "Politics in the Classroom," which quoted anthropology professor Gerry Erchak to this effect: "In the hiring process you'd probably be wise not to mention your political views. If you say, 'Oh, hey, I really think Reagan was great,' or, 'I'm a Bush guy,' I can't say a person wouldn't be hired, but it's like your pants falling down. It's just horrible. It's like you cut a big fart. I just don't think you'll be called back."[46]

The faculty prejudices reflected in Erchak's comment are a pervasive fact of academic life. In the same spring, Professor Timothy Shortell was elected by his peers to the chair of the sociology department at Brooklyn College. His election became a news item when it was discovered that he had written an article referring to religious people as "moral retards" and was on record describing senior members of the Bush administration as "Nazis." The recent eruption of the Churchill controversy in Colorado had made Shortell's extreme attitudes newsworthy, as they would not otherwise have been. The

---

[45]This and the following anecdote were related to the author on a visit to the University of Delaware.
[46]"Politics in the Classroom," *The Skidmore News*, April 29, 2005

same attitudes had not impressed his department peers as the least bit unusual. Departmental chairs at Brooklyn College exercise veto powers over faculty hiring decisions. Is it reasonable to think that someone with views like Shortell's would approve the hiring of a sociology candidate with religious views or Republican leanings?

According to the survey of 1,700 academics by Professor Daniel Klein and Andrew Western, the ratio of Democrats to Republicans in sociology departments nationwide is 28–1.[47] As in the case of Ward Churchill, the public airing of Shortell's prejudices generated a reaction strong enough to persuade the president of Brooklyn College to block his appointment to the departmental chair to avoid further embarrassment to the college. On the other hand, left to itself the university process would have placed Shortell in a position to determine the composition of faculty for a generation to come. Criminology professor Michael Adams of the University of North Carolina, Wilmington, has reported an incident reflecting similar prejudice. A colleague on a search committee for the Criminology Department remarked to him that a candidate they were reviewing should not be hired because he was "too religious."[48] Too religious to study crime? Among his search committee colleagues, only Adams thought this peculiar.

The prejudice against conservatives is so ingrained and commonplace that academics do not see it as a problem at all. To them it is just the order of things. When an anthropology professor at Rollins College, an elite private school in Florida, was asked whether he was concerned that there were no conservatives in his department, he explained why he wasn't in these words: "Anthropology is the study of other cultures and requires individuals who are compassionate and tolerant." When confronted, the professor

---

[47]Klein and Western, op. cit.

[48]Mike Adams, "Fear and Loathing in Faculty Recruitment," *Townhall.com*, June 2, 2004, http://townhall.com/columnists/ mikeadams/2004/06/02/fear_and_loathing_in_faculty_recruitment/page /full. Adams was placed on the committee when he was still a self-described "liberal."

was completely oblivious of the intolerance of his own state-ment.[49] David French, the president of the Foundation for Individ-ual Rights in Education and a graduate of Harvard Law School, spent two years as a lecturer at Cornell Law School: "During my second interview with the director of the program I was applying to join, she asked the following question: 'I note from your *cur-riculum vitae* that you seem to be involved in religious right issues. Do you think you can teach gay students?' How many gay applicants at Cornell have been asked: 'Do you think you can teach Christian students?'"[50] When a conservative student publi-cation at Duke University published an article showing that con-servatives were a rarity on the Duke faculty, the chairman of the Duke philosophy department, Professor Robert Brandon, explained: "We try to hire the best, smartest people available.... If, as John Stuart Mill said, stupid people are generally conservative, then there are lots of conservatives we will never hire."[51]

During a recent conflict over diversity at the Harvard Law School, a candid acknowledgment of the hiring bias against con-servative candidates was made by Professor Alan Dershowitz, a faculty liberal. When the Harvard crisis came to a head, the administration created a "Committee on Healthy Diversity" to assuage left-wing students who wanted more women and racial minorities hired. While there were already a considerable number of women and minority professors at Harvard Law, there were only a handful of identifiable Republicans out of a faculty of 200.[52]

---

[49]The anthropology professor is Robert Moore and I asked the question on a visit to Rollins in November 2005.

[50]David French, "More on Viewpoint Discrimination," *Fire's The Torch*, April 6, 2005, http://www.thefire.org/more-on-viewpoint-discrimina-tion/.

[51]Cindy Yee, "DCU Sparks Varied Reactions," *The Chronicle Online*, Feb-ruary 9, 2004, http://www.dukechronicle.com/articles/2004/02/10/dcu-sparks-varied-reactions#.VKMETcNuVA.

[52]Andrew Peyton Thomas, *The People v. Harvard Law*, Encounter, 2005; David Horowitz, *Campus Blacklist* (booklet), Students for Academic Freedom, Washington, D.C., 2003.

Seizing the opportunity the left had seemingly provided, conservative students appealed to the Committee on Healthy Diversity to hire more conservatives, but their pleas went unanswered. Professor Dershowitz explained why their request fell on deaf ears: "The true test for diversity for me is would people on the left vote for a really bright evangelical Christian, who was a brilliant and articulate spokesperson for the right to life, the right to own guns ... anti-gay approaches to life, anti-feminist views? Would there be a push to get such a person on the faculty? Now, such a person would really diversify this place. Of course not. I think blacks want more blacks, women want more women, and leftists want more leftists. Everybody thinks diversification comes by getting more of themselves. And that's not true diversity."[53] Of course, thanks to the relative scarcity of faculty conservatives, there is no significant constituency for hiring more of them.

Academic Freedom

The activist agendas of today's academics are not only a departure from academic tradition; they are violations of established principles of academic freedom dating back to 1915. These principles, which were developed by the American Association of University Professors, have been universally embraced by American colleges and universities and are elaborated in official faculty guidelines, while remaining unenforced. Rule APM 0-10 of the University of California's *Academic Personnel Manual*, written in 1934 by its president Robert Gordon Sproul, states:

> The function of the university is to seek and to transmit knowledge and to train students in the processes whereby truth is to be made known. To convert, or to make converts, is alien and hostile to this dispassionate duty. Where it becomes necessary, in performing this function of a university, to consider political, social, or sectarian movements, they are dissected and examined,

---

[53]Thomas, op. cit. pp. 126–127.

not taught, and the conclusion left, with no tipping of the scales, to the logic of the facts.... Essentially the freedom of a university is the freedom of competent persons in the classroom. In order to protect this freedom, the University assumed the right to prevent exploitation of its prestige by unqualified persons or by those who would use it as a platform for propaganda.

On July 30, 2003—sixty-nine years after this statement was written—the passage was removed from the Berkeley personnel manual by a 43–3 vote of the Faculty Senate.[54] This was an eloquent and disturbing expression of the new academic culture, which had accommodated itself to the intrusion of partisan agendas into the academic curriculum. The Sproul clause was replaced by one that omitted any distinction between indoctrination and education, and which made faculty the arbiter of the standard: "Academic freedom requires that teaching and scholarship be assessed only by reference to the professional standards that sustain the University's pursuit and achievement of knowledge," the new passage stated. "The substance and nature of these standards properly lie within the expertise and authority of the faculty as a body.... Academic freedom requires that the Academic Senate be given primary responsibility for applying academic standards...." In other words, academic freedom is whatever the faculty says it is. Gone is the injunction against making converts to political,

---

[54]Martin Trow, "Californians Redefine Academic Freedom," *Academic Questions*, Summer 2003, http://www.cshe.berkeley.edu/sites/default/files/shared/publications/docs/ROP.Trow.AcademicFreedom.3.0 5.pdf; David Horowitz, "California's Betrayal of Academic Freedom," *FrontPageMag.com*, September 14, 2004, http://archive.frontpagemag.com/readArticle.aspx?ARTID=11409; One of incidents that precipitated the change in UC policy on academic freedom was the complaint of a student at UC Berkeley that her Middle Eastern studies lecturer had told students that the notorious Czarist forgery, *The Protocols of the Elders of Zion*, was true. The *Protocols* describes a Jewish plot to control the world and was a document used by the Nazis to justify the extermination of Jews. The student's complaint was dismissed by university authorities. An official of the UC Academic Senate defended the professor's preposterous and bigoted statement as coming under the protection of "academic freedom."

social or sectarian agendas; gone, too, the admonition not to exploit the prestige of the university as a platform for political propaganda.

With this rewriting of university guidelines, the principle of academic freedom, which had been created to protect scholarship, had now become a substitute for it—a license for professors to do what they liked. This ominous event in the life of American universities passed virtually unnoticed—an indication of how completely this core principle of university governance had fallen into disregard, and how profoundly the university culture had changed. The removal of the Sproul clause was the Faculty Senate's response to a dilemma created the previous year, when a radical lecturer named Snehal Shingavi announced that his section of a freshman writing course would be titled, "The Politics and Poetics of Palestinian Resistance." In describing the course, which was required of all freshman whose writing skills did not meet the university's standard, Shingavi wrote: "The brutal Israeli military occupation of Palestine, [ongoing] since 1948, has systematically displaced, killed, and maimed millions of Palestinian people.... This class will examine the history of the [resistance] and the way that it is narrated by Palestinians in order to produce an understanding of the *Intifada*." The course description Shingavi had placed in the official university catalogue ended with a warning: "Conservative thinkers are encouraged to seek other sections."[55] When Fox News Channel hosts jumped on this attempt to exclude conservative students, the public reaction prompted university officials to remove the warning from the catalogue. But they allowed the course—a blatant exercise in political propaganda—to continue as announced.

The only academic rationale for the freshman English course was to teach incoming students the elements of style—the

---

[55]Roger Kimball, "The Intifada Curriculum," *Wall Street Journal*, May 9, 2002; Marc J. Rauch, "America-Hating Professors," *FrontPageMag.com* October 14, 2002, http://archive.frontpagemag.com/readArticle.aspx? ARTID=21875.

grammatical construction of topic sentences, paragraphs, and the like. This was why the course was offered by the English Department and not the department of Political Science or Middle Eastern Studies. But instead of confronting an egregious abuse of the classroom for political purposes, the Berkeley Faculty Senate chose to conceal its hypocrisy by eliminating the section of its academic freedom code specifically designed to draw the distinction between education and indoctrination and to prevent such abuses. The misuse of freshman writing courses is common at many universities, where sections are regularly built around themes like feminism, radical environmentalism and radical perspectives on race.[56] At the same time, there are academic freedom guidelines still nominally in force at these schools, which were written to prevent such practices. The Faculty Handbook of Ohio State University (to take a fairly typical example) instructs professors as follows: "Academic freedom carries with it correlative academic responsibilities. The principal elements include the responsibility of teachers to ... differentiate carefully between official activities as teachers and personal activities as citizens, and to act accordingly." Policy HR 64 in the Penn State Policy Manual is even more explicit: "No faculty member may claim as a right the privilege of discussing in the classroom controversial topics outside his/her own field of study. The faculty member is normally bound not to take advantage of his/her position by introducing into the classroom provocative discussions of irrelevant subjects not within the field of his/her study."

Behind these guidelines lies a liberal philosophy of education in which it is the professional responsibility of educators to teach students *how* to think, rather than *what* to think. This is what distinguishes democratic systems of education from their totalitarian counterparts. Under academic freedom guidelines, teachers are expected to instruct students how to assemble data from the

---

[56]I have personally interviewed students about such courses on scores of college campuses.

evidential record, how to evaluate the data and how to construct an argument using the data. They are expected to refrain from using the authority of the classroom to impose on students their personal conclusions about questions to which the answers are not verifiable or are beyond their professional expertise. It is the difference, as Stanley Fish wrote, between teaching *about* controversial issues and "urging them as commitments."

There are no "correct" answers to controversial issues, which is the very reason they are controversial. There are no factually determined answers to controversial questions that any current expertise can resolve, for the same reason. It is precisely because the answers to such questions are inherently subjective and opinion-based that teachers should not use the authority of the classroom to force students to adopt the position they themselves favor. To do so is not education but indoctrination. These principles are still enshrined in the academic freedom guidelines of many large university systems, like the ones in Pennsylvania, Ohio and, until recently, California. But they are widely disregarded by activist professors in university liberal arts programs, and there are no institutional mechanisms for calling such professors to account.

These observations were inspired by my own educational experience at Columbia University in the 1950s. I was a Marxist at the time and wrote my classroom papers, as a seventeen-year-old, from that perspective. Even though this was the height of the Cold War and my professors were anti-communist liberals, they never singled me out for comment the way many conservative students I have encountered are singled out today. No professor of mine ever said in the course of a classroom lecture, "Horowitz, why don't you explain why Communists kill so many people?" Yet last year, a Christian student at the University of Rhode Island, Nathaniel Nelson, was singled out by his political science professor who interrupted a class discussion in a course on political philosophy from Plato to Machiavelli to ask, "Nathaniel, why do Christians hate fags?" I do not know how my education would have been affected if my professors had become my adversaries in the classroom, but I am sure the effect would not have been positive. If my professors had made me an object of their partisan passions, the trust between teacher and student would have been irreparably ruptured, and with it the ability of the teacher to provide his student with the full benefits of his experience and expertise.

I am grateful to my Columbia professors for not becoming my adversaries in the classroom in the way that has become common in the classrooms of activist professors today. I am grateful to them for treating me as a seventeen-year-old who was their student, and to whom they had the same professional obligation they had to students who might agree with them on contemporary controversies. I am grateful for their professionalism and for the respect they showed to their academic calling; and I am grateful for their concern for my vulnerability as a young man. In twenty years of schooling up through the graduate level, I never heard one teacher or professor, on one occasion, in one classroom, ever express a political opinion. Not one. It is my hope that the integrity exhibited by my teachers in that politically troubled era will be restored one day to American institutions of learning, so that future generations of students can receive as full a benefit from their educational experience as I did.

PART II

The Campaign for Fairness and Inclusion

The Decline of Academic Discourse
(A Speech to the Modern Language Association)

I can't say I'm exactly pleased to be here. As a father and grand-father, I know I am attending the convention of an organiza-tion hostile to the family when its convention is held at the one time of the year that is reserved for family gatherings and reunions. But I am on hostile terrain in other ways as well. Peter Collier and I would not have called our magazine *Heterodoxy* if we thought our perspective would fit in with the dominant dis-course of its target audience, members of the American academy. We are the counterculture, and this convention is the Trilateral Commission of the academic ruling class. Just so we know where we stand.

My appearance here is best seen, then, as an in-your-face ges-ture, a showing of the flag of dissent in the camp of an oppressive orthodoxy. But perhaps we can all learn something from it. Thirty years ago I was a master's student in English literature at Berkeley and wrote a book on Shakespeare. It is, in fact, the only book I authored in my 25 years as a radical that I can comfortably read today. And that in itself is a commentary on the current fashion-able view that literature has no transcendent value, that there are no themes that are timeless, no expressions that escape the nar-row, reductive, and ultimately uninteresting strictures of class, race, and gender politics. What could be more inane and boring, for example, than a misreading of *The Tempest* as a text about British

---

Paper delivered at the annual meeting of the Modern Language Associa-tion in Toronto, December 1993.

imperialism, with Caliban as a prototype for Third World revolutionaries?

As a former practitioner in this profession, my greatest complaint against the Modern Language Association is not even its bad politics and out-of-date social analysis, although one surely has to wonder about the judgment of people who remain faithful to a worldview long after its bankruptcy has been demonstrated at incalculable human cost. What provokes my ire at the current profession is its assault on literature and its abandonment of the educational task, which is to expose the next generation to the enriching wonders of the literary text; and finally its burial of the literary subject under a mountain of feminist, Marxist, deconstructionist *Kitsch*.

One has only to compare the scholarly contributions of past presidents of the Modern Language Association—Marjorie Nicholson, Henri Peyre, Maynard Mack, and Germaine Brée come to mind—with the empty files of ideological poseurs like Catharine Stimpson and Houston Baker to measure its descent into intellectual mediocrity and political attitudinizing. Literature is not politics, nor even a preparation for politics.

Historians of the future will wonder in amazement at the domination of academic thinking in post-cold war America by ideas that were first made fashionable by Nazis and Communists and their intellectual teachers. What do Heidegger, Foucault, DeMan, Althusser, Gramsci, Nietzsche and Marx have in common but their popularity among American academics and their place in an intellectual tradition that gave rise to Lenin and Stalin, Mussolini and Hitler?

Of course, the academic left that everywhere else insists on the connection between theory and "praxis" in this case can find no connection between the anti-liberal and nihilist agendas to which they pay intellectual homage, and the dreadful acts committed by the communists and fascists who were actually guided by them. "Is it possible," asks David Hirsch, an eloquent critic, "that there should be no connection between the Nazis' effort to murder God in Auschwitz and Heidegger's attempt to deconstruct the meta-physical tradition in Western philosophy, which is to say his attempt to destroy that fusion of Hellenism and Hebraism which is Christianity? In fact, are we not bound in all honesty to say that the real-world end-point of [the] deconstruction of the logocentric tradition is precisely Auschwitz?"

But why stop at Auschwitz? Aren't the theories that underpin the intellectual flights of Fredric Jameson, Houston Baker, Terry Eagleton and other stars of the academic left precisely the ideas that led to the creation of the Soviet gulag, with its tens of millions of victims whose only crime was to be politically incorrect? There are, in fact, two intellectual traditions that lie at the back of current academic theory: Marxism and nihilism. Is there any thinker in all of history whose ideas have been as wrong—and with such destructive consequences—as those of Marx? His plan for a kingdom of freedom turned into a blueprint for oppression and murder, while his dream of a planned economy resulted in mass poverty and starvation. There is one Marxist proposition—and only one—that has stood the test of time, and he lifted even this from Hegel: History repeats itself, the first time as tragedy, the second time as farce.

How else explain that after the Ministries of Truth have been dismantled in the capitals of the communist and fascist empires, after the commissars of thought control and the *Gauleiters* of political purity have been turned out to pasture, the totalitarian fantasy of a world without dissidents is being revived by American academics? In the English departments and "Student Life" centers of our nation's universities, we can see a renewal of the totalitarian project to create a "new man" and "new womon" [sic] free from the taint of attitudes that are reactionary and incorrect, capitalist and patriarchal, and otherwise "oppressive." In administrative "Diversity Offices" and in Women's Studies classrooms we see resurrected the discredited Marxist theory that human beings are "socially constructed," along with the impossible dream that a vanguard can reconstruct them so that they will be transformed into citizens who are pure in mind and politically correct.

The numbing mediocrity of what passes for present academic discourse is a direct consequence of these agendas, which have led to an almost complete lack of intellectual diversity on American faculties in the liberal arts. Political correctness, speech codes, and sensitivity re-education sessions are but pale imitations of their totalitarian originals. The oppressive apparatus of the new campus thought control is justified by the prospect of "eliminating racism, sexism, and classism"—that is, by the same fantastic vision of a liberated future that inspired the Nazi and Communist disasters.

Of course, there are many intellectual orphans of the left who can no longer believe in the Marxist future and have not been able to figure out how a social minority—blacks, gays or women—can achieve a liberation that would be inclusive for all. Towards the liberated future they suspend disbelief. The left's path is a nihilistic option taken by deconstructionists, relativists, and most postmodernists. Is it mere accident that relativism and nihilism should have become favored outlooks of the academic left during the period of socialism's collapse—that is, at the precise moment that the ideas of the left were being refuted by historical events? Relativism and nihilism are, in fact, the ways in which the left has managed to avoid the painful facts of its own past—of its complicity in the great crimes of this century's failed utopias. The "deconstructionist turn" can be seen as the necessary answer to the radical's dilemma: How to avoid the truth of a history that has punctured its social illusion? How to maintain the destructive passions of the radical project?

Utopianism and nihilism, of course, are two sides of the same intellectual coin, as biographically linked as euphoria and depression, as semiotically joined as "nowhere" and "no how." The revolution, as conceived by the secular messianists of the modem left, is really a vision of heaven on earth, of paradise regained. But, as everyone knows, the great creative work of revolution invariably begins as a work of destruction. Marx himself identified the radical's affinity with the Great Destroyer, invoking Mephistopheles's dictum: "All that exists deserves to perish." What is the radical's imperative except the devil's choice? To sever the past from the future, to annihilate what is in exchange for what will be. The Hegelian term for "transformation" (now reformulated as "social change," a value embedded in the official definition of the university's mission) is *Aufhebung*—to deconstruct, to de-structure, to demystify, to dissolve, to demolish, to deny, to defame, to debase—out of something, to create nothing. Nowhere.

And what is this something that is to be denied and destroyed by the contemporary left with its deconstructionist and nihilist agendas, but once again the liberal democratic societies of the capitalist West? *Plus ça change, plus c'est la meme chose.* Is it an accident, then, that the seminal thinkers of the postmodern left are the 20th century's destructive utopians, Communists and Nazis? Or that their 19th-century intellectual godfathers are Nietzsche and Marx? "Every anti-liberal argument influential today," as Stephen Holmes observes, "was vigorously advanced in the writings of European fascists" like Giovanni Gentile and Carl Schmitt, including the critique of "its atomistic individualism, its myth of the pre-social individual, its scanting of the organic, its indifference to community . . . its belief in the primacy of rights, its flight from 'the political,' its decision to give abstract procedures and rules priority over substantive values and commitments, and its hypocritical reliance on the sham of judicial neutrality."[1]

Or, to look at it from the other side, the academic left's positive agendas—"cultural determinism, the reduction of all social relationships to issues of power; the idea that one's identity is centered in one's ethnicity or race; the rejection of the concept of the individual—...all of these ideas," as Gene Veith observes, "are direct echoes of the fascist theorists of the 1930s."[2] Of course, to compare the agendas of the tenured left with the radical projects of Nazis and Communists is to aggrandize the professors with an

---

[1] David Horowitz, "The Left After Communism," in *The Politics of Bad Faith,* Free Press, 1998, p. 33, fn23.
[2] David Horowitz, "The Left After Communism," in *The Politics of Bad Faith,* Free Press, 1998, p. 33, fn 24.

historical potential they mercifully lack. It is true that university intellectuals were among the first groups to enlist with Hitler and Lenin; but America is not Weimar Germany or Czarist Russia, and the current political trend on American campuses is a wave of the past rather than the future.

A more precise image of our present academic malaise was provided by Houston Baker's presidential address to this convention last year. Baker is head of the African American literature department at the University of Pennsylvania, salaried at the level of a corporate executive, and an artfully malicious practitioner of radical chic. Professor Baker's most recent contribution to scholarship is a book that celebrates and defends rap music, including its most violent and gangster-oriented expressions, as one of the premier art forms of the 20th century. Baker is, in fact, the chief academic apologist for a violent and criminal culture that most black leaders—less detached from the actual community of black Americans than himself—have begun to identify and reject as a threat to their children.

The centerpiece of Baker's address, which typically had nothing to do with literary scholarship and everything to do with striking the right political pose, was a diatribe against 300 members of fraternity houses situated on "Locust Walk," a campus thoroughfare at the University of Pennsylvania. According to Professor Baker, "These exclusive inhabitants have made life miserable, violent, and dangerous for women and minorities for decades. To walk through campus ... is to journey through the heart of fraternal darkness where 300 uncivil and privileged white occupants hold a community of 22,000 hostage."

Not content with this ludicrous charge, Baker extended his indictment of the white males on Locust Walk to include the alleged criminal oppression committed by white males generally, against West Philadelphia, the United States, and the world: "The Locust Walk fraternities ... have not only been an enduring source of violence and insult against black, women, Hispanic, gay, and lesbian students in West Philadelphia. They have also been a metonymic [he means synecdochal] inscription at the center of everyday campus life, of American—indeed global—maps of white, male power and privilege.... Locust Walk [is] a devastating emblem of general cartographies of white, male-centered legitimacy and control."

Here, then, was a rococo performance of the professorial mission as understood by today's academic commissars: the demonization of American culture and of the white male minority as a prelude to the work of revolutionary deconstruction. The real crimes of these tenured literati are their betrayals of culture and common sense. More than that, it is their failure to fulfill the obligation of teachers, which is to transmit the hard-won lessons of previous generations. In our time this means the importance of those values and beliefs that have gone into the making of the most successful multi-ethnic society in history—the understanding of and respect for those institutions, laws, and traditions that have made American democracy possible.

The intellectual level of the American university is at the lowest ebb in its 300-year history, less academically free than when colleges were run by religious puritans. The mission of the modern research university was once the disinterested pursuit of knowledge and the education of moral character. Today that mission has been redefined by a generation of radicals, and its tasks have become political indoctrination and cultural deconstruction. The American university is now a major part of the nation's cultural crisis, and we have organizations like the Modern Language Association and its current leadership to thank for that.

2

Campus Repression

H uey Long was once asked whether he thought fascism could ever come to America. His answer was, "Yeah, but it'll come calling itself anti-fascism." America isn't close to such a future, but I couldn't help thinking about Long's comment in connection with an episode that occurred recently at my alma mater. The occasion was a conference at Columbia University scheduled by a conservative organization called Accuracy in Academia. The conference title was "A Place at the Table: Conservative Ideas in Higher Education;" its purpose was to highlight the lack of intellectual diversity in the highly politicized environments of academic institutions like Columbia. Among the announced speakers were two university trustees, Ward Connerly and Candace DeRussy, as well as Dinesh D'Souza, the urbane author of *Illiberal Education.* The ceremonies were to begin with a Friday evening dinner addressed by Connerly, who is currently heading a national civil rights campaign. Connerly was coming off an important victory at the polls November 3, when Washington became the second state (after California) to ban racial preferences. According to Accuracy in Academia president Daniel Flynn, 140 students and professors attended the dinner, which was held in the East Room of Columbia's Faculty House.

But guess who else came to that dinner? The mere presence of Connerly, who expresses ideas the campus left doesn't want to

Originally published as "Fascism By Any Other Name," December 7, 1998, http://www.salon.com/1998/12/07/nc_07horo/

hear, was enough to spur 100 raucous radicals into action. They threw up a picket line outside the dinner and hurled obscenities and racial epithets at those entering the building. Keep in mind that these students, like Columbia itself, had previously welcomed such rabid anti-Semites and racial demagogues as Khalid Muhammad, and had honored unrepentant Communists like Angela Davis, who in a recent appearance at Michigan State told students that the main problem in the world was white people. Columbia not only welcomes such race-haters but pays them handsomely out of student funds to propagate their bigotry.

By contrast, the conservative conference featured no rabble-rousers, no hate agendas, and actually paid the university $11,000 to hold its event on campus. In a healthy academic environment, a university administration might be expected to respond to the outrage that took place at Columbia by disciplining the students who abused the free-speech privileges of others, and who posed a threat to public safety. But these days, such thoughts are far from the minds of university administrators whose profiles, as Peter Collier has observed, are a cross between Saul Alinsky and Neville Chamberlain. In fact the decision taken that very night by Columbia's president, who is also chairman of the Association of American Universities, was exactly the opposite of what it should have been. President George Rupp's solution to the problem created by the presence of the rioters was to ban those who had registered for the conference from attending the sessions the following day. As security guards were placed at the entrance to Columbia's Faculty House, its director, John Hogan, piously explained that the action was wholly consistent with free speech because only the audience members—not the speakers—were subject to the order. It's a nice distinction: You can talk, but nobody will be allowed to listen.

Evicted by the university, the event organizers decided to move the conference to neighboring Morningside Park, but the Ivy League mob followed them there. The first speaker, D'Souza, was shouted down by chants of "Ha! Ha! You're Outside/We Don't Want Your Racist Lies." Demonstrators held up signs that read:

ACCESS DENIED, WE WIN: RACISTS NOT ALLOWED AT COLUMBIA, and THERE'S NO PLACE AT THE TABLE FOR HATE.[1] Which shows just how out of touch the protesters were with their own reality. But then so was the Columbia administration. An official brochure tells visitors that "Columbia University prides itself on being a community committed to free and open discourse and to tolerance of differing views." Orwell couldn't have framed it better.

A distressing aspect of the Columbia incident has been the absence of almost any public commentary on the event from civil libertarians, from public officials or from the nation's press. Imagine the uproar if Randall Terry and his Operation Rescue squads had surrounded a campus abortion clinic and attempted to harass and intimidate those who entered; or if the president of an Ivy League school had ordered his security forces to block the entrance to the clinic, while a college official explained that no one was interfering with the right of anyone to perform an abortion, just barring anyone who wanted one from entering.

The demonstrators had their intended effect. The attack was designed to strike fear into the hearts of the student community, and to further marginalize the ideas of conservatives in the academic world, which it effectively did. One student who registered for the event, but decided not to attend, explained to the organizers, "I did not attend the conference for a number of reasons, the most important being that I did not feel it would be good for my academic future and safety." Elsewhere, similar intimidations have produced similar results. While 55 percent of Californians voted to end racial preferences in the state two years ago, the faculty senate of the University of California at Berkeley, in a public vote, lined up 152–2 in support of such discrimination. Does anyone imagine that the fear of collegial ostracism did not play a role in this otherwise unfathomable ratio?

---

[1] "Twelve Cases of Campus Censorship," Dan Flynn, *FrontPageMag.com*, March 14, 2001, http://archive.frontpagemag.com/readArticle.aspx? ARTID=22229

The incipient fascism that erupted at Columbia did not spring from the heads of a few campus idiots. It was a logical consequence of decades of university pandering to radical intimidators and campus criminals who regularly assault property, persons and reputations, and almost always get what they want. In the last 30 years, under the pressures of the left, campuses have moved a long way toward endorsing the proposition that the ends justify the means. If the cause is considered just, it's all right to ruin reputations with loose charges of racism, sexual harassment or rape. If the goal is racial equality, it's all right to discriminate. If the ideas are correct, it's okay to silence anyone who disagrees. This brownshirt activism is intellectually supported by the spread of anti-liberal ideas in the academic curriculum by the postmodernists of the tenured left. As I have pointed out in a newly published book, *The Politics of Bad Faith*, the most powerful intellectual influences in the academy derive from the intellectual traditions of Marxism and European fascism. Identity politics, coupled with fashionable Nietzschean clichés about the will to power, form the core of current ideological fashions among campus radicals. But what is this if not the fascist politics of the *Volk*? The intellectual left of the '90s, it turns out, owes more to Mussolini than to Marx.

There is even a schism within the left over these issues—between the identity racialists and "postmodern" irrationalists on the one hand, and an older generation of "neo-Enlightenment" leftists who have been manfully defending class analysis and—*mirabile dictu*—reason itself. The most prominent of these critics are Alan Sokal, Todd Gitlin, Eric Hobsbawm and Michael Tomasky. But at the political ground level they are a beleaguered force—Cassandras crying in the wilderness amid the fiercer and outnumbering passions of the young. In the ideological war zone, as the Columbia outrage shows, "identity politics" rules. And identity politics, based on racial and gender categories and on nihilistic assumptions that power is all, culminate in a posture in which the rules of civility and democratic process are dismissed as so much mystification, mere obstacles to the coming social redemption. This is the stuff totalitarian dreams are made of.

Ironically, and despite the continental provenance of much of its *Weltanschauung*, identity radicalism also incorporates a profound element of American mischief. At its heart is an American individualism of the solipsistic, arrogant, community-be-damned kind. The intellectual currents of identity politics began to blossom, after all, during the Me Decade, so it should hardly be surprising if they give expression to a conquering, devouring American ego unrestrained by any social contract. Me, me, my, my—my rights, my pain, my rage *über Alles*. So blinded are these campus bands of the self-righteous and the self-absorbed that they don't even notice the cognitive dissonance in a bunch of privileged white guys and gals hurling racial epithets at a Ward Connerly—in origin a poor black from the segregated South—or at a Dinesh D'Souza—an Indian immigrant to these shores.

All this in the name of social justice for people of color! Huey Long would recognize it for what it is, and so would George Orwell.

3

Post-Modern Professors and Partisan Politics

When the dust has finally settled on this lost year of American politics, there may be consolation in the fact that much of the damage is reparable, and that most of the scars inflicted on the nation will be readily healed. As a new election cycle rolls around, fresh faces will become the focus of public attention. Bill Clinton, along with his seductions and prevarications, will be gone. There will be renewed respect for the privacy rights of public figures. Even Congress will come together and, in a bipartisan moment, undo the Special Prosecutor Law that liberals contrived as a weapon against conservatives and conservatives turned into a weapon—first against liberals, then against themselves. Larry Flynt will slither back under his rock.

But there is one institution, whose corruptions have thrust themselves to the fore in this presidential crisis, whichwill not be so easy to repair. That institution is the American university, which in the midst of the presidential impeachment battle volunteered a battalion of scholars to serve the Clinton cause. As the House Judiciary Committee was gearing up for its impeachment inquiry in October, a full-page political ad appeared in *The New York Times* calling itself "Historians in Defense of the Constitution." The signers declared that in their professional judgment there was no constitutional basis for impeaching the president,

Originally published as "Postmodern Professors and Partisan Politics," January 31, 1999, http://archive.frontpagemag.com/Printable.aspx?ArtId= 24281 and to do so would undermine our political order. The statement was eagerly seized on by the president's congressional defenders, and deployed as a weapon against his congressional accusers. In the none-too-meticulous hands of the pols, the signers became four hundred "constitutional experts" who had exposed the Republicans' attempt at a *"coup d'état."* One of the three organizers of the statement, Professor Sean Wilentz, even appeared before the House Judiciary Committee to warn Republicans ominously that "history will hunt you down" for betraying the American founders. On the day his Senate trial began, the president himself referred reporters to the "constitutional experts" who had gone on record that he should not have been impeached.

The signers of the statement were not constitutional experts at all.[1] One of them, Julian Bond, was not even a historian, though two universities, Maryland and Virginia, had made him a "professor of history." Now head of the NAACP, Bond is a leftist with a failed political career whose university posts were in effect political appointments. Another signer, Henry Louis Gates, is not a historian but a talented essayist and a professor of literature. A third, Orlando Patterson, is a first-rate sociologist. Perhaps the three are affirmative-action signers designed to increase the African American presence on the list. All three, of course, are men of the left. Sean Wilentz is himself a *Dissent* socialist. A second organizer, C. Vann Woodward, is a distinguished historian of 19th- and 20th-century America, but not a historian of the Constitution. The third, Arthur Schlesinger, Jr., is a partisan Democrat who has written adoring books on Andrew Jackson, Franklin Roosevelt and the Kennedy brothers, but not on the American Constitution.

Indeed, the same could be said for almost all the "historians in defense of the constitution"—with a handful of exceptions like Pauline Maier, who has indeed studied and written about the

---

[1]"Historians' Statement on Impeachment," *Washington Post*, October 28, 1998, http://www.washingtonpost.com/wp-srv/politics/special/clinton/stories/petition102898.htm

Founding, and Clinton partisan Garry Wills. Others on the list have even less credentials than the organizers to pontificate on these matters. Todd Gitlin is a professor of sociology and cultural studies, whose only contribution to historical knowledge is a tendentious book justifying the radical Sixties from the perspective of a former president of SDS. Jonathan Weiner is a writer for *The Nation* whose major publication is a book on John Lennon's FBI file. Michael Kazin is another *Nation* writer whose work as a historian is on American populism. John Judis is a *New Republic* editor who wrote a biography of William Buckley and a book on 20th-century conservatives. Jeffrey Herf's expertise is modern German history; Robert Dallek and Bruce Kuklick are 20th-century diplomatic historians who have also written books on Lyndon Johnson and Comiskey Park. Maurice Isserman is another *Nation* regular and a historian of the 20th-century American left with no claim to expertise on the Constitution or the impeachment process. Another signer, Ellen Du Bois, can be taken as typical of a large cohort in what have become the thoroughly politicized humanities. She is a professor of women's history at UCLA and a militant feminist. She is joined as a signer by other zealous feminists whose academic work has been the elaboration of feminist themes, not constitutional issues. These include Gerda Lerner, Linda Gordon, Ruth Rosen, Sara Evans, Christine Stansell (Wilentz's wife) and Alice Kessler-Harris. Two months after the *Times* ad appeared, while the House was pursuing its impeachment vote, a notice was posted on the Internet announcing that Du Bois would be a speaker (along with two other well-known leftists) at a "Reed College Symposium on the Joy of Struggle." The symposium, a presentation of the Reed College Multiculturalism Center, was co-sponsored by the Feminist Union, the Queer Alliance, Earth First, Amnesty at Reed, the Latino/a Student Association, and the Reed student activities office.

To be sure, not all the signers are ideologues, but the statement they have signed reflects the longstanding political corruption of the American academy, and is itself a form of political deception.

By mobilizing 400 historians "in defense of the Constitution," the organizers imply that these well-known left-wing academics are defending the document's original intent. Since when, however, have leftists become defenders of the doctrine original intent? Are any of the signers on record as opposing the loose constructionism of the Warren Court? Were any of the scholars exercised when the Brennan majority inserted a non-existent "right of privacy" into the Constitution to justify its decision in Roe v. Wade? Were any of them outspoken defenders of Judge Robert Bork, the leading theorist of "original intent," when a coalition of political vigilantes set out to destroy his nomination to the Supreme Court and even solicited his video-store purchases to see if he had rented X-rated films? Not only is the answer to all these questions negative, but dozens of the same historians, including organizers Arthur Schlesinger, Jr. and Sean Wilentz, are "veterans of the politicized misuse of history" (as Ramesh Ponnuru put it in a recent *National Review*), having previously signed an equally tendentious "historians' brief" to the Supreme Court in support of abortion rights. Concern for the intent of the Constitution apparently enters these academic hearts only when it can be deployed against Republicans and conservatives. This probably explains why the office address listed at the bottom of the advertisement is the Washington address of People for the American Way, a national lobby for the political left.

Partisan political pronouncements by groups invoking the authority of a profession are treacherous exercises. They misrepresent what scholarship can do, such as deciding questions that are inherently controversial. More importantly, they cast a chill on academic discourse by suggesting there is a historians' party line. When Jesse Lemisch, a notable left-wing historian, tried to organize a counter-statement supporting the impeachment of Clinton over his "wag-the-dog" policy in the Gulf, he received vicious e-mails from his academic colleagues.

The kind of politicization reflected in these episodes is, in fact, a fairly recent development in academic life. Its origin can be traced to a famous battle at the annual meeting of the American Historical Association in 1969. At that meeting, the Radical Caucus, led by Staughton Lynd and Arthur Waskow, attempted to have the AHA pass an official resolution calling for American withdrawal from the Vietnam War and an end to the "repression" of the criminal gang known as the Black Panther Party. Opposition to the resolution was led by radical historian Eugene Genovese and by liberal historian H. Stuart Hughes. Four years earlier, Genovese had become a national cause célèbre when he publicly declared his support for the Communist Vietcong. He nonetheless opposed the radical call for such a resolution as a "totalitarian" threat to the profession and to the intellectual standards on which it was based, since it imposed a political orthodoxy on scholarship. H. Stuart Hughes, who had been a peace candidate for Congress, joined in asserting that any anti-war resolution would "politicize" the AHA, and in urging the members to reject it.

Hughes and Genovese narrowly won the battle but eventually lost the war. The AHA joined other professional academic associations in becoming institutions of the political left. In a *Nation* editorial ("Scholars on the Left," February 1, 1999), Jon Wiener, one of the signers of the historians' statement, boasted that "three members of the *Nation* family" had just been elected to head three powerful professional associations—the American Historical Association, the Organization of American Historians, and the Modern Language Association—with a combined membership of 54,000 academics.

Eric Foner is president-elect of the American Historical Association. He is the scion of a family of well-known American Communists, a supporter of the Rosenbergs, a sponsor of Communist Party stalwarts Angela Davis and Herbert Aptheker, a life-long member of the radical left and, recently, an organizer of the secretaries' union at Columbia and the would-be architect of an alliance between intellectuals and the working class. David Montgomery, the new president of the Organization of American Historians, is described in *The Nation* as "a factory worker, union organizer, and Communist militant in St. Paul in the Fifties ... Montgomery's ties to labor remain strong: He was active in the Yale clerical workers strike and other campus and union struggles." Edward Said, president of the Modern Language Association, is a former member of the Palestine Liberation Organization's governing council and was the most prominent apologist in America for PLO terrorism until he fell out with Yassir Arafat over the Oslo peace accords, which Said regarded as a "sellout" to the Israeli imperialists. A living legend in the leftist academy, Said's overrated work is little more than warmed-over Marxism.[2]

That is the bad news. The good news is more modest. The historians' statement was not an official resolution of either the AHA or the OAH, and neither Montgomery nor Eric Foner signed it. When asked why, Foner said he did not think it was appropriate for him to do so because of his position as head of an organization representing 15,000 members, many of whom might not agree with its sentiments. That was the right idea, but unfortunately he was unable to extend it to the problem at hand. Thus he did not think a volatile political statement by 400 professors, invoking the authority of their profession, was itself inappropriate, even though almost all of them lacked professional competence in the subject at hand.

The deeper problem exposed by this episode is the serious absence of intellectual diversity on university faculties. Such diversity would provide a check on the hubris of academic activists like Wilentz and his co-signers. The fact is that leftists in the university, through decades of political hiring and promotion, and through systematic intellectual intimidation, have virtually driven conservative thought from the halls of academe. It is a fact that a Marxist ideologue like Angela Davis can be officially invited

---

[2]Keith Windschuttle, "Edward Said's 'Orientalism' Revisited," The New Criterion, January 1999, http://www.newcriterion.com/articles.cfm/ Edward-Said-s—ldquo-Orientalism-rdquo—revisited-2937; Also, Ibn Warraq, Defending the West: A Critique of Edward Said's Orientalism, Prometheus, 2007

to speak at a quality institution like Brandeis and be paid $10,000 for her effort, while a Jeanne Kirkpatrick, invited to the same institution, was asked by administrators not to come because they were unable to guarantee her safety. It is a fact that Columbia University will host an official reception honoring Herbert Aptheker, a Communist Party apparatchik and its chief apologist for the Soviet rape of Hungary, but will close down a conference featuring University of California trustee Ward Connerly because of his politically incorrect view that racial preferences violate the Constitutional guarantee of equal rights before the law.[3]

---

[3]See chapter 2 above.

4

My Visit to Bates

Spring is the season when high school graduates, parents in tow, set out on their tours of ivied campuses in search of the right investment for their education dollar. This April I made a parallel tour. Speaking at colleges in Chicago, Boston, Lewiston, New Haven, Quinnipiac, Houston, Dallas and College Station, Texas, I conducted my own hands-on survey to see how American colleges have changed since I was an undergraduate in the 1950s. Or, to be more precise, to check conclusions I had already drawn about these matters on the basis of previous trips I had made to over 100 campuses in the last decade.

When I was an undergraduate, the political censors attacked the university from without. Now they were entrenched in university faculties and administrations. Then, the university defined itself as an institution dedicated "to the disinterested pursuit of knowledge." Now, every term of that definition is under siege by post-modernists and deconstructionists who have become the new academic establishment and have redefined the university as an institution dedicated "to social change." That is one reason the academy, once a redoubt of intellectual freedom and cutting-edge discourse, has become the butt of snickering jokes about political correctness, and a cornucopia of Kafkaesque tales about bureaucratic censorship and administrative obtuseness.

Originally published as "Enemy of the people," Salon.com, April 26, 1999, http://www.salon.com/1999/04/26/bates/

In Chicago I encountered a very bright second-year graduate student enrolled in the famous Committee on Social Thought program. He had previously completed four years of undergraduate work at Harvard, where he had never heard the name "Friedrich von Hayek." In a way, it was the most shocking anecdotal evidence I retrieved in my forays into the halls of learning. It's not just that Hayek won a Nobel Prize for economics in 1973; or that he is the author of a classic text of the modern era, *The Road to Serfdom*, which was required reading for students at Columbia when I went there in the 1950s; or that he is one of the three or four greatest social thinkers of the 20th century. Any of these would have been enough to make such a student's ignorance dismaying. But Hayek is also one of the handful of social scientists who demonstrated more than 60 years ago why the socialist system could not work and, thus, why it would eventually collapse, as it did in 1989.

It was not the first time I had encountered such ignorance of Hayek or conservative intellectuals on university campuses, nor was it accidental. It was a direct consequence of the tenured left's dominance of liberal-arts institutions after the 1960s—its politicization of the curriculum and the faculty-hiring process. This was the subject of the lectures I gave at the campuses I visited.

At Bates College in Maine, for example, I spoke in defense of the following proposition: "The Intellectual Tradition of the Left is Bankrupt and Its Hegemony at Bates Is an Abuse of Academic Freedom."[1] In a preview of the situation I would encounter at this pricey liberal-arts college, I received an e-mail from a professor at Smith College, a comparable institution, when I challenged the faculty there about such academic abuses: "I would gladly crush you in a debate on students' so-called 'right not to be ideologically indoctrinated in the classroom,'" Professor E. C. Graf wrote me. "Your phrase 'students' academic freedom' is already a laughable oxymoron, as if students ever had such a thing or ever should.... As for

---

[1]"Best-selling Author to Discuss Popular Culture at Bates," *Bates News*, January 2, 1999, http://www.bates.edu/news/1999/01/02/david-horowitz/

admitting that I 'indoctrinate' my students instead of teaching them, tell me my friend, when has there ever been a difference?"

In a rare departure from the norm, I received an invitation to Bates from the dean of the College, who informed me shortly after introducing himself that he was a "leftist." Out of 100 or so colleges I have spoken at in the last several years, it should be said, I have only been officially invited to four and never by a faculty member. The college administrations will roll out no red carpets, nor provide honoraria or airfares for a conservative like me, as they will for my former political comrades on the left; nor will faculty members offer credit to students for attending my lectures, a common practice for left-wing visitors as well. Even on this visit to Bates, where I had to take my hat off to the dean who invited me, my reception proved to be a little unusual.

When I arrived at the airport in Portland the night before my scheduled evening lecture, a university-provided driver picked me up and deposited me at the door of an apartment that the university had also made available. But there the hospitality ended. Until my evening lecture the next day, no one called or greeted me, and I was left to my own devices. In this odd interregnum, I found myself wondering whether the dean who invited me was even going to contact me before my lecture. As the noon hour approached, I decided to drop in on the dean to thank him for my invitation and inquire if he would like to have lunch. When I got there, a secretary informed me that he was unavailable. Instead, a student escort was provided to take me to the school cafeteria, where I ate by myself. Eventually the dean did show up to take me back to his office. He was entirely cordial, while volunteering that he had taken some criticism from members of his faculty for inviting me. (Later, when I had returned to California, I received a somewhat testy letter from him because of a full-page ad I had run in the school paper on the day of my lecture, which he had not seen at the time. The ad announced that the dean was inviting students to attend my evening talk, and continued with the following headline: "Marxism Is a Resurgent Doctrine in the Former Soviet

Empire and Apparently on American Campuses Too." Below this headline was a reminder to students that the false doctrines of Marxism had led to the deaths of 100 million people. Below that was list of books written by authors like Thomas Sowell, David Gress and myself, offered as antidotes to what students were being taught by their professors at Bates.

In all fairness the dean had a point, which I readily conceded. I had undoubtedly made his life more difficult. Still, his anguish was just another indication of the pressure he was under from his leftist faculty because of my visit. How far left? Well, in the Bates catalogue, one course listed was "The Cuban Revolution: Problems and Prospects," which included a two-week on-site visit to Cuba's police state. Aviva Chomsky, daughter of the MIT professor, had taught the course until she left Bates for a more "working-class" school, as the dean informed me when I asked.

Since I had a whole day available before my scheduled talk, I decided to sit in on one of Bates' political science courses to check my general impressions of the academic curriculum. It was a course about industrialized societies. I asked students for directions to the building in which political science courses were taught, and went to the department office on the ground floor. I was informed that I could audit the class if the professor didn't object. Accordingly, I approached the professor as she was entering her classroom and asked permission to attend.

She was an Indian woman in her thirties and spoke with an English accent. She seemed pleased at the prospect of having an adult in her audience, and did not hesitate before inviting me in. All through the class hour she smiled at me, talked in my direction, and even encouraged me to answer a question when the rest of the class could not. She taught from a single text, and it was obvious from her remarks that the class consisted in reading through the text a chapter at a time. In the college courses I had attended at Columbia some forty years ago, there was rarely an "official" text for the course, and if there was one, my professors seldom referred to it. Any text included was more as an aid to students. The real text for the course was the professor's lecture notes, and students were expected to read several books, usually by leading contributors to the subject and usually with strongly differing views. A political-science course devoted to modern industrial societies, as this one was, would have had required readings by Weber, Marx, Durkheim, Tönnies, and even Hayek.

In this course, however, there was a single 600-page text called *Modernity*, edited by the well-known English leftist, Stuart Hall. Like Hall, every contributor to the text was a Marxist. There was no lecture. The teacher guided the students page by page, paragraph by paragraph, through the textbook she had assigned. She taught her class as though it were a science course, based on an accepted body of knowledge, where a single explanatory text is the norm. Except that this norm was the discredited intellectual tradition of Marxism. I asked the student next to me what the acronym ACS, staring out of the page of her text, stood for. She said, "Advanced Capitalist Society." I noticed another acronym, MIBTC, and was told it stood for "Military-Industrial-Bureaucratic-Technocratic-Complex." The teacher was admonishing the students to pay attention to the main points in the authors' arguments and to take note of the way they supported their conclusions, whether by references to authorities or facts. Then she had the class break up into small groups, each of which was to apply this technique to a different section and assess whether the author of that section satisfactorily proved his or her point.

My group was assigned a section on "American militarism." The question put by the text was whether militarism—its existence was assumed—had emerged out of the capitalist economic structures of ACSs, or whether it became systemic only after it had emerged. No question was raised as to whether this was a justifiable description of American society. One young woman in my little group wondered aloud whether the author—merely by pointing out that cell phones made by AT&T were used by the army in the Gulf War—had actually proved that there was a "Military-Industrial-Bureaucratic-Technocratic-Complex." I stepped out of my role as observer to tell her to hold onto that thought.

When I was able to buy a copy of *Modernity* and read it, I found that the passage about militarism was typical rather than exceptional. The viewpoints in the text ranged from classical Marxism to feminist Marxism to post-modernist Marxism. No opposing views were introduced except to be refuted. In the book's index there was not a single reference to the name Hayek. On the other hand, there were plenty of discussions of obscure Marxists like Nicholas Poulantzas, who wrote a book on the "ruling class" in the 1960s before jumping out of a window at age 29.

After the class, I went up to the teacher and said that I admired her pedagogy in advising the students that she wasn't there to tell them *what* to think, but to teach them *how.* On the other hand, I thought that assigning a single text written only by Marxists worked at cross-purposes with that goal. The smile disappeared from her face. She said: "Well, they get the other side from the newspapers." Education like this costs the Bates' students' parents $30,000 a year in tuition alone.

This was not to be the end of my auditing adventure. After I left her class, the lecturer complained about me to the dean, and the dean called me at my apartment to tell me in an irate voice that I should have gone through his office if I wanted to sit in on a class. I explained that I was unable to find him; that the departmental office had encouraged me; and that the lecturer herself had welcomed me into her classroom until my question caused her to have a change of heart. My words failed to appease him. Obviously she had given him a hard time, and there was no way he was going to sympathize with me or my view of what had transpired. I realized that this intimidation was similar to the intimidation over the ad, and the criticism he had received for inviting me at all. It served a purpose, which was to minimize the contact that professors and students might risk with conservatives like myself—even conservatives invited to campus by their dean.

That, no doubt, why the little reception with faculty he arranged for me before my talk was confined to the handful of older professors at Bates who shared my views, or at least were not ideologically repelled by them and who were protected by tenure. I admired their courage, nonetheless, in attending my event, while cognizant of the fact that even in the darkest days of the McCarthy era, Communist faculty were not so threatened with ostracism by their peers.

I gave my speech to about 60 students, among whom seven or eight formed a very unhappy contingent of campus leftists. Had I not been officially invited, it is more than likely that even these few would not have been there. I spoke about the religious ideas that had led to the destruction of 100 million people in our century, killed by progressive missionaries in order to realize their impossible dreams. I described revolutionary leftists as modern Manichaeans, who believed that the world was ruled by alien powers of darkness. Even democracies were not free societies but were dominated by these powers, which Marx called "ruling classes" against whom those who believed in social justice were permanently at war.

Even though these Marxist fantasies had led to unprecedented ruin for all the societies that eventually came under their sway, their currency was evident throughout the Bates curriculum. Now the alien powers were called the "patriarchy" or the "white male oligarchy" or, more obliquely, "institutional racism." But they were just as fantastic, and belief in them inspired passions potentially as destructive as the passions of traditional Marxists. No one, I said, was oppressed in America, except perhaps children by their abusive parents.

I give the leftist students credit for waiting until the end of my talk to vent their outrage over the blasphemies I had uttered. One young woman got so emotional she decided to leave the building to save herself from further contamination. Another young woman stood up, and with tremendous urgency sputtered: "But what about the hierarchies? You didn't mention the hierarchies!" She was referring, of course, to the hierarchies of race, gender and class that were the staples of her Bates education. Her politicized professors had undoubtedly schooled her in the idea that these hierarchies oppressed people of color, women, and wage-slaves in America. In America! In the year 1999!

Of course I had actually mentioned the hierarchies (though not by name), dismissing them as left-wing illusions, no more substantial than the idea that somewhere behind the Hale-Bopp comet a space ship was waiting to take the enlightened to heaven. So I tried another tack.

"Let me ask you this question," I said. "Where do you put Oprah Winfrey in your hierarchies?" I knew that Oprah Winfrey was at the bottom of any oppressive hierarchy chain as conceived by leftists. As a woman born in Mississippi to a black sharecropper, she had been sexually abused, the oppressed of the oppressed. But Oprah had risen by dint of her own intelligence, effort, and talent to become a mother-confessor and authority figure to millions of lower-middle-class white females who had never been through a sensitivity-training course. The fortune she was able to amass through these efforts cast her among the super-rich of America's ruling class as one of the *Forbes* 400, with a net worth of $550 million before the recent stock-market boom.

"She's a token," the young woman said.

"Sorry, she's not a token," I replied. "Cornel West is a token."

I chose Cornel West, an intellectual of modest talents, whose skin color had catapulted him into academic stardom with a six-figure income at Harvard. Cornel West was a token because the university is a feudal institution run somewhat like the Communist Party, where the elect raise people up by exercising the same kind of arbitrary *droit de seigneur* that was the privilege of rulers in pre-democratic and pre-capitalist times. There was no tenure committee or central committee, however, to lift Oprah out of the societal mud. No one to say to Phil Donahue, the reigning afternoon talk show sovereign, "Move over, Phil, we need a person of color to put in prime time for diversity's sake." The *earned* power Oprah Winfrey has been able to acquire refutes every cliché of the political left. Her psychological power over her mainly white audience has made her the first individual in history able to create a best-seller by fiat and the millions in revenues that go with it. She is a filmmaking industry in herself. She has shown that the barriers of race, class and gender are not insuperable obstacles to advancement in America, any more than residual anti-Semitism or prejudice against the Irish create impenetrable "hierarchies" of oppression to bar those groups' ascent.

But such a perspective is politically incorrect at places like Bates, so dangerous that the faculty commissars are constantly on guard to prevent students from risky contact with conservative ideas.

5

Ann Coulter at Cornell

L ast month an episode occurred at Cornell University which the world took little note of, but which speaks volumes about the state of higher education and of an academic culture that is anything but. On April 30, Ann Coulter—best-selling conservative author, lawyer and well-known TV commentator— returned to her *alma mater* to speak about the Confederate flag controversy. She came as the guest of the Cornell College Republicans and *The Cornell Review*, a conservative student paper that she had helped to found seventeen years earlier.

Cornell is one of the most segregated institutions in the United States. Its black students live in all-black dorms—a privilege officially denied to other ethnicities and races at the school. Most black students attend classes at the Africana Studies Center at the north end of campus, where they never have to mix with the general student population. At Africana, they are taught by a faculty infused with the humors of political correctness—anti-white racism and a pseudo-Marxist contempt for American institutions and principles. Here they learn that "only whites can be racist" because only whites have power, and that slavery in Africa was not really bad because it wasn't "capitalist" and the slaveholders were black.

The politicization of the academic curriculum at Cornell began in 1969 with the most disgraceful occurrence in the history of

Originally published as "Ann Coulter at Cornell," May 21, 2001, http://archive.frontpagemag.com/Printable.aspx?ArtId=24430; http://www.salon.com/2001/05/21/coulter_4/

American higher education. That year, black radicals armed with shotguns took over the Cornell administration building.[1] From this high ground, they issued a set of demands as a ransom for not carrying their mayhem further. In a denouement that more than any other event may be said to have given birth to the contemporary politicized university, the Cornell administration capitulated to the terrorists' demands to set their own curriculum and appoint their own professors.

Since then, the triumph of the political left at Cornell has been challenged only via pin-pricks administered by the conservative *Cornell Review* and the sporadic appearances of conservative speakers such as Coulter. Unlike leftists who are invited to speak at Cornell, Coulter's appearance had to be underwritten by outside sources—in this case by the Washington-based Young America's Foundation, since the student funds available for such programs at Cornell as elsewhere are firmly in the grip of the political left. Faculty and student conservatives at Cornell—as at other elite campuses—are routinely subject to harassment, persecution and an insecurity of place and employment completely unknown to other minorities, including gays and blacks. Out of more than a thousand members of the Cornell faculty, for example, there are only three openly conservative professors available to sponsor organizations like the College Republicans and *The Cornell Review.* Such sponsorship is a requirement for receiving student funds. When I spoke at Cornell six years ago, one of the three faculty conservatives, a botany professor, was under siege by both the administration and the student left—barred from his own classes and waiting to see if he would be fired—for expressing a politically incorrect opinion on the subject of homosexuality.

The faculty sponsor of *The Cornell Review* who introduced Coulter was Jeremy Rabkin, the same conservative professor who had introduced me on my visit. At every "liberal" campus in

---

[1] Donald Alexander Downs, *Cornell '69: Liberalism and the Crisis of the American University,* Cornell University Press, 1999

America there tends to be a lonely and courageous intellectual like Rabkin available for this duty. Harvey Mansfield famously fulfills this role at Harvard. In the ten years that I have been visiting college campuses, not a single so-called liberal, of the 100 or so with which I am directly familiar, has shown the Voltairean spine to actually stand up and defend the conservative students' right to hear speakers of their choice by offering to sponsor their organizations and events. Either respect for basic democratic principle is so low among the academic elite, or fear of career consequences from the left so great, that this simple act of decency never seems to happen.

In normal circumstances, a conservative coming to speak to the two conservative groups at Cornell would be ignored by campus media and silently boycotted by the other officially recognized and funded political student organizations, of which there are many—all of them on the left. Flyers announcing the talk would be torn from campus bulletin boards; leftist professors would advise their students to avoid the occasion; and the event itself would be attended by a small contingent of those willing to be publicly identified as conservatives and to accept the social and educational consequences of that fact. But this spring—if my own tour of a dozen campuses is any indication—it has become almost obligatory for campus radicals to attend these events and attempt to obstruct them in the name of progressive ideas. Since Coulter's topic was the Confederate flag, which had become a national controversy, a confrontation of some sort was inevitable. Previously Coulter had written a column on the flag which pointed out that slavery had existed longer under the Stars and Stripes than under the Stars and Bars—that the flag symbolized more than the slavery cause, and that, in any case, there were no visible pro-slavery advocates around to make leftist concerns about the implications of its presence valid.[2]

---

[2]Ann Coulter, "A Confederacy of Dunces," February 1, 2000, *Jewish World Review*, http://www.jewishworldreview.com/cols/coulter020100.asp

These mildly expressed views were a call to arms to the Cornell vigilantes. Even before her arrival, campus Democrats had
already sent out a flyer calling on students to protest Coulter's
talk, while another flyer from the more ardent left aggressively
linked her with Adolf Hitler and the neo-Nazi David Duke. The
link was a series of anti-affirmative action quotes attributed to
each.

Like other college administrations, the one at Cornell is hyper-
sensitive about perceived slights directed towards ethnic minorities or the political left, but turns a blind eye to these groups'
efforts to demonize conservative students and shut down their
side of the debate. As at other schools, Cornell's administrators are
not at all oblivious to the threat the left represents to civil dialogue and free speech, and thus assigns security police to watch
over events like the Coulter speech. University administrators do
not want an incident, such as an injured speaker, which might
cause bad publicity and alert a wider public to the little tyrannies
the administration allows to thrive on campus. At the same time,
administrators have no intention of reining in these campus hooli-
gans or restoring an atmosphere appropriate to an institution of
higher learning. The police may remove obstructers and thugs, but
the administration will not discipline them. It knows the organizations and individuals who are the source of the problem but will
take no action against them because they are either ethnic minorities or "progressives" or both. This tolerance has the effect
of encouraging the delinquent behavior that requires the
police, while keeping conservatives a harassed minority in campus
community.[3]

Coulter was heckled by the left throughout her speech, but in a
way that she found peculiar. "It was not arguments they were
reacting to. I could have been talking to a stone wall, so closed—or
empty—were these young minds. It was isolated words that set

---

[3]For details, see my *Uncivil Wars: The Controversy Over Reparations For
Slavery*, 2001

them off." It was not a confrontation of views, but an encounter between a witch-hunting mentality and its intended target. The left is faced with a serious problem when it actually goes into these battles, because its radical paradigm requires a fight with "white supremacists"—hence the flyers with references to Hitler and Duke. But once leftists arrive at the scene of battle, it is quickly apparent that there are no actual white supremacists present; certainly not conservatives like Ann Coulter. Consequently, it becomes necessary to invent them or—better—to *discover* them, hiding behind the masks of conservative tolerance and compassion. Congressman Charles Rangel once described Republicans as supporting tax cuts instead of poll taxes and wearing suits instead of sheets, conveniently forgetting it was his own party that was the political home of slavers and Klansmen. The same mentality prompts leftists to complain about "subtle forms of racism" when there are no obvious bigots to point to. And to play "gotcha" with isolated words that only a leftist would regard as culpable. One anti-Coulter outburst was triggered in mid-sentence while she was pointing out that European slave traders bought Africans who were already enslaved: "It wasn't as if the traders ran into the jungle and kidnapped their victims." The word "jungle" triggered an audience uproar. *Jungle? Aha! We knew, behind the smile, you were a racist all the time.*

Coulter managed to make it to the question period, but only just. During the discussion, the podium and stage were pelted with oranges while one champion of the people after another got up to talk about racist oppression they knew about personally. Victimhood is perhaps the only thing these students have actually been taught in college. From orientation on, minority students are told: you are oppressed; you are victims. This is their romance and their power. It is not something they are about to give up. One man in the audience stood up and, after ranting about his "slave ancestors," lunged at the platform where Coulter stood. The police managed to grab him just before he reached her, and removed him. The lunatic was white, his slave relatives allegedly Scots. Finally, an older black man got up and began a rant he refused to end. Campus police are not about to arrest older black men; they risk being photographed and subsequently denounced as a "racist Gestapo," a practice common among campus radicals. So, as the rant continued, Coulter simply left.

6

Missing Diversity on Campus

In the fall of 2001, I spoke at a large public university in the eastern United States. It was one of more than 30 colleges I had visited during the school year and, as usual, my invitation had come from a small group of campus conservatives who also put together a modest dinner for me at a local restaurant. Our conclave reflected the current state of conservatism in the American university. Not only were our numbers small; there were no deans or university administrators present, and only one professor. Open conservatives are an isolated and harassed minority on today's college campuses, where they enjoy little respect and almost no support from institutional powers.

Although I am a nationally known public figure, the author of books that have been best-sellers and nominated for a national book award, a Fox News contributor and one of America's 100 leading "public intellectuals" according to a recent study of the subject, the absence of administration representatives at these events is wholly predictable.[1] In nearly 200 campus appearances, I can think of only two exceptions—my appearances at Bates University and at Old Dominion. When I spoke at the University of Michigan to 1,000 students, there were three university vice presidents in the balcony, but none thought to introduce himself to

---

Originally published as "Missing Diversity On America's Campuses," September 03, 2002, http://archive.frontpagemag.com/ReadArticle.aspx? ArtId=24464
[1]Richard A. Posner, *Public Intellectuals: A Study Of Decline*, Harvard University Press, 2002

me. Occasionally a professor will attend these dinners, but rarely more than one. My experience as a conservative is not unique. On the other hand, if I were an anti-American radical like Angela Davis, deans of the college would wait on me and professors would confer academic credits on students for attending my appearances. On many occasions my speech would be an official campus event.

Among those invited to the dinner was a silver-haired history professor who served as the faculty sponsor of the club inviting me. This man represented a dying breed of faculty conservatives who had become tenured in an era when hiring committees were not yet applying a litmus test to exclude those whose political views were not suitably to the left. The transformation that followed was succinctly described a decade ago by the distinguished intellectual historian, John P. Diggins, at an annual meeting of the American Studies Association in Costa Mesa, California. Diggins told the assembled academics: "When my generation of liberals was in control of university faculties in the Sixties, we opened the doors to the hiring of radicals in the name of diversity. We thought you would do the same. But you didn't. You closed the doors behind you."

To illustrate how ingrained the new attitude has become and how casually it is deployed to justify the suppression of conservative ideas, let me cite an e-mail I received from a professor at Emory University. The professor was responding to an article I had written about the abuse of conservative students by administrators at Vanderbilt and the exclusion of conservatives from the Vanderbilt faculty. He was not especially radical, yet he did not have so much as a twinge of conscience at the picture I drew of a faculty cleansed of conservative opinions. "Why do I and other academics have little shame here?" he asked and then answered the question: "We are not the only game in the marketplace of ideas. We are competing with journalism, entertainment, churches, political lobbyists, and well-funded conservative think tanks."

In other words, academics like this Emory professor see themselves not primarily as educators, but as agents of an "adversary culture" at war with the world outside the university. But the university was not created—and is not funded—to *compete* with other institutions. It is designed to train employees, citizens and leaders of those institutions, and to endow them with appropriate knowledge and skills. Because of its strategic function as an educator of elites, however, it can be effectively used to subvert other institutions too. There is an organic connection, for example, between the political bias of the university and the political bias of the press. It was not until journalists became routinely trained in university schools of journalism that mainstream media began to mirror the perspectives of the adversary culture. Universities have become a power base of the political left, and the Emory professor's argument only makes sense, really, from the vantage of someone so alienated from his own society as to *want* to subvert it. His suggestion that universities somehow balance conservative think tanks of the wealthy is patently absurd. "Well-funded" conservative think tanks may stand in intellectual opposition to subversive agendas, but don't have captive student audiences they are supposed to be educating. Moreover, there are no wealthy think tanks that can compete with Harvard, its centuries of tradition, its thousands of faculty members, its government subsidies and its $18 *billion*, tax-free endowment.

When academics are imbued with a sense of social mission that requires ideological cohesion, the result is inevitably an intellectual monolith. How monolithic? Last spring I organized college students to investigate the voting registrations of university professors at more than a dozen institutions of higher learning. The students used primary registrations to determine party affiliation. Here is a representative sample:

- At the University of Colorado—a public university in a Republican state—94 percent of the liberal arts faculty whose party registrations could be established were Democrats and only 4 percent Republicans. Out of 85 professors of English who registered to vote, zero were Republicans. Out of 39 professors of history—one. Out of 28 political scientists—two.

How Republican is Colorado? Its governor, two senators and four out of six congressmen are Republican. There are 200,000 more registered Republicans in Colorado than there are Democrats. But at the state-funded University of Colorado, Republicans are a fringe group.

- At Brown University, 94.7 percent of the professors whose political affiliations showed up in primary registrations last year were Democrats; only 5.3 percent were Republicans. Only three Republicans could be found on the Brown liberal arts faculty. Zero in the English Department, zero in the History Department, zero in the Political Science Department, zero in the Africana Studies Department, and zero in the Sociology Department.
- At the University of New Mexico, 89 percent of the professors were Democrats, 7 percent Republicans and 4 percent Greens. Of 200 professors, ten were Republicans, but zero in the Political Science Department, zero in the History Department, zero in the Journalism Department and only one each in the Sociology, English, Women's Studies and African American Studies Departments.
- At the University of California, Santa Barbara, 97 percent of the professors were Democrats, with 1.5 percent Greens and an equal 1.5 percent Republicans. Only one Republican professor could be found.
- At the University of California, Berkeley, of the 195 professors whose affiliations showed up, 85 percent were Democrats, 8 percent Republicans, 4 percent Greens and 3 percent American Independent Party, Peace and Freedom Party and Reform Party voters. Out of 54 professors in the History Department, only one Republican could be found; out of 28 Sociology professors zero, out of 57 English professors zero, out of 16 Women's Studies professors zero, out of nine African American Studies professors zero, out of six Journalism professors zero.

- At the University of California, Los Angeles, of the 157 professors whose political affiliations showed up, 93 percent were Democrats, only 6.5 percent were Republicans.
- At the University of North Carolina, the *Daily Tar Heel* conducted its own survey of eight departments and found that, of the professors registered with a major political party, 91 percent were Democrats while only 9 percent were Republicans.

In an ideological universe in which university administrators claim that diversity is their priority, these are striking facts. How can students get a good education if they're only being told half the story? The answer is, they can't. The present academic monolith is an offense to the spirit of free inquiry. The hiring practices that have led to the present situation are discriminatory and illegal. They violate the Constitution, which prevents hiring and firing on the basis of political ideas, and patronage laws that bar state institutions from servicing a particular political party. Yet university administrators have not shown any inclination to address this problem, or to reform the practices that perpetuate it. Nor have self-identified "liberal" professors, who are themselves the source of the problem. If there is to be reform, it will have to come from other quarters.

7

Wake Up America:
My Visit to Vanderbilt

Vanderbilt University is a venerable institution and the premier seat of higher learning in the state of Tennessee. Like every one of the nearly 200 colleges I have visited in the last ten years, Vanderbilt has long ceased to be a liberal institution in the meaningful sense of that term. In the hiring of its faculty and in the design of its liberal arts curriculum, in the conduct of its communal dialogue and in the shape of its public square, Vanderbilt is for all intents and purposes an intellectual monolith—an ideological subsidiary of the Democratic Party and the far side of the political left.

No aspect of the university system exposes this bias as readily as the process by which tribunes of the nation's culture wars are invited to speak at college forums. When students seek to invite speakers, only authorized groups with faculty sponsors can extend invitations. Moreover, they must come up with funds to underwrite travel and lodging arrangements, along with an honorarium that can range from $1,000 to $20,000 or more, depending on the speaker's celebrity. If the speaker is a political activist, these appearances can provide a substantial supplement to personal income and a significant subsidy to the speaker's political cause.

I spoke at 23 universities this spring, appearing at Vanderbilt on April 8. The invitation came from a conservative student group called Wake Up America, which was formed three years earlier for

Originally published as "Wake Up America: My Visit To Vanderbilt," September 4, 2002, http://archive.frontpagemag.com/ReadArticle.aspx?ArtId=22923

the purpose of bringing speakers to campus. Despite its express purpose, Wake Up America has only managed to put on four events in the three years of its existence. This is not because of a scarcity of conservative speakers ready to speak on college campuses. It is because Vanderbilt University refuses to provide funds to Wake Up America to underwrite its aspirations. Vanderbilt's attitude towards Wake Up America is in fact anything but supportive. Vanderbilt officials have treated the group like an alien presence from the moment of its conception.

When Wake Up America's founder, Dan Eberhart, approached the assistant vice chancellor and head of Student Life, Michelle Rosen, to gain approval for his group, she told him: "There is no need for your organization because a student group already exists, namely the Speakers Committee." This was a transparent subterfuge. The assistant vice chancellor knew that the Speakers Committee was a partisan student group dedicated to bringing left-wing speakers to the Vanderbilt campus. James Carville, Ralph Nader, Kweisi Mfume and Gloria Steinem have been recent visitors, courtesy of the Committee. These are pricey celebrities, and the Vanderbilt student activities fund has granted the Speakers Committee $50,000 a year in the past to make their wish list a reality. This year the Student Finance Committee, which administers the fund, has increased the Speakers Committee grant to $63,000. By contrast, in its entire three-year existence, Wake Up America has never been granted a single cent to bring conservatives to the Vanderbilt campus.

The Speakers Committee is actually only one of an array of left-wing groups that are the beneficiaries of Vanderbilt funds, which can be used to subsidize on-campus visits by political figures. In a recent press release announcing the disbursement $1,143,963 to student groups, the Student Finance Committee defined its purpose in these noble words: "to fund activities that will have broad campus appeal and that will guarantee a diversity of activities within our community." Not surprisingly, a glance at the roster of funded groups reveals that this diversity principle does not extend to the realm of ideas.

While Wake Up America receives no funds, the Vanderbilt Feminists receive $10,620; the Vanderbilt Lambda Association (a group of gay leftists) receives $12,000; the (left-wing) Middle Eastern Student Association receives $4,700; the (left-wing) Black Students Alliance receives $12,400; the (left-wing) Organization of Black Graduate & Professional Students receives $13,120; the (left-wing) Vanderbilt African Student Association receives $1,500; the Vanderbilt Association of (left-wing) Hispanic Students receives $14,200; and the (left-wing) Vanderbilt Asian American Student Association gets $15,000.

How do I know that these ostensibly ethnic associations are left-wing? I know it as a result of my inquiries at Vanderbilt, and by my own broad range of experience with similar groups on campuses across the country. They are not only political and to the left, but they are more often than not at the extreme end of that spectrum as well. For example, when I spoke at Denison College in Ohio a few weeks before my Vanderbilt appearance, I had been preceded by Angela Davis, who was Denison's official Martin Luther King Day speaker the month before, sponsored by the recognized ethnic minority organizations on campus. Davis is a life-long Communist apparatchik who received a Lenin Prize from the East German police state during the Cold War, and remained a party member after the fall of the Berlin Wall. The official Denison website, on the other hand, describes her as "known internationally for her ongoing work to combat all forms of oppression in the United States and abroad." The university closed its offices during her speech so that the entire campus could hear her unreconstructed Marxist views.

My appearance at Michigan State had been preceded by columnist Julianne Malveaux, who had been that university's official Martin Luther King Day speaker. Malveaux received $15,000 in student funds, supplied in part by the Black Student Association.

As in the case of Davis, Malveaux's views are antithetic to King's. She is a crude racial Marxist who once asserted that there were "200 million white racists in America" and on another occasion expressed her wish that Supreme Court Justice Clarence Thomas would have a heart attack. Her speech, called "Economic Justice: The Struggle Continues," included attacks on Ward Connerly, on Laura Bush, and on the idea of a colorblind society with Dr. King as its prophet. (Malveaux was subsequently appointed president of Bennett College.)

At Duke, I had been preceded by Aaron Magruder, a black cartoonist who had gained fame through his strip "Boondocks" and notoriety for attacking America after the destruction of the World Trade Center on 9/11. Magruder likewise had been the university's official Martin Luther King Day speaker. In his speech, Magruder noted that 90 percent of the American people supported the war against the Islamic terrorists and said, "I would like to believe the 10 percent leftover is black." He then told the students: "Your vote means nothing; you can protest if you want, they'll throw you in jail." Davis, Malveaux and Magruder reflected the extremist sentiments of the black student groups on campus without whose imprimatur no Martin Luther King Day speaker could be selected.

Vanderbilt University annually provides roughly $130,000 for left-wing agitations, including the visits of left-wing speakers. This is balanced by $0 for conservative groups and speakers. Ironically, the faculties of these schools are strong proponents of campaign finance reform in the political world they don't control.

The situation at Vanderbilt is completely normal in the academic world, with the exception of a relative handful of small conservative and religious schools like Hillsdale and Bob Jones University. At the University of Wisconsin, the Multicultural Student Center, upset over an ad I placed in the school paper, attacked its liberal editors for running "a racist propaganda machine"—an absolutely unfounded smear—and attempted to shut it down. The following fall the MSA was rewarded for its bad behavior with a grant of $1 million to fund its radical activities. At the same school, the campus organization Students for Objectivism receives $500 in student program funds to support its activities. At Duke University, in the wake of my placing an ad opposing reparations and the demonstrations that attended it, President Nan Keohane announced a grant of $100,000 in additional funds for student groups.[1] When I spoke at Duke, a day after my visit to Vanderbilt, $50,000 of Keohane's grant had been disbursed—$500 to the Duke Conservative Union and $49,500 to left-wing groups.

Because university funds were unavailable, my Wake Up America hosts had to raise the money from outside contributions, not an easy task for students. They managed to secure funding from three individuals and two conservative organizations— Young America's Foundation, which underwrites the lion's share of my tours, and the Leadership Institute. The money they raised allowed them to bring me to campus, house me and provide about one-fifth the honorarium I would have received if I were a left-wing ideologue like Julianne Malveaux. Left-wing activists working the campus circuit with modest celebrity can make six-figure incomes, courtesy of university largesse.

A frustrating but typical trait of college conservatives is that they don't—as a rule—complain about the inequities that are routinely inflicted on them. Inequitable funding is only one of the injustices that conservative students suffer and take for normal. Obtaining a faculty sponsor for Wake Up America was even more difficult than getting the vice chancellor to approve its formation.

The founder of Wake Up America, Dan Eberhart, scoured the campus for a professor who would sponsor his club. He put letters of request in professors' mailboxes. He approached them directly. In the end, out of approximately one thousand faculty members at Vanderbilt, he was able to come up with only one who would

---

[1] I have written about these events in "Uncivil Wars: The Controversy Over Reparations for Slavery," 2001 and in Volume 6 of this series, *Progressive Racism*.

sponsor a group whose intention was to bring conservative speakers to a college campus. Vanderbilt is not only an old and traditional institution; its home is a state with a Republican governor, two Republican senators, and a citizenry whose majority voted Republican in the last presidential election. The successful purge of conservatives from the faculty of Vanderbilt is thus a sobering commentary on the politically debased condition of the university, which has fallen victim to an academic McCarthyism more insidious (because incomparably more effective) than the academic witch-hunts of the past.

The lone faculty member willing to sponsor a non-left student group at Vanderbilt was a business school professor from outside the Vanderbilt community. Because his primary occupation is actually business rather than teaching, this professor flies from his home in San Francisco to Nashville twice a week to teach his course. In other words, there were really no conservative professors in residence at Vanderbilt University who were willing to publicly sponsor a group whose purpose is to bring an under-represented viewpoint to the Vanderbilt community—even though it is a viewpoint shared by a majority of Tennessee voters and half the American public.

My Vanderbilt talk was scheduled for Monday, April 8. Wake Up America had reserved the room where it would be given. On Thursday, April 4, the Vanderbilt administration informed Dan Eberhart that a professor now needed the room for a review class and that my speech would have to be cancelled. Vanderbilt is a very large university, and even the building I gave my speech in seemed virtually deserted the night I spoke. Yet this kind of obstruction was not unusual. I had similar experiences on at least three other occasions during this spring tour alone. The University of Oregon cancelled my appearance the day I arrived in state, on grounds that a request for security for the event made two weeks earlier had been one day too late, and that the room had been given to another event—although my sponsors were not informed until one day before my announced appearance. NYU cancelled the room for my talk there the day I arrived in New York, also because of an alleged room-scheduling problem; and James Madison University cancelled my talk, as I was about to depart for Virginia, for the same reason.

In other circumstances, a young and well-mannered conservative like Eberhart might have capitulated to this petty harassment and terminated the event. Fortunately, he held his ground. He was perhaps strengthened in his resolve by the fact that my office had been able to arrange a C-Span taping of the event. Eberhart's resistance resulted in permission to proceed, but not until he had agreed to pay for the wear and tear to the carpet of the foyer of the hall where the speech took place. A $100 cleanup fee was also added, though no food or beverages were served and there was no refuse to clean up.

Despite a downpour, about 250 people showed up for the speech in Wilson Hall and listened civilly while I described "How the Left Undermined America's Security Before 9/11." The attendance was gratifying because the student paper, the *Vanderbilt Hustler,* did not inform the campus community that the speech was taking place (or report on it after it was given). Afterwards I signed books and answered the questions of those who stayed to ask them. One was a professor of philosophy who handed me a yellowing copy of my very first book, *Student,* published exactly forty years earlier. In it, I described the first student demonstrations of the 1960s at Berkeley, where I was pursuing a graduate degree. I didn't realize at the time that New Leftists like myself were going to transform American universities into politicized institutions where only approved ideas would be welcome. I hope I would have had second thoughts about my activities then if I had realized this would be the outcome.

When I asked this professor what kind of philosophy he taught at Vanderbilt, he said with a smirk, "Marxist philosophy." Then he asked me to inscribe his book: "To my political enemy, from a foaming-at-the-mouth right-wing ideologue." A sense of humor is apparently not a radical asset. I signed the book, but with a different inscription from Euripides—"second thoughts are best"—and he left.

I was then approached by a group of undergraduates who were not politically conservative. A young woman with a diffident demeanor asked, in an earnest tone, what I thought of racial profiling. Her question was inspired by a portion of my talk that addressed the problem of airport security. I had pointed out that nine of the World Trade Center terrorists were actually stopped by airport security on 9/11 because they had faulty I.D.s. But they had been allowed to board the planes anyway. I said that the Clinton Administration's failure to institute adequate security measures prior to the attack was due in part to an ideological aversion to profiling Muslim terrorists.

I tried to explain to the student the difference between factoring race into a profile and using race as the profile itself. I referred her to Heather MacDonald's article in the conservative magazine *City Journal*, "The Myth of Racial Profiling"—fully realizing that this undergraduate would never have heard of Heather MacDonald or the *City Journal*. Nor would she be familiar with the writings of virtually any living conservative writer, including myself. I gave her the name of the website where MacDonald's article was posted and could be located. But I did so with a heavy heart, because I knew that the student had many questions, not one; that her parents were paying $30,000 a year to give her a good education, but that at Vanderbilt she would only be getting one side of the story and only one perspective on the ideological conflicts that would affect her life.

I had met students like this throughout my campus sojourns. The encounters were the saddest memories I took away with me. Millions like this young woman would pass through universities like Vanderbilt, which would routinely betray their trust. They would be given decks that were stacked, and instruction that was partisan, and there was nothing that I, or a small contingent of conservatives, could do in one hour or during one event to alter these facts.

8

The Campus Blacklist
and a Ray of Hope

The most successful and pervasive blacklist in American history is the blacklist of conservatives on American college campuses, their marginalization in undergraduate life and their virtual exclusion from liberal arts faculties, particularly those that deal with the study of society itself. Because it is a blacklist enforced by academics, there has been no academic acknowledgment of the problem. Consequently, the evidence regarding its mode of operation and the extent of its impact is anecdotal or confined to research that is incomplete. Nonetheless, only its beneficiaries will deny the reality.

This spring I have spoken at more than a dozen universities, conducting my own inquiries into this problem. In my speeches I always try to cover a broad menu of subjects, hoping that in the hour or two available I will be able to jar students who may be encountering their first conservative adult on campus into thinking in new ways about issues that affect them. These include the war, race relations, and the pervasive influence on campus of leftist viewpoints. In my speeches, I always make it a point to begin with the subject of the university blacklist, and open my remarks with these words: "You can't get a good education if they're only telling you half the story—even if you're paying $30,000 a year." This is the slogan I created for the Campaign for Fairness and Inclusion in Higher Education when I launched it two years ago.

Originally published as "The Campus Blacklist," April 18, 2003, http://archive.frontpagemag.com/ReadArticle.aspx?ArtId=18634

One of the institutions I visited this spring, Tulane Law School, has not a single Republican or conservative faculty member; the Duquesne Law School—where I also spoke—has only one. The conservative students I met with at the University of Michigan could not identify a single conservative on their faculty, although they could name several Marxists. When I visited Bowling Green University, conservative professors were isolated in a research center that has no teaching responsibilities. Out of 15 professors in the Department of Political Science at the University of Richmond, a private school with a decidedly conservative student body, there is one identifiable Republican.

The Center for the Study of Popular Culture, which I head, is presently conducting a survey of the voting registrations of professors in the social sciences at 40 universities. The results already confirm these impressions, as did surveys by Frank Luntz and the *American Enterprise* magazine, which were initiated by the Center. An independent study of 20 law schools by John McGinnis and Matthew Schwartz also confirms the absurdly unbalanced ratio disclosed by our efforts. At a recent lunch with Michael Parks, the dean of the Journalism School at the University of Southern California, I asked him if he could name a single conservative on his faculty. He confessed he could not. You could throw a dart at a list of all American universities and be virtually certain of hitting one where Republican and conservative faculty members constitute less than a dozen members of a liberal arts faculty made up of hundreds, even thousands. After the United States and Great Britain had liberated Iraq and the streets of Baghdad were filled with Iraqis celebrating their freedom, the Academic Senate at UCLA voted to "condemn America's invasion of Iraq" by a vote of 180–7. This, in a nation where 76 percent of the population supports the war.

The absurd under-representation of conservative viewpoints on university faculties obviously does not happen by random process. It is the result of systematic exclusion and/or repression of conservative viewpoints. In state universities the political bias against conservatives in hiring amounts to an illegal political patronage operation, which provides huge advantages to the Democratic Party and to the political left, whose activists are subsidized and provided with platforms to influence others. Allegedly scholarly reports on capital punishment, racism, poverty and other volatile political issues that make their way into the national media are virtually guaranteed to have a left-wing spin. Left-wing political journalists are themselves provided sinecures in the form of university professorships, while politically left journals are often underwritten by university presses. Leftist journalism schools provide a steady stream of cadre to the nation's media institutions. Campus funds available for political activities are inequitably distributed to student groups with left-wing agendas, at ratios that often reach 50–1. These fees underwrite an army of radical speakers and agitators who operate nationally, while skewing the politics of the campus strongly to the left. Among other effects is the spread of political hypocrisy. The same people who demand campaign finance reform in national politics enjoy the benefits of a system in which students are taxed to provide funds almost exclusively to one side of the political debate.

How has this monopoly of the academic campus come about? To begin with, universities are feudal institutions whose organizational structures are hierarchical and collegial and thus closed to scrutiny and oversight. Michael Parks, the dean of the USC journalism school, agreed with me that a faculty without conservatives is antithetical to the idea of a university and good journalistic training. But he confessed that there was absolutely nothing he could do to alter the situation. Senior members of the faculty control faculty hiring. Unless they bound by ethical scruples, as they most evidently are not, they will hire only people who agree with them and share their prejudices. The prestigious journalism schools at Columbia and New York University also feature conservative-free faculties, and there are others too numerous to mention.

That is how sociological flat-earthists—Marxists, socialists, post-modernists and other intellectual radicals—whose ideas have been discredited by historical events, can still dominate their academic fields. In the Sixties and Seventies, centrist liberals dominated academic faculties. Because they were committed to pluralistic values, they opened the door to Marxists and other political ideologues. As soon as the ideologues reached a critical mass, they closed the doors behind them. The feudal hierarchies of the university made it relatively easy to create the closed system that exists today.

Now it is virtually impossible for a vocal conservative to be hired for a tenure-track position. Conservative faculty members who have achieved this feat invariably tell me that they were forced to keep their political views to themselves until they achieved tenure. But the blacklist really begins with the politicization of the undergraduate classroom (also a post-Sixties phenomenon) and the systematic political harassment of conservative students by their radical professors. The chief effect of this harassment is to discourage conservatives from pursuing academic careers. Leftist professors think nothing of intruding their political passions into the classroom in a manner that is inappropriate and abusive. Professorial remarks denigrating conservative ideas and personalities—often in the most inappropriate context imaginable—powerfully convey the message that conservative ideas are unacceptable in the academic community. While reading lists are stripped of conservative texts, professorial expectations are defined as agreement with the ideology and political biases of the instructor. Grades often are employed to make the bias stick. These are all daunting facts to any conservative undergraduate contemplating continuing his or her studies with the idea of pursuing an academic career.

In informal interviews conducted at the universities I visited, I met with students who had been called "fascists" by their own professors—in one case, for inviting Fox TV host Oliver North to campus. At the University of Oregon, one of the students told me he had been labeled a "neo-Nazi" in class for expressing the view that former Senate Majority Leader Trent Lott had been the victim of a political double standard. At the University of Richmond, I encountered a student whose Spanish Language professor referred to President Bush as a "moron" in the classroom. At each venue I generally interview a dozen or more conservative students personally. I ask them whether they have been subjected to this kind of classroom abuse. Invariably the majority have. Far from being aggressive in the manner of campus leftists, the students who come to my events are dressed in suits and ties and have a scrubbed, honor-scout deportment. It is usually left to me to point out to them that they have been abused and should think about protesting the abuse.

Leftist professors create a hostile environment by posting anti-Bush or anti-Israel cartoons on their office doors and bulletin boards, which students cannot avoid seeing when they come for consultation and guidance. Left-wing faculty also recruit students to political demonstrations and will lead campus political protests, making no secret of their political passions. What does this communicate to the students in their class who do not share their political views? What adverse impact does this have on the responsibility of teachers to teach all their students, not just those who share their political prejudices?

To address these issues, I have devised an "Academic Bill of Rights" that stresses intellectual diversity, demands the inclusion of divergent viewpoints in reading lists, and recognizes that political partisanship by professors in the classroom is an abuse of students' academic freedom. The bill of rights also declares that partisan funding of student organizations and visiting speakers is unacceptable. In my visits to college campuses, I have found that conservative students respond to this message enthusiastically and that even liberal students are concerned when it is brought up. Fairness, equity and inclusion are American values, and will be supported by the American public whenever they are at issue. In my campus campaign I have begun to receive the kind of responses to these agendas that offer some hope.

My visit to the University of Missouri provides an illustrative case. Before I had even arrived in Columbia, where the university is located, the students informed me that a leftist biology professor named Miriam Golomb was offering her students credits to come and protest my speech. One of Professor Golomb's students had asked if she would provide credit merely for attending my speech. Golomb replied, "No, why would I, since I don't like what he has to say? He's a racist." Then Professor Golomb had a second thought. "But I will give you twice as many credits if you go to protest." Golomb, who is white, then went to the black students association, officially known as the "Legion of Black Collegians," to try to incite the group to protest my appearance. Her appeal backfired; several of the students present reported what had happened to their friends among the College Republicans. Professor Golomb also sent an email to students urging them to protest my appearance; a leaflet with my picture was created (my student sources are convinced that Professor Golomb was the creator), calling me "a real live bigot" and accusing me of being "on the payroll of a right-wing foundation."

The immediate impact of this professorial agitation was to cause the university to increase its security and assign seven armed guards to the event. I was thus transformed into a "controversial" speaker whose very appearance was a public danger. The left-wing college TV station ran promotional ads describing me as "an extreme right-wing conservative" to complete the effect.

As soon as I arrived in Columbia and learned of these developments, I had the students take me to the university office of the Vice Chancellor of Administrative Affairs. When the vice chancellor appeared, I expressed my outrage at being slandered by one of her professors and wondered whether this treatment of a visiting speaker was appropriate to an institution that billed itself as a center of higher learning. I pointed out that I was a nationally known and respected commentator, that my views were representative of at least half the population, and that I had been a civil rights activist for fifty years. I said I would like an apology from Professor Golomb and a university statement deploring her actions, which were harmful to the principle of academic freedom, to the free exchange of ideas and to the educational mission of the university. How could students feel free to express themselves in such an atmosphere? I pointed out that I was the ostensible target of these attacks, but that the real victims would be the students who invited me. I would only be at the university a couple of hours. But the stigma the professor's slander imposed on this event would stay with the students throughout their college careers. They would be known as students who had invited a racist to campus, however false and malicious that accusation might be.

The vice chancellor listened to what I had to say, then blandished me with typical bureaucratic assurances. I did not get the impression that any action would be taken (and that proved to be the case). Since I was only there for a few hours, I was forced to content myself with having made the point.

My speech was delivered two hours later in the theater of the business school. When I walked into the room, it was packed with 500 people, many of whom were not students, who gave me a standing ovation. I was introduced by Professor Richard Hardy, faculty advisor of the College Republicans. He waved the obscene attack-leaflet and began to describe what Professor Golomb had done. It turned out that she was present in the audience, and rose—according to her own account later—to protest his "misrepresentation" of what she had done. She said she had not offered the credits to her students to protest the event but to attend it. This version was contradicted by her own students, but neither Professor Hardy nor I were able to hear what she saying above the din from the audience. Professor Hardy thought she was apologizing for the slander and asked me if I accepted. I said I did.

When I walked to the podium to speak, the audience again rose to its feet and gave me a second ovation. I began by describing who I was, since the attacks had put me on the defensive. I recalled how I had marched on my first civil rights demonstration for American blacks in 1948, when I was nine years old, and had continued my efforts for civil rights ever since. To bring matters to the present, I told them how the previous week I had gone to San

Diego to receive an award from an organization called Operation Hope, headed by a charismatic black leader named John Bryant. Bryant had formed Operation Hope in 1992, in the wake of the Los Angeles riots. Since then he had brought tens of millions of dollars in investments and loans into five inner cities, had helped hundreds of poor black and Hispanic families to purchase their own homes, and had taught economic literacy skills to more than 100,000 inner-city residents. I have been working with John Bryant since 1996, and the award recognized my efforts in behalf of Operation Hope. I have raised half a million dollars for the organization and have opened doors for John in Republican Washington after his Democratic patrons were turned out of office. As a result of these efforts, John was welcomed at the Bush White House, where he extended an invitation to the president to come to South Central Los Angeles. The event took place on the 10th anniversary of the Los Angeles riots, and the president was given a warm welcome by community activists at an event hosted by John and Operation Hope.

In the past, I had been reticent to talk about these efforts, but Professor Golomb's "protest" prompted me to break my silence. I wanted the students who invited me to have ammunition to defend themselves, and those attending to see just how malicious the attacks were. After establishing my *bona fides*, I launched into the opening set piece of every speech I give on college campuses. I said, "You can't get a good education if they're only telling you half the story, even if you're paying $8,000 a year," which was their tuition. I talked about the longest, most successful blacklist ever conducted in America. I talked about the political harassment of conservative students, the creation of a hostile learning environment, and the need to get representation for under-represented viewpoints on their campus. I talked about the need for intellectual diversity.

I then related these observations to the war in Iraq. I spoke about the role of the left-wing university in undermining American self-respect and self-confidence at a time when the nation was facing enemies who were deadly. I showed them another way to look at America, using the history of black Americans as an example. I pointed out that slavery had existed and been accepted for thousands of years in black Africa and in every society—until a day came at the end of the 18th century, when dead white Christian males in England and the United States concluded for the first time in human history that slavery was immoral and should be abolished. I reminded them how a white slave-owner named Thomas Jefferson put into the founding document of this nation the revolutionary idea that all men are created equal; and how within a generation, as a direct result of the efforts of England and America, slavery had been abolished in the Western world.

I said the proper way to look at America is not just that it shared in the crimes of all nations, but—more importantly—that it became the pioneer of human equality and freedom for all nations; that as a result of America's efforts to realize the ideals of equality and freedom, blacks in America are now the freest and richest black people anywhere on the face of the earth, including all the nations that are ruled by blacks. I pointed out that our Islamo-fascist enemies are supporters of slavery in Libya and the Sudan, and of tyranny and oppression everywhere; that we are in a civil war which pits the forces of freedom led by the United States against the forces of darkness and oppression who rallied to the defense of the regime in Iraq. I pointed out that it was important for them to learn to be proud of their country, because if they were not proud of their country they could not defend themselves.

That was the end of my speech and it resulted in another ovation. The response—particularly after the attacks—was rewarding. But my greatest gratification came afterwards, as the conservative students were taking me back to my hotel. One of them had a roommate who was a member of the Legion of Black Collegians and who had attended my talk. As a black student in a left-wing educational system that extended back to the very first grade, she was the most focused target and most vulnerable victim of the left's campaign of slander against America's heritage, and thus against her heritage as an African American. What this black student told her roommate when my speech was concluded was how much she had learned by coming to the event. "Everything I have been told all my life," she said, "has been a lie."

PART III

The Campaign for an Academic Bill of Rights

The Academic Bill of Rights

1. All faculty shall be hired, fired, promoted and granted tenure on the basis of their competence and appropriate knowledge in the field of their expertise and, in the humanities, the social sciences, and the arts, with a view toward fostering a plurality of methodologies and perspectives. No faculty shall be hired or fired or denied promotion or tenure on the basis of his or her political or religious beliefs.

2. No faculty member will be excluded from tenure, search and hiring committees on the basis of their political or religious beliefs.

3. Students will be graded on the basis of their reasoned answers and appropriate knowledge of the subjects and disciplines they study, not on the basis of their political or religious beliefs.

4. Curricula and reading lists in the humanities and social sciences should reflect the uncertainty and unsettled character of all human knowledge in these areas by providing students with dissenting sources and viewpoints where appropriate. While teachers are and should be free to pursue their own findings and perspectives in presenting their views, they should consider and make their students aware of other viewpoints. Academic disciplines should welcome a diversity of approaches to unsettled questions.

Originally published in September 2003. Stephen Balch, president of the conservative National Association of Scholars, read and amended my draft, and provided some of its key formulations.

5. Exposing students to the spectrum of significant scholarly viewpoints on the subjects examined in their courses is a major responsibility of faculty. Faculty will not use their courses for the purpose of political, ideological, religious or anti-religious indoctrination.

6. Selection of speakers, allocation of funds for speakers programs and other student activities will observe the principles of academic freedom and promote intellectual pluralism.

7. An environment conducive to the civil exchange of ideas being an essential component of a free university, the obstruction of invited campus speakers, destruction of campus literature or other effort to obstruct this exchange will not be tolerated.

8. Knowledge advances when individual scholars are left free to reach their own conclusions about which methods, facts, and theories have been validated by research. Academic institutions and professional societies formed to advance knowledge within an area of research, maintain the integrity of the research process, and organize the professional lives of related researchers serve as indispensable venues within which scholars circulate research findings and debate their interpretation. To perform these functions adequately, academic institutions and professional societies should maintain a posture of organizational neutrality with respect to the substantive disagreements that divide researchers on questions within, or outside, their fields of inquiry.

What Has Happened
to American Liberals?

American liberals once supported intellectual liberty, academic freedom, and the right to express one's views without being tarred and feathered through guilt-by-
association. Their great villains were businessmen Babbitts who
wanted to interfere with the free exchange of ideas at the universities they funded, and political McCarthyites who wanted to stifle
the opinions of professors they found objectionable.

But now it seems academic freedom and intellectual liberty are
"conservative" issues, and a governor who supports them is "pandering to the far-right crowd." At least that is what *The Denver
Post* has charged in a remarkable lead editorial, titled "Absurdity
in Higher Ed," that appeared in its September 13 edition.[1] Joining
liberal columnists at the Denver *Rocky Mountain News*, the Boulder *Daily Camera* and its own editorial cartoonist, the *Post* has
weighed in on one side of a public debate in Colorado over "The
Academic Bill of Rights"—a measure that Governor Bill Owens
and Senate leader John Andrews have been discussing as a suggested remedy for observed abuses in the academic system. As proposed, this measure would protect professors of all political
persuasions—left and right—from being fired or hired on the basis
of their political views.

Originally published as "What Has Happened To American Liberals?,"
September 15, 2003, http://archive.frontpagemag.com/ReadArticle.aspx?
ArtId=16379

[1]"Absurdity in Higher Ed," *Denver Post*, September 14, 2003, http://
  archive.frontpagemag.com/readArticle.aspx?ARTID=16372

According to the *Post:* "The flap began in January, when Gov. Bill Owens told KOA-Radio listeners that far too many political science professors were liberal lefties. Since then, he and other GOP lawmakers have met with David Horowitz, the conservative leader of Students for Academic Freedom, which pushes for political diversity in academic hires. Horowitz, for his part, says his bill of rights has nothing to do with quotas."

I do say that. But so does the Academic Bill of Rights. Its provisions expressly *prohibit* quotas or even potential "affirmative action" attempts to provide political balance in hiring. You cannot impose quotas or promote balance under the provisions of a bill that says in so many words: "No faculty shall be hired or fired or denied promotion or tenure on the basis of his or her political or religious beliefs."[2]

Could anything be clearer? Yet, in its editorial, *The Denver Post* ignores the plain meaning of these words in order to accuse the governor and the Republican Party of promoting the Academic Bill of Rights as a means to stack university faculties with Republicans: "The same party that's been squawking over race-based college admissions now apparently wants universities to check voter-registration rolls when hiring faculty to ensure more conservatives are added to the ranks."

The Republican Party and conservatives want no such thing, nor is there a shred of evidence to suggest that they do. In mentioning "voter-registration rolls," the *Post* editorial is here referring to a report issued by the Center for the Study of Popular Culture which showed that 94 percent of the faculty at Colorado University (Boulder) whose political affiliation the Center was able to identify were registered Democrats, as were 98 percent of the faculty of Denver University. These statistics were offered by the Center to demonstrate a *prima facie* case that there is political

---

[2] "Academic Bill of Rights," *Students For Academic Freedom*, http://www.studentsforacademicfreedom.org/documents/1925/abor.html

bias in the hiring process at these schools. At no time did we suggest that this process was a good thing or that its bias should be reversed. We are unalterably opposed to hiring professors on the basis of their political views, which is why we have proposed the Academic Bill of Rights.

So the real issue is this: Are liberals in the state of Colorado willing to endorse an Academic Bill of Rights that guarantees professors the right to be hired without regard for their political beliefs and students the right to have access to a diversity of views fairly presented? Or are liberals going to persist in their efforts to thwart a measure that would guarantee that the principles of academic freedom will be observed?

3

A Libertarian's Odd Dissent

L ibertarians have a reputation for focusing too much on principle and ignoring real world contexts. Jesse Walker's attack on the Academic Bill of Rights in the current issue of *Reason Magazine* comes close to fitting the stereotype. Walker, who is himself an editor of *Reason,* suggests that the Academic Bill of Rights could have "chilling effects" on academic freedom.[1] The missing context is this: What academic freedom, in connection with what existing university, could he possibly be referring to?

Two years ago I was invited by conservative students to speak at the University of California Berkeley. The university administration assigned 30 armed guards to keep order at the event. I was picketed by the International Socialist Organization, the Spartacist League and assorted left-wing thugs with menacing taunts and signs calling me a "racist ideologue"—a photo of which wound up in *Newsweek.* Previously, the *Daily Cal* had apologized for allowing an ad written by me to be published in the student newspaper. The reason for these attacks? I had the temerity to suggest that paying reparations for slavery 137 years after the fact might be a bad idea. Not a single administrator or professor at Berkeley rose to my defense, or to the defense of my right to speak without fear of bodily harm or reckless slander. This is the state of

---

Originally published as "The Academic Bill of Rights: A Debate on the Right," September 18, 2003, http://archive.frontpagemag.com/ReadArticle.aspx?ArtId=16287
[1]Jesse Walker, "Chilling Effects," *Reason,* September 17, 2003 http://reason.com/archives/2003/09/17/chilling-effects

"academic freedom" on our campuses today. There are 16,000 Marxist professors—or so a professional association of Marxist professors has claimed—but faculty libertarians and conservatives are as rare as unicorns. An intellectual waterfly like Cornel West is one of the 100 most cited public intellectuals in academic journals, according to Richard Posner's recent study.[2] The eminent libertarian scholar Richard Epstein, on the other hand, does not even make the list.

This is the context into which I have introduced the Academic Bill of Rights as a step towards remedying the situation. Walker might have mentioned that Eugene Volokh, a libertarian who vetted the Academic Bill of Rights for me, and one of the nation's foremost legal experts on First Amendment rights, has found nothing to object to in the document. It would have been nice to have had some acknowledgment of facts like these from Walker before he joined our opponents. If libertarians choose not to support our cause, it will be gravely weakened. One would hope, therefore, that a decision to withhold support would be made on strong intellectual grounds.[3] Unfortunately, Walker offers no such grounds.

Walker draws an invidious comparison between our bill and Hubert Humphrey's affirmative action legislation, which Humphrey swore would not lead to racial preferences but did. This analogy is inapt. There is absolutely nothing in the Academic Bill of Rights about affirmative action for conservatives. The rights the bill delineates are negative rights—limits on what authorities in the university community and outside it may do. The appropriate analogy would have been the American Bill of Rights. Would Walker argue that because so-called liberals have managed to pervert the clear meaning of the 14th Amendment, we should there-

---

[2]"Public Intellectuals: A Study Of Decline," op. cit.

[3]As it turned out, *Reason* continued its unscrupulous attacks on our campaign for the next several years with the effect that it was indeed gravely weakened, receiving little support from conservatives and none from libertarians.

fore reconsider our support for it and regard it as having "chilling effects" on our freedom?

Second, Walker claims that the Academic Bill of Rights "extends the concept of academic freedom to students," and that this is a problem. This argument came as something of a surprise to me—a libertarian objecting to too many freedoms! In fact, the Academic Bill of Rights does not extend any more rights to students than are implicit in the existing academic-freedom tradition—a fact to which we draw attention in the preamble to the document. Walker suggests that "contradictions" between professors' rights and students' rights "could be resolved in unfortunate ways." He offers the example of "a biology student lodging an official complaint because her professor gave short shrift to Creationism." Well, such a complaint is conceivable, but under the Academic Bill of Rights it would be dismissed. Article 4 of the bill states: "While teachers are and should be free to pursue their own findings and perspectives in presenting their views, they should consider and make their students aware of other viewpoints."

The meaning is clear. The professor has a right to teach the course any way he or she wants. If the professor is an evolutionary biologist, then that's what he or she should teach. All that the Bill of Rights stipulates is that students should be made aware of other viewpoints. There is no conflict here. The Bill of Rights clearly recognizes that teachers have the right to teach their courses as they see fit.

The only limit to this right is article 5: "Exposing students to the spectrum of significant scholarly viewpoints on the subjects examined in their courses is a major responsibility of faculty. Faculty will not use their courses for the purpose of political, ideological, religious or anti-religious indoctrination." Having audited a course at one of the premier liberal colleges in the country, where a 600-page Marxist textbook on "modern industrial society" was taught as though it were a text in Newtonian physics, I can testify that this is a necessary right to protect students' academic freedom.

Walker's next argument is a tangential attack on articles posted to the Students for Academic Freedom website that reflect attitudes he finds disturbing. One such is about Cornell antiwar faculty teach-ins, and raises the question of whether it is appropriate for professors to participate in non-academic events aimed at converting students whom they teach to a politically partisan viewpoint and on a subject they may not be professionally qualified to pontificate on. This question is touched on by one of the principles of the Academic Bill of Rights, which reflects the views of a notable liberal professor, Stanley Fish. The principle reads: "Academic institutions and professional societies should maintain a posture of organizational neutrality with respect to the substantive disagreements that divide researchers on questions within, or outside their fields of inquiry."[4] The purpose of this principle is to preserve an academic attitude of uncertainty towards truth as opposed to a dogmatic political one. But the bottom line is that articles on the site to which Walker refers are irrelevant to the Academic Bill of Rights itself.

Walker takes his discussion of this matter, which is really a side-discussion, into two substantive areas. One is the issue of private institutions, for which he hopes I am not recommending a legislative solution. He is right to hope, since I am not making such a recommendation. The Academic Bill of Rights explicitly says: "These principles only fully apply to public universities and to private universities that present themselves as bound by the canons of academic freedom. Private institutions choosing to restrict academic freedom on the basis of creed have an obligation to be as explicit as is possible about the scope and nature of these restrictions."

Walker draws an analogy between the Academic Bill of Rights and the Fairness Doctrine, which required radio and TV outlets to

---

[4]Stanley Fish, "Save the World on Your Own Time," *Chronicle Of Higher Education*, January 23, 2003, http://chronicle.com/article/Save-the-World-on-Your-Own/45335/; Stanley Fish, *Save the World on Your Own Time*, Oxford University Press, August 2008

balance the views of their broadcasts, and worries that this is what is intended. He need not worry. The Academic Bill of Rights strictly forbids hiring on the basis of political or religious views, and thus contravenes legislated balancing of any kind. I agree with Walker that there is no such thing as a perfectly balanced debate, but I reject his insinuation that I have set out to create one. On the contrary, I have drawn up the Academic Bill of Rights in a manner explicitly designed to prevent such balancing.

4

The Battle for the
Academic Bill of Rights

I spent the beginning of September visiting universities in the state of Colorado, where I had gone to promote the Academic Bill of Rights, a document designed to take politics out of the university curriculum and to protect the right of students to get an education rather than an indoctrination. In practice, this meant that I was throwing down the gauntlet to the tenured leftists who have colonized the faculties of American colleges and turned American campuses into their political base. Not coincidentally, in the weeks preceding my trip, the Academic Bill of Rights had become the focus of a fierce political battle in Colorado and the chief education issue in the state.

The cause of the furor was a media leak which revealed that I had met months earlier with Governor Bill Owens and Senate Majority Leader John Andrews; and that Senator Andrews was planning legislation based on the bill. The mischief started with a news feature that appeared on September 6 by *Rocky Mountain News* reporter Peggy Lowe, called "GOP Takes on Leftist Education." Lowe reported: "Top Republican legislators are working on a plan that would require Colorado colleges and universities to seek more conservatives in faculty hiring, more classics in the curriculum and more 'intellectual pluralism' among campus speakers." The only truth in these claims was the last one. The Academic Bill of Rights does call for pluralism in the selection of

---

Originally published as "The Battle for the Bill of Rights," October 15, 2003, http://archive.frontpagemag.com/Printable.aspx?ArtId=15907

speakers. It does not call for affirmative action for conservatives. In fact, it stipulates that academic hires should be made on merit and strictly forbids the hiring of any faculty on the basis of their political viewpoints: "All faculty shall be hired, fired, promoted and granted tenure on the basis of their competence.... No faculty shall be hired or fired or denied tenure or promotion on the basis of his or her political or religious beliefs."[1]

Contrary to the *Rocky Mountain News* story, the Academic Bill of Rights does not call for more classics in the curriculum either. Instead it clearly states that "curricula and reading lists in the humanities and social sciences should reflect the uncertainty and unsettled character of all human knowledge in these areas by providing students with dissenting sources and viewpoints where appropriate.... Academic disciplines should welcome a diversity of approaches to unsettled questions." In other words, assigned reading texts should *not* reflect only one point of view.

The Academic Bill of Rights is an *anti*-quota bill, designed to challenge quotas presently imposed by an academic establishment dramatically skewed to the left of the political spectrum. How dramatically? Two reports recently released by the Center for the Study of Popular Culture reveal that 93.6 percent of the faculty at Colorado University (Boulder) and 98 percent of the faculty at Denver University who registered in political primaries were Democrats, a distribution that clearly suggests bias in the system of training and hiring academic faculty.

On September 9, the other major Colorado news source, *The Denver Post*, followed the *Rocky Mountain News'* distorted account with a lead editorial called, "Absurdity in Higher Ed," which began by asking, "When is a quota not a quota? When it benefits Republicans, it seems." According to the *Post* editors, "The same party that's been squawking over race-based college admissions now apparently wants universities to check voter-

---

[1]Academic Bill of Rights; see Part III, Chapter 1 of this text.

registration rolls when hiring faculty to ensure more conservatives are added to the ranks."[2]

Not only was this utterly false, but the *Post* editors had gotten the facts exactly backwards. Republicans and conservatives were opposed both to liberal race quotas *and* to liberal quotas that restricted non-liberals and their ideas to marginal representation on college campuses. The Academic Bill of Rights was designed to promote equal opportunity and thus intellectual diversity. The same day the *Post* editorial appeared, the *Rocky Mountain News* ran a story headlined "Democrats call Academic Bill of Rights McCarthyism." The false story was replicating itself. "Democrats lashed out Monday at a GOP plan to get more Republicans on Colorado's college campuses, calling it academic McCarthyism and quotas for conservatives," the article began.[3] The Democrats' Senate Minority Leader, Joan Fitz-Gerald, denounced the bill as "affirmative action for conservative Republicans, to get them into universities," and warned: "There is something chilling and troubling about a movement like this. They're going to create a climate of fear in our universities, fear of being the professor who says the wrong thing."[4] The Academic Bill of Rights does just the opposite: it explicitly *defends* professors' absolute right to say the wrong thing, and forbids administrations or legislatures from punishing them for their political opinions.

For an entire week, liberal columnists across Colorado had a field day attacking the "quotas" allegedly required by the Academic Bill of Rights. Meanwhile, a hundred faculty members demonstrating for a faculty union at Metro State Denver College added the bill to their grievance list. Their leader, Joan Foster, who was also head of the Metro Faculty Senate, called for an investigation into the "secret meeting" I was alleged to have had with Governor Owens to discuss the bill. This secret meeting was as

---

[2]David Horowitz, *Reforming Our Universities: The Campaign for an Academic Bill of Rights*, Regnery, 2010, p. 57
[3]Op. cit. p. 55
[4]Ibid.

mythological as the quotas which were supposed to be embedded in the bill itself. My office had made an appointment with the governor and I walked in the front door of his gubernatorial office in the Capitol to spend a half-hour with him, a privilege of ordinary citizens.

This surreal media circus was interrupted on September 16 by an editorial appearing in the *Rocky Mountain News.* Written by Vince Carroll, it was titled "Tone the Rhetoric Down" and actually attempted to set the record straight. After rehearsing the Democrat charges against the Academic Bill of Rights, Carroll pointed out that, in fact, it would do "none" of the things claimed: "The Academic Bill of Rights advocates precisely the opposite of political litmus tests," he explained. The *News* then printed excerpts from the Academic Bill of Rights to prove the point. But this dose of reality had almost no effect on the bill's opponents, who continued their scorched-earth tactics and bizarre attacks.

Two weeks after the *Rocky Mountain News* editorial appeared, I arrived in Denver to give a speech at Metro State College. As is often the case, the left at Metro State had organized an event to illustrate exactly the problem I had come to speak about. When I reached the campus, a demonstration to protest my speech—in advance of my speech—was already in progress. The leader of the demonstration was a leftist named Felicia Woodson, who also served as the Metro State student body president. Woodson appealed to the crowd: "Why was he even allowed to come to campus to speak?" To which a heckler responded, "Free speech."[5]

The Auraria campus of the Colorado university system is built on the site of a defunct gold mining camp and houses three colleges—Metro State College, Colorado University (Denver) and Colorado Community College. These public institutions are presumably dedicated to educational pursuits—opening minds and exposing them to a marketplace of ideas. Yet here was a protest to

---

[5]Op. cit., p. 59

close down that marketplace for a speaker who been invited by students—and in fact by the official student activities board—to talk about academic freedom. That students should think it appropriate to protest a speech they hadn't heard was itself a problem. But where were the adults? In fact, they were on the platform leading the protest. Most prominent among them were Joan Foster, the head of the Faculty Senate, and Jim Martin, a trustee of the University of Colorado system. Their presence as leaders and sponsors of the protest showed just how confused some educators have become about the educational mission.

This spectacle naturally provided the text of my talk to the 800 students assembled in the Metro Student Union. "One would expect an educator to encourage students to listen to an invited speaker," I told them. "The same educator might be expected to say, 'If you disagree with what you hear, prepare a reasoned and civil answer to it.' That is what an education is about. Or should be. Using one's brains, instead of just one's tongue. Learning to use logic instead of relying on raw emotions. This is a university, not the *Hannity and Colmes* show." This comment drew laughs of recognition.

I had conducted a study of the Metro State campus which showed that, among 85 members of the social science departments, 41 were registered Democrats and none were registered Republicans in a state which was majority Republican. In fact we had missed two Republicans on the faculty, one of whom introduced himself to me at the event. Far more important than the distribution of faculty and the possibility of bias in the hiring process was the university culture itself. If the leader of the Faculty Senate and a university trustee could not distinguish the educational mission of the university from that of the political arena, how many teachers at the institution could? And, if many did not, what were the implications for the quality of education on the Auraria campus?

To illustrate the politicized culture of the academy, I described a visit I had made before my speech to the Political Science department of Colorado University, one of the three schools on the

Auraria campus. The Political Science department is a narrow hallway flanked with offices whose solid wood doors are sandwiched between bulletin boards that are used for professorial announcements. The only times students come to the department offices are when they are seeking guidance and help from their professors. Perhaps they are falling behind in their grades and want advice that would aid them in improving their scores. Perhaps they are contemplating a professional career and want guidance in pursuing it. Whatever the reasons for their visits, they are seeking a counselor, someone they need to be able to trust.

Yet every bulletin board in this narrow hallway, and two-thirds of the wooden office doors that students would have to open in order to visit their professors, were plastered with anti-Republican, anti-Bush, anti-conservative cartoons and political messages in the same vein. There were no counterbalancing postings in sight. Such political propagandizing has no place in this academic setting. Do professors feel so impotent that they have to hector a captive audience of students who are placed in their professional charge, and over whom they exercise enormous institutional power? Does it not occur to them that inflicting their partisan viewpoints on students whose education has been put in their trust is a form of harassment and a betrayal of their professional obligations? And if they do not, even in this limited but instructive setting, how do they teach their actual courses? How do they insure that their students will get an education and not an indoctrination?

I recalled to my audience the time President Reagan was shot. When he was brought to the hospital and put on the operating table, just before he was put under the anesthetic, he looked at his doctors and said with a wink, "Are you guys Republicans or Democrats?" We can all laugh at Reagan's humor because we trust our doctors to follow their Hippocratic Oath and treat us equally, without regard to our political affiliations or religious beliefs. It is a basic professional responsibility to do so. But while we can still trust our doctors in this regard, the same cannot be said of our teachers. And that is a serious institutional problem which the academic freedom movement has set out to address.

Just how bad the situation was in the classrooms of the Metro State campus was brought home to me the day after I left, when I received the following email from a student who had come to hear my speech.

Dear: Mr. Horowitz

I am a Special Forces soldier, former Marine, and currently a student at Metro State University. Today I heard your speech. While your views are not popular ones, I do feel they are the right ones, in regards to making the American education system more equally representative in the viewpoints it offers. I have witnessed first hand the abuse of a teachers' political rhetoric in classes at Metro State.

As a service member I have served in Panama (Just Cause), Gulf War I, Somalia, Bosnia, Kosovo, and most recently Afghanistan and Iraq. I have been told in classes by my professors that my views are aggressive, violent, racist, and offensive in regards to my opinions on world politics. I have even been told that the wearing of my uniform in class is inappropriate, and offensive.

My current duties are with the state of Colorado as an Officer Candidate School instructor. I try to conduct myself as a professional at all times whether in or out of my classroom. The service has taught me to respect others, and their opinions, no matter what they are. I try to instill that in my students. Yet as a student myself in college I am forced to endure hours of political rhetoric about past wars which I have fought in, and lost friends in.

Most recently I had to endure hours of liberal rhetoric on how badly this administration is doing in the war on terrorism, and how the troops in Iraq are the reason other countries hate us. These viewpoints come from individuals who have never served their nation in a time of war, or had friends die in these wars they talk so knowingly about.

I endure this attitude, and grief in order to get my degree. Like other veterans I am trying to improve myself by going back to school and getting a higher education. Or as I like to call it, a low education. I am proud of my veteran brothers who take on the challenge of raising a family and improving their knowledge base. I feel we have only learned not to spit on our vets as was done during the Vietnam War. We have not learned that their opinions may hold merit, or that maybe they have some real world knowledge we can learn from.

I would like to thank you Mr. Horowitz for trying to improve the system and make it a better place to learn and not just a liberal indoctrination program. On behalf of all my veteran friends serving and not, I would like to say you have our support, and thank you.

SFC Mark J. Elrod USARMY 10TH SFG(A) Special Forces.[6]

During my stay in Colorado, I learned that the excessively politicized debate over the Academic Bill of Rights was partly the aftershock of a bitter redistricting fight that Democrats had lost. This posed the question, which several people raised in the course of my visit, as to why I had not gone directly to universities with my proposal instead of the legislature. In fact, I had. Of course, the ideal way to introduce the Academic Bill of Rights would be for universities themselves to adopt it. The problem is that universities have themselves become political institutions and their entrenched political forces will reject the bill in order to preserve their own dominance.

I was made aware of this fact when I first came up with the idea of an Academic Bill of Rights in the course of discussions with the chairman of the board of regents of the State University of New York (SUNY), one of the largest public university systems in the United States. The chairman was enthusiastic about the bill and assured me he would make it the policy of his institution. He was particularly encouraged because he could see no objection to its particulars that might be raised from any quarter. In fact, not a

---

[6]Op. cit., p. 62

single individual opposing the Academic Bill of Rights has identified a single clause or statement in the bill as being objectionable.

I also brought the proposal to the chancellor of the University
of Denver, a private university, but to no avail. Again there was no
objection to any specifics in the bill itself. Instead, like the chairman of the state university, the chancellor was really afraid of his
leftist faculty. The leader of a university—whether private or public—is a fund-raiser first and foremost. To achieve his goals, he
needs to assemble the best faculty talent in order to produce the
best student product. The one thing a university head can't afford
is to have an institution in turmoil because his faculty—or the
activist wing of his faculty led by professors like Joan Foster—has
launched a revolt against him. The fear induced by such a prospect
is paralyzing. It is difficult to fight a political faction waging an
unprincipled battle under the cloak of educational neutrality and
academic professionalism. It is doubtful that there are many college presidents who are up to this challenge. Yet the problem and
its inequities persist. This makes the intervention of an overtly
political institution like the legislature necessary if the interests of
students, of scholars who are not political, and of the general public are to be served.

It is my view that the majority of university professors—particularly those on whom institutional prestige is based and who are
situated in professional schools like medicine, engineering, business and the hard sciences—will welcome the Academic Bill of
Rights. They will directly benefit from strengthening academic
integrity and thwarting the agendas of political ideologues. However, it is still the case that in the politics of university administration a minority of ideologues can dominate a majority that is
composed of scholars who are politically inactive.

After I left Colorado, the president of Metro State College
rejected the request by Faculty Senate president Joan Foster to
have my meeting with Governor Owens "investigated." But he
went on—in the words of the *Rocky Mountain News*—to say that
"the Academic Bill of Rights is not needed on Metro State's cam-

pus because the Board of Trustees has committed to academic freedom in [its] personnel handbook and policy manual." It was classic bureaucratic subterfuge. This is what the Metro State manual says: "The Board of Trustees endorses the principle of academic freedom, which means the freedom to discuss academic subjects fully, engage in research and publish the results of research, and write or speak as citizens without fear of institutional censorship or discipline, provided individuals do not represent themselves as speaking for the College." Even the casual reader of this statement will note that it is about academic freedom for professors, not students. There is not a word in it that would protect students from the abuses of ideological faculty who confuse the university with a political platform and education with indoctrination. This is why the Academic Bill of Rights is necessary and why only the actions of legislators will begin the necessary process of reform.

5

The Professors' Orwellian Case

The American Association of University Professors prides itself on being a guardian of academic freedom. There is a sound historical basis for this pride, beginning with its famous 1915 report, which launched the academic freedom tradition. Through the 1970s the Academic Freedom Committee of the AAUP developed principles and guidelines that have been adopted by American universities to protect the intellectual independence of their faculties. In the 1915 report, the AAUP also recognized the academic-freedom rights of students. However, as it is a guild organization whose members are professors, it is not surprising that the AAUP has not been so solicitous of the academic rights of students. Not surprisingly, the same is true of university administrations, whose academic-freedom policies are generally modeled on AAUP guidelines.

In fact, when student rights have been widely infringed by faculty and university administrations, the AAUP has tended to overlook the infringements and even defend them. This is not a small problem. In the name of "political correctness," student speech rights have been curtailed and students' academic freedoms abused across the country on an unprecedented scale. Indoctrination courses masquerading as education have spread through the curriculum and become objects of public ridicule. The outrage

Originally published "The Professors' Orwellian Case," December 5, 2003, http://archive.frontpagemag.com/Printable.aspx?ArtId=15136; Professors Stephen Balch and Philip Klinkner provided advice on the text.

over political correctness and "speech codes," however, did not come from the AAUP or academic faculties but from the public at large. Moreover, curbing these excesses has been the work of legislatures and the courts more than of academic institutions or associations.

This year a criminology class at a Colorado university was given an assignment to write a paper on "Why George Bush Is a War Criminal." Bad enough. But a student who chose to submit a paper on "Why Saddam Hussein Is a War Criminal" received a failing grade.[1] At Augustana University, a Lutheran private college, a student was attacked by his own professor as a "neo-fascist" in front of his classmates for the sin of inviting a Fox News Channel host to speak on the campus. At Metro State College in Denver, a student who was a Special Forces instructor and had served his country in Panama, the Gulf War, Somalia, Afghanistan and Iraq was told by his professor that he was a "racist" and "violent" and that his uniform was an "offense to the class." At Texas University, students complained about professors who used their classrooms as political soapboxes, including one journalism professor who instead of teaching journalistic skills lectured on racism, alleged American imperialism in Iraq and ruling class control of the media. I myself attended a class in "Modern Industrial Societies" at Bates College a few years ago, in which the sole text was a 500-page tract put together by the editors of *New Left Review* with a range of authorities restricted to Marxists. When I asked the professor about the educational appropriateness of so one-sided a text, she replied: "They get the other side from the newspapers."

A series of recent studies by independent researchers has shown that, on any given university faculty in America, professors

---

[1]Spokesmen for the AAUP, with the assistance of a compliant education press, attacked this particular claim, both disregarding and distorting the facts in order to discredit the idea that any abuses exist. I have reviewed this case in detail in my book *Reforming Our Universities: The Campaign for an Academic Bill of Rights*, Regnery, 2010, pp. 81–91, and set the record straight.

to the left of the political center outnumber professors to the right of the political center by large margins. At some elite schools like Brown and Wesleyan, the ratio rises to 28–1 and 30–1. Yet neither the Brown administration, nor the American Association of University Professors, or any academic association has thus far indicated the slightest interest in—let alone concern about—these troubling facts.

In this educational climate, it seemed like a reasonable idea to devise an Academic Bill of Rights that would focus on *student* academic rights, while protecting the integrity of academic institutions. Consulting with several academics, both conservative and liberal, I drew up a formal bill based on the tradition of academic freedom that had been initiated by the American Association of University Professors in its better days. The bill emphasizes the importance of intellectual diversity to a free education and codifies protections for students that are currently being systematically neglected. It was initially designed for adoption by university administrations but was also made available to legislators, several of whom—including Colorado Senate Majority Leader John K. Andrews and U.S. Representative Jack Kingston, R-GA—have taken steps to codify the bill in law.

About all these developments, the AAUP remained silent until I recently contacted them to solicit their support for the Academic Bill of Rights. Their response airbrushes me out of the picture and addresses the question of pending legislation supporting the bill with the bill itself, without distinguishing the two issues or mentioning my role in either.[2] What I proposed was not statutory legislation—as their statement suggests—but a bill to be adopted by universities or by the AAUP itself.[3]

---

[2]"Academic Bill of Rights," *American Association of University Professors*, December 2003, http://www.aaup.org/AAUP/comm/rep/A/abor.htm

[3]All the legislation associated with the Academic Bill of Rights took the form of non-binding resolutions in support of its principles.

I had previously submitted a draft of the Academic Bill of Rights to four noted liberal academics—Stanley Fish, Michael Bérubé, Todd Gitlin and Philip Klinkner—as well as to Stephen Balch, the head of the National Association of Scholars; Alan Kors a noted professor and defender of individual rights; and Eugene Volokh, a distinguished libertarian law professor. Each suggested amendments to the original draft; the bill was edited and altered to meet their concerns. With the revised bill in hand, I contacted Mary Burgan, the head of "Committee A"—the AAUP's Committee on Academic Freedom—and was told they were considering it, but never heard from back from her. Finally, in response to a repeated request, I received a curt email referring me to the AAUP website, where an official AAUP statement on the bill had already been posted.

A group of scholars might have been expected to respond to my request for support in the spirit in which it was offered, suggesting amendments to formulations in the bill they found objectionable. The AAUP could have proposed different wordings of the text, or asked that specific clauses be dropped. In response to concerns expressed by Professor Todd Gitlin, I had dropped an entire provision from the original draft. But instead the AAUP responded with the ferocity of a partisan political body, calling the Academic Bill of Rights "a grave threat to fundamental principles of academic freedom," and saying it was to be "strongly condemn[ed]."

Instead of a reasoned, fair-minded response, the professors issued an intemperate, misleading and at times incoherent denunciation. If any act might serve as a symbol of the problems that have beset the academy in the last thirty years—its intense politicization and partisanship and consequent loss of scholarly perspective—it is this unscholarly assault on a document whose philosophy, formulations and very conception have been drawn from its own statements and positions on academic freedom.

The AAUP's statement begins by attacking what it calls the bill's requirement that "universities ... maintain political pluralism." Bad way to start. The Academic Bill of Rights calls for no such requirement and does not employ the term "political pluralism." This is not merely a careless reading of the text; it is a substantive misrepresentation. The AAUP insinuates that the bill requires political balance, which it does not. It calls for the fair representation of conflicting viewpoints on issues that are controversial—for intellectual standards to replace the existing political ones.

Having misrepresented the principle promoted by the Academic Bill of Rights, the AAUP dismisses the problem addressed by the bill by simply declaring that current protections of intellectual fairness and scholarly discipline "work well" and therefore that the bill is "not only . . . redundant, but also infringes academic freedom in the very act of purporting to protect it." In other words, we already have the protections you are proposing and, by the way, as proposed by you these protections are actually threats.

The AAUP then elaborates its conclusion by continuing to distort what the bill actually says. "The proposed Academic Bill of Rights directs universities to enact guidelines implementing the principle of neutrality [the AAUP's own term, not one found in the bill] by requiring that colleges and universities appoint faculty 'with a view toward fostering a plurality of methodologies and perspectives.' The danger of such guidelines is that they invite diversity to be measured by political standards that diverge from the academic criteria of the scholarly profession."

The Academic Bill of Rights does no such thing. It expressly rules out measuring anything academic by political standards. Article 1 of the bill states quite clearly: "No faculty shall be hired or fired or denied promotion or tenure on the basis of his or her political or religious beliefs." In other words, the bill *forbids* use of the very political categories that the AAUP claims it invites. However, having created this straw man, the AAUP proceeds to demolish it: "No department of political theory ought to be obligated to establish 'a plurality of methodologies and perspectives' by appointing a professor of Nazi political philosophy, if that philosophy is not deemed a reasonable scholarly option within the discipline of political theory." But Article 1 of the Academic Bill of

Rights explicitly states that "all faculty should be hired, fired and promoted and granted tenure on the basis of their competence and appropriate knowledge in their fields of expertise." Hence the appointment of a professor with specific political views would be forbidden by the bill. There is no excuse for such careless reading of a text under attack. If the AAUP can't be counted on to represent fairly a viewpoint with which it disagrees, how can it be so sanguine that the faculty it represents can be relied on to do so?

Over and over, the AAUP statement implies that political standards would be substituted for academic standards under the Academic Bill of Rights. "Advocates for the Academic Bill of Rights ... make clear that they seek to enforce a kind of diversity that is instead determined by essentially political categories, like the number of Republicans or Democrats on a faculty, or the number of conservatives or liberals." As already noted, this is blatantly false. The first article of the Academic Bill of Rights explicitly forbids the use of political categories in appointing faculty, which rules out enforcing diversity through such standards.

The AAUP argument stands the reality of the bill on its head. The reality is that the Academic Bill of Rights is an *anti*-quota bill; its intention is to remove the political quotas that exist at the present time, not to institute new ones, which it expressly forbids. The Academic Bill of Rights does not threaten true academic standards or decision-making. It merely codifies the principles of academic freedom with which the AAUP says it agrees. Here is the way the Academic Bill of Rights formulates faculty responsibility for establishing a pluralism of views: "Exposing students to the spectrum of significant scholarly viewpoints on the subjects examined in their courses is a major responsibility of faculty." The operative phrase is *"significant scholarly viewpoints."* What is it that the AAUP doesn't understand about these words? And why does it insist on representing the Academic Bill of Rights as advocating the opposite of what it says?

The distortion continues and is compounded: "Because there is in fact little correlation between these political categories and disciplinary standing, the assessment of faculty by such explicitly political criteria, whether used by faculty, university administrations, or the state, would profoundly corrupt the academic integrity of universities. Indeed, it would violate the neutrality principle itself." In addition to misrepresenting what the Academic Bill of Rights proposes—the bill does not promote the assessment of faculty by political criteria but *forbids* it—the AAUP statement ignores the academic reality. In American universities today, there is actually a huge correlation between political categories and academic standing. The Academic Bill of Rights is designed to correct this corruption of academic integrity, which the AAUP has been content to preside over and defend.

The AAUP indictment goes on, as repetitious as it is inaccurate, asserting that "the bill seeks to distinguish indoctrination from appropriate pedagogy by applying principles other than relevant scholarly standards, as interpreted and applied by the academic profession." The short answer is that it does not. Moreover, no evidence is supplied by the AAUP to suggest that it does.

In addition to its false allegation that the Academic Bill of Rights attempts to introduce political criteria into academic judgments, the AAUP statement charges that it would transfer existing academic responsibilities to college administrators and the courts. But the Academic Bill of Rights does not do this any more than is already done through existing employment contracts and affirmative action procedures. Any contested tenure decision is likely to wind up in the courts, while a vast apparatus of quasi-judicial procedures involving university administrations in oversight of the classroom has been set up to comply with federal laws on discrimination and ethnic diversity imperatives adopted under pressure from special interest groups. Has the AAUP declared that racial diversity programs are a "grave threat to fundamental principles of academic freedom," because they remove some autonomy from academic faculties? Of course it has not.

More disconcerting than its inconsistency on basic issues of academic governance is the AAUP's incoherence on the philosophical underpinnings of academic freedom. The AAUP statement singles out a phrase in the Academic Bill of Rights that refers to "the uncertainty and unsettled character of all human knowledge," and claims that "this premise . . . is antithetical to the basic scholarly enterprise of the university, which is to establish and transmit knowledge." This statement is puzzling, to say the least. Major schools of thought in the contemporary academy—post-modernism, deconstructionism and pragmatism, to name three—are anti-foundationalist in their epistemologies and build their disciplines on exactly the premise that knowledge is uncertain. Has the AAUP condemned these philosophical outlooks as threats to scholarship?

Why, moreover, should there be a conflict between regarding knowledge as "unsettled" and also transmitting it? Does knowledge have to reflect absolute truth in order to be knowledge? Doesn't the purpose of the university encompass the *pursuit* of knowledge in addition to its transmission? Can it be said that scholars in any field agree on all issues in their field? On most issues? What interpretive issues in the field of English literature, history, sociology, the law—for example—could be said to be universally agreed on by scholars in the field? Probably none. Are there no outstanding unsolved issues even in the scientific disciplines, to take the most difficult case? What can the AAUP be thinking?

The AAUP statement continues with a hairsplitting distinction and another false assertion: "Although academic freedom rests on the principle that knowledge is mutable and open to revision, an Academic Bill of Rights that reduces all knowledge to uncertain and unsettled opinion, and which proclaims that all opinions are equally valid, negates an essential function of university education." First the split hair: What is the difference between the statement that "knowledge is mutable and open to revision" (the AAUP's formulation) and the Academic Bill of Rights statement that human knowledge is unsettled, i.e., that claims to absolute truth are to be treated with skepticism? There is none, and the AAUP's assertion of the contrary is sophistry.

Now the falsehood: "[The Academic Bill of Rights] proclaims that all opinions are equally valid." It does not proclaim any such thing—another pure invention. Nor does the statement that human knowledge is open to challenge imply that every challenge is worthy of consideration, as the AAUP states. That would be absurd, and there is nothing in the Academic Bill of Rights to suggest it. In fact, as already noted, the Academic Bill of Rights states quite the opposite: "Exposing students to the *spectrum of significant scholarly viewpoints* on the subjects examined in their courses is a major faculty responsibility." In other words, the Academic Bill of Rights specifically states that the opinions which ought to be considered should be drawn from the spectrum of significant scholarly viewpoints, not from polls taken of the man in the street. Since this is explicitly stated in the Bill of Rights, one wonders again how the AAUP Academic Freedom Committee could have arrived at such a preposterous conclusion.

The AAUP's claim that academic standards and established disciplines rule the academic world, and that the AAUP supports them, does not stand up to scrutiny. The AAUP is not on record, for example, objecting to fields that are overtly political, such as Women's Studies, Queer Studies and Labor Studies—each of which emerged by overtly rejecting the judgments of its academic superiors and peers. If the AAUP's standards had prevailed, programs like these would never have gotten off the ground.

The AAUP statement analyzes legislation based on the Academic Bill of Rights that is pending or shortly to be pending in Colorado and other state legislatures, and in the U.S. Congress. The AAUP is concerned about a possible threat this legislation might pose to academic autonomy. The short answer to this is that if they are so concerned, there is an available remedy. By recognizing that the Academic Bill of Rights reflects their own unenforced academic-freedom guidelines, they would obviate the need for legislation and preclude any governmental intrusion—more accurately, any *further* governmental intrusion than they already accept to enforce racial and gender diversity.

Presently, however, universities to whom the Academic Bill of Rights has been proposed are taking the position that their existing academic-freedom policies duplicate the protections provided in the Academic Bill of Rights, which is therefore redundant. Ironically, the very fact that universities like Duke and Colorado are presently claiming this redundancy refutes the AAUP's argument that the Academic Bill of Rights is a threat to academic freedom. Why would universities claim to be already embracing its tenets if that were the case?

The real issue is that current academic practices do not protect students because the academic freedom guidelines to which lip service is paid are not enforced. The resistance of universities to the academic freedom protections for students which we are proposing is the heart of the problem. If a professor with leftist views has a ten- or thirty-to-one advantage of being hired over a conservative, what does that say about the ability of faculties to judge what constitutes indoctrination versus what constitutes education? How can faculties that have demonstrated such bias in the selection of their academic peers be presumed to be fair-minded in their treatment of students who are their academic inferiors? Notwithstanding this serious problem, the Academic Bill of Rights does not call for interference by legislatures in these matters. Its guidelines, as the AAUP statement itself acknowledges, are drawn explicitly from the AAUP's own academic-freedom policies but are extended to cover students as well.

As a final matter, the AAUP statement finds article 8 of the Academic Bill of Rights especially objectionable. Article 8 states that "academic institutions and professional societies should maintain a posture of organizational neutrality with respect to the substantive disagreements that divide researchers within or outside their fields of inquiry." The AAUP finds "the implications of this requirement ... truly breathtaking." It is hard to see why. What academic rationale can there be for a university or an academic association to declare itself against the war in Iraq, as more than few have done?

In fact, the AAUP's comments on Article 8 hide through ellipses the fact that the principle refers to academic institutions and professional societies—not to academic departments—and refers to disagreements within "or outside" professors' scholarly fields of expertise. The AAUP further distorts what the bill actually says by suggesting that Article 8 refers to "judgments of quality," which it absolutely does not. It refers only to "substantive disagreements." The AAUP's distortion of the article obscures the fact that it is referring to issues that are politically divisive. Article 8 was actually inspired by Stanley Fish's essay, "Save the World on Your Own Time," which argues that there is a conflict between political concerns and professional inquiry, and that to protect the latter universities should remain institutionally neutral on controversial questions of the day.[4]

Perhaps Article 8 should have explained further what it means by "substantive disagreements," and issues "outside" the fields of professors' scholarly expertise. If so, this could be easily fixed by revisiting the wording of the text and revising it. But the AAUP has not suggested that. Instead it has distorted the meaning of the text to reach its Orwellian conclusion that "the Academic Bill of Rights undermines the very academic freedom it claims to support." On the contrary, it is the partisan dishonesty of the AAUP's assault on these missing protections that does just that. No better case could be made for the need of academic reform than the AAUP's own behavior in this matter.

---

[4]Stanley Fish, "Save The World On Your Own Time," *The Chronicle of Higher Education*, Jan. 23, 2003, http://chronicle.com/article/Save-the-World-on-Your-Own/45335/

6

In Defense of
Intellectual Diversity

I am the author of the Academic Bill of Rights, which many student governments, colleges and universities, education commissions, and legislatures are considering adopting. Already the U.S. House of Representatives has introduced a version as legislation, and the Senate should soon follow suit.[1]

State governments are also starting to rally around efforts to protect student rights and intellectual diversity on campuses. In Colorado, the State Senate president, John K. Andrews Jr., has been very concerned about the issue, and State Rep. Shawn Mitchell has just introduced legislation requiring public institutions to create and publicize processes for protecting students against political bias. Lawmakers in four other states have also expressed a strong interest in legislation of their own, based on some version of the Academic Bill of Rights. Students for Academic Freedom is working to secure the measure's adoption by student governments and university administrations on 105 member campuses across the country.[2]

Originally published February 10, 2004 in *The Chronicle of Higher Education*—one of the rare times I had access to the university community to present our case. In fact, all the "legislation" mentioned was in the form of resolutions supporting the principles of academic freedom embodied in the bill. None was in the form of statutory laws with penalties for violations.

[1] The fate of these efforts, which ultimately failed, is recounted in David Horowitz, *Reforming Our Universities: The Campaign for an Academic Bill of Rights*, op. cit.; http://www.studentsforacademicfreedom.org/documents/1925/abor.html

[2] This was an organization I created to promote the Academic Bill of Rights, http://www.studentsforacademicfreedom.org/. None of these efforts was successful.

The Academic Bill of Rights is based squarely on the almost 100-year-old tradition of academic freedom that the American Association of University Professors established. The bill's purposes are to codify that tradition; to emphasize the value of "intellectual diversity" already implicit in the concept of academic freedom; and, most important, to enumerate the rights of students not to be indoctrinated or otherwise assaulted by political propagandists in the classroom or any educational setting.

Although the AAUP has recognized student rights since its inception, most campuses have rarely given them the attention or support they deserve. In fact, it is safe to say that no college or university now adequately defends them. Especially recently, with the growing partisan activities of some faculty members and the consequent politicization of some aspects of the curriculum, that lack of support has become one of the most pressing issues in the academy. Moreover, because I am a well-known conservative and have published studies of political bias in the hiring of college and university professors, critics have suggested that the Academic Bill of Rights is really a "right-wing plot" to stack faculties with political conservatives by imposing hiring quotas. Opponents of legislation in Colorado have exploited that fear, writing numerous op-ed pieces about alleged right-wing plans to create affirmative-action programs for conservative professors.

Nothing could be further from the truth. The actual intent of the Academic Bill of Rights is to remove partisan politics from the classroom. The bill that I am proposing explicitly forbids political hiring or firing: "No faculty shall be hired or fired or denied promotion or tenure on the basis of his or her political or religious beliefs." The bill thus protects all faculty members—left-leaning critics of the war in Iraq as well as right-leaning proponents of it, for example—from being penalized for their political beliefs. Academic liberals should be as eager to support that principle as conservatives.

Some liberal faculty members have expressed concern about a phrase in the bill that singles out the social sciences and humanities and says hiring in those areas should be based on competence and expertise, with a view toward "fostering a plurality of methodologies and perspectives." In fact, the view that there should be a diversity of methodologies is already accepted practice. Considering that truth is unsettled in these discipline areas, why should there not be an attempt to nurture a diversity of perspectives as well? Perhaps the concern is that "fostering" would be equivalent to "mandating." The Academic Bill of Rights harbors no intention, implicit or otherwise, to mandate or produce an artificial balance of intellectual perspectives. That would be impossible to achieve and would create more mischief than it would remedy. On the other hand, a lack of diversity is not all that difficult to detect or correct.

By adopting the Academic Bill of Rights, an institution would recognize scholarship rather than ideology as an appropriate academic enterprise. It would strengthen educational values that have been eroded by the unwarranted intrusion of faculty members' political views into the classroom. This corrosive trend has caused some academics to focus merely on their own partisan agendas and to abandon their responsibilities as professional educators with obligations to students of all political persuasions. Such professors have lost sight of the vital distinction between education and indoctrination. The latter—as the AAUP recognized in its first report on academic freedom, in 1915—is not a legitimate educational function.

Because the intent of the Academic Bill of Rights is to restore academic values, I deliberately submitted it in draft form to potential critics who did not share my political views. They included Stanley Fish, dean of the College of Liberal Arts and Sciences at the University of Illinois at Chicago; Michael Bérubé, a professor of English at Pennsylvania State University at University Park; Todd Gitlin, a professor of journalism and sociology at Columbia University; and Philip Klinkner, a professor of government at Hamilton College. While their responses differed, I tried to accommodate their criticisms, for example deleting a clause in the

original that would have required the deliberations of all committees in charge of hiring and promotion to be recorded and made
available to a "duly constituted authority." I even lifted wholesale
one of the bill's chief tenets—that colleges and professional academic associations should remain institutionally neutral on controversial political issues—from an article that Dean Fish had
written for *The Chronicle* ("Save the World on Your Own Time,"
January 23, 2003). He has also written an admirable book, *Professional Correctness* (Clarendon Press, 1995), which explores the
inherent conflict between ideological thinking and scholarship.

Since the Academic Bill of Rights is designed to clarify and
extend existing principles of academic freedom, its opponents
have generally been unable to identify specific provisions that they
find objectionable. Instead, they have tried to distort the plain
meaning of the text. The AAUP has been part of that effort, suggesting in a formal statement that the bill's intent is to introduce
political criteria for judging intellectual diversity and thus to subvert scholarly standards. It contends that the bill of rights "proclaims that all opinions are equally valid," which "negates an
essential function of university education." The AAUP singles out
for attack a phrase that refers to "the uncertainty and unsettled
character of all human knowledge" as the rationale for respecting
diverse viewpoints in curricula and reading lists in the humanities
and social sciences. The AAUP claims that "this premise ... is
antithetical to the basic scholarly enterprise of the university,
which is to establish and transmit knowledge."

The AAUP's statements are incomprehensible. After all, major
schools of thought in the contemporary academy—pragmatism,
postmodernism, and deconstructionism, to name three—operate
on the premise that knowledge is uncertain and, at times, relative.
Even the hard sciences, which do not share such relativistic
assumptions, are inspired to continue their research efforts by the
incomplete state of received knowledge. The university's mission
is not only to transmit knowledge but to pursue it—and from all
vantage points. What could be controversial about acknowledging

that? Further, the AAUP's contention that the Academic Bill of Rights threatens academic standards by suggesting that all opinions are equally valid is a red herring, as the bill's statement on intellectual diversity makes clear: "Exposing students to the spectrum of significant scholarly viewpoints on the subjects examined in their courses is a major responsibility of faculty."

As the Academic Bill of Rights states, "Academic disciplines should welcome a diversity of approaches to unsettled questions." That is common sense. Why not make it university policy?

The only serious opposition to the Academic Bill of Rights is raised by those who claim that, although its principles are valid, it duplicates academic-freedom guidelines that already exist. Elizabeth Hoffman, president of the University of Colorado System, for example, has personally told me that she takes that position. But with all due respect, such critics are also mistaken. Most universities' academic-freedom policies generally fail to make explicit, let alone codify, the institutions' commitment to intellectual diversity or the academic rights of students. The institutions also do not make their policies readily available to students—who, therefore, are generally not even aware that such policies exist.

When I met with Elizabeth Hoffman, she directed me to the University of Colorado's website, where its academic-freedom guidelines are posted. Even if those guidelines were adequate, posting them on an Internet site does not provide sufficient protection for students, who are unlikely to visit it. Contrast the way that institutions aggressively promote other types of diversity guidelines—often establishing special offices to organize and enforce all sorts of special diversity-related programs—to such a passive approach to intellectual diversity.

At Colorado's website, one can read the following: "Sections of the AAUP's 1940 Statement of Principles on Academic Freedom and Tenure have been adopted as a statement of policy by the Board of Regents." Few people reading that article or visiting the site would suspect that the following protection for students is contained in the AAUP's 1940 statement: "Teachers are entitled to freedom in the classroom in discussing their subject, but they should be careful not to introduce into their teaching controversial matter which has no relation to their subject." Is there a college or university in America—including the University of Colorado—where at least one professor has not introduced controversial matter on the war in Iraq or the Bush White House in a class whose subject matter is not the war in Iraq, or international relations, or presidential administrations? Yet intrusion of such subject matter, in which the professor has no academic expertise, is a breach of professional responsibility and a violation of a student's academic rights.

We do not go to our doctors' offices and expect to see partisan propaganda posted on the doors, or go to hospital operating rooms and expect to hear political lectures from our surgeons. The same should be true of our classrooms and professors, yet it is not. When I visited the Political Science department at the University of Colorado at Denver this year, the office doors and bulletin boards were plastered with cartoons and statements ridiculing Republicans, and only Republicans. When I asked President Hoffman about that, she assured me she would request that such partisan materials be removed and an appropriate educational environment restored. To the best of my knowledge, that has yet to happen.

Not everyone would agree about the need for such restraint, and it should be said that the Academic Bill of Rights makes no mention of postings and cartoons—although that does not mean to suggest that they are appropriate. I refer to them only to illustrate the problem that exists in the academic culture when it comes to fulfilling professional obligations that professors owe to all students. I would ask liberal professors who are comfortable with such partisan expressions how they would have felt, as students seeking guidance from their own professors, if they had had to walk a gantlet of cartoons portraying Bill Clinton as a lecher, or attacking antiwar protesters as traitors.

The politicized culture of the university is the heart of the problem. At Duke University this year, a history professor welcomed his class with the warning that he had strong "liberal" opinions, and that Republican students should probably drop his course. One student did. Aided by Duke Students for Academic Freedom, the young man then complained. To his credit, the professor apologized. Although some people on the campus said the professor had been joking, the student clearly felt he faced a hostile environment. Why should the professor have thought that partisanship in the classroom was professionally acceptable in the first place?

At the University of North Carolina at Chapel Hill, a required summer-reading program for entering freshmen stirred a controversy in the state legislature last fall. The required text was Barbara Ehrenreich's socialist tract on poverty in America, *Nickel and Dimed: On (Not) Getting By in America.* Other universities have required the identical text in similar programs, and several have invited Ehrenreich to campus to present her views under the imprimatur of the institution and without rebuttal. That reflects an academic culture unhinged. When a university requires a single partisan text of all its students, it is a form of indoctrination, entirely inappropriate for an academic institution. If many universities had required Dinesh D'Souza's *Illiberal Education: The Politics of Race and Sex on Campus* or Ann Coulter's *Treason: Liberal Treachery From the Cold War to the War on Terrorism* as their lone freshman reading text, there would have been a collective howl from liberal faculties, who would have immediately recognized the inappropriateness of such institutional endorsement of controversial views. Why not require two texts, or four? My stepson, who is a high-school senior, was required to read seven texts during his summer vacation.

The remedy is so simple. Requiring readings on more than one side of a political controversy would be appropriate educational policy and would strengthen, not weaken, the democracy that supports our educational system. Why is that not obvious to the administrators at Chapel Hill and the other universities that have instituted such required reading programs? It's the academic culture, stupid.

7

Marching Through Georgia

L ast week I went to Atlanta to attend hearings before the Higher Education Committee in the Georgia legislature and to testify about Senate Majority Leader Eric Johnson's legislation to pass the Academic Bill of Rights. A final hearing will be held this week. In Colorado the Education Committee of the House just passed academic- freedom legislation based on the Academic Bill of Rights.[1] A professor attempted to intimidate one of the students testifying at the hearing in Colorado, proving the need for a remedy. Academic bullies of the left do in fact attempt to coerce students into following their party line. To restore the integrity of our higher educational system, something needs to be done. An Academic Bill of Rights is a good place to start.

The political left, which has instituted an informal thirty-year blacklist against conservatives on college campuses, has declared war on academic freedom and on the Academic Bill of Rights, which has been attacked by the American Association of University Professors as a "grave threat to academic freedom." What could be more Orwellian? The AAUP supported speech codes that defended terrorist Sami al-Arian while not lifting a finger to help a leftist anthropologist who is currently being crucified, along with the entire anthropology department at Emory, for an ill-considered

---

Originally published as "Marching Through Georgia," February 27, 2004, http://archive.frontpagemag.com/ReadArticle.aspx?ArtId=13977
[1]Specifically, a resolution supporting the principles of the Academic Bill of Rights and encouraging universities to adopt them; http://www. studentsforacademicfreedom.org/documents/1925/abor.html

and self-referent metaphor that some black professors didn't like. In fact they waited two months to be offended by her remark, which is the time it took them to figure out they could turn a profit on the incident by demanding a new hire and expanding resources for themselves as an expiation for the offense.[2]

Objections have been raised that the Academic Bill of Rights is legislation, and that legislators might abuse any power it gives them. This is pure hypocrisy on the part of those who do not oppose the vast bureaucratic machinery of affirmative action and diversity—which is the effect of far more ambitious and intrusive legislation than I have encouraged. All the legislative developments on behalf of the principles of the Academic Bill of Rights are non-binding resolutions. Of course they also serve notice on the intolerant left that its time may have come. This is a sufficient cause for the animus.

In the second place, the remedy for concerns about legislation is obvious. If universities adopt the policy themselves, there will be no legislation. In fact, the principal utility of the legislative moves so far has been to get the problem noticed. Two weeks ago *The Chronicle of Higher Education*—the most important journal in the field—ran a large spread on the Academic Bill of Rights. You can bet that the entire administrative establishment of the higher education system has discussed it as a result. So far, not a single administrator has contacted me to discuss it. That is an indication of the problem—and of the battle we are facing. But I have news for these administrators, and for the intolerant politically left faculty whose abusive practices they are protecting: every conservative legislator in the country has been subjected to your abuse, and sooner or later they are going to act to put as much legislation in force as is necessary to end that abuse.[3]

---

[2]Erin O'Connor, *Bates College Update*, February 27, 2004, http://erinoconnor.org/2004/02/
[3]This turned out to be sheer bravado on my part. The abuses have not been reduced, and there are today no effective protections for students against classroom indoctrination.

What kind of abuse? The students whom I met with, and who testified in Atlanta, had these stories (among others) to tell. In a course on the Constitution required by state law for all Georgia freshmen, a professor harangued his class for the full hour-long session on the necessity of socialized medicine. In a psychology course, a professor ranted about the evils of Republicans and the Bush administration. In a speech communications course, the teacher asked if there were any Republicans in the class. A female student raised her hand. She was summoned to the head of the class. The lecturer asked her to tell the class why she was a Republican. She replied that Republicans were for smaller government, lower taxes and a strong defense. The teacher then proceeded to lecture the class on why Republicans are stupid.

After the legislative session, I went to dinner with a group of Emory students. I had been invited to speak at Emory by the College Republicans 18 months before. At that time, I was the first stand-alone conservative speaker the College Republicans had been able to invite in four years. My predecessor was University of California regent Ward Connerly, who was driven off the stage by a raucous and threatening leftist mob and never finished his speech. Before I even got to Emory, the Emory Black Student Alliance fought to prevent me from coming. They tried to stop the Collegiate Council from voting me funds. They tried to impose restrictions on what I could say. When I got there I spoke on academic freedom. Naturally I used the left's attacks on me during my reparations campaign as an example of the lack of academic freedom on college campuses.

When I left, the Black Student Alliance complained to the college administration and the College Council. They said I had strayed from the topics I was allegedly allowed to talk on because I had mentioned reparations. They demanded an apology from the College Republicans and they demanded that the College Republicans give back the money they had paid me. They actually succeeded in changing the rules for speakers so that "controversial speakers"—i.e., conservative speakers—could only appear if there was someone else on the platform to refute them, or if there was a moderator to put them in their place if they "strayed" from their approved topic.

A week or so before my dinner with the College Republicans on my Georgia visit, they tried again to invite me. As a result, they were summoned to appear before five deans and administrators who told them what a bad idea it would be if I spoke; that it would divide the community; that minority students wouldn't apply for admission to Emory if I spoke on campus again. Apparently no argument was too unprincipled or too low if it could be effective in intimidating the College Republicans from inviting me.

The Black Student Alliance circulated a paper saying that I was a "white Republican" whose hobby was "bashing blacks" and that my speech a year and a half before had exhibited "racism and classism." The associate director of Student Life warned that it would have "a massive potential to get ugly, ugly" if the Council voted to fund my speech, and referred to the students requesting the funding as "haters." The College Council was duly intimidated by these efforts and voted 11–4 to reject the request. The week before, they had voted $7,500 to fund a speech by Jello Biafra. The same council recently voted to turn down funds for a lecture by radio talk show host and author Dennis Prager because he would be the "second pro-Israel speaker" that year.[4] I have asked the Emory students to write a full account of the episode in which I was involved, so others may understand why our campuses are so racially polarized. At Emory black students, Asian students and white students are all self-segregated. In my view, much of the racial tension on college campuses is a consequence of the heightened racial consciousness that administrators have fostered.

We are only at the beginning of this battle, and we will not let up until we have restored educational values to these universities. Among these values is ending the status of conservative students as second-class citizens in their university communities.

---

[4] Erin O'Connor, *Much Ado at Emory*, March 16, 2004, http://www.erinoconnor.org/archives/2004/03/much_ado_at_emo.html

8

Betraying Academic Freedom

D
o instructors use college classrooms for political indoctrination? There is ample testimony that they do, including a recent book by UCLA graduate Ben Shapiro,
Brainwashed: How Universities Indoctrinate America's Youth.
The evidence is available to anyone who takes time to look at
UC's own websites. This year's UCLA online catalogue includes a
course called the "Fiat Lux Seminar: Honors Collegium 98"
which, according to the catalogue, incorporates "History 19" and
"Public Policy 1284."

The Fiat Lux Seminar is subtitled "Re-Reading Democracy in
America: Politics Before and After 9/11." It is taught by Professor
Vinay Lal, a member of the UCLA History Department. According
to the catalogue, there are two requirements for students to complete the course: a paper on one of the two class texts and an in-
class presentation. Here is how the presentation is described in the
UCLA catalogue: "Each student will also do a succinct class presentation of no more than ten minutes accompanied by a handout
(1 pg.). In this presentation, the student will draw upon some
aspect of American political, cultural, or social life, which has a
bearing on the subject matter of the course. For example, a presentation might focus on what the election to California's governor-
ship of a movie star who has been charged by a dozen women with

Originally published as "California's Betrayal of Academic Freedom,"
September 14, 2004, http://archive.frontpagemag.com/ReadArticle.aspx?
ArtId=11409

sexual molestation, drives perhaps the most environmentally unfriendly vehicle in the world, and appeared not to have a single idea about governance says about American 'democracy.' Other presentations can focus on corporate ownership of the media, the rise of Fox News, the MTA and grocery chain strikes in Los Angeles, the trade union movements, the presence of African-Americans and Latinos in the US army, the film 'Bowling For Columbine,' the assault on civil liberties, the indefinite detention of hundreds of Muslims without any accountability to notions of justice, or thousands of such phenomena."

The mere fact that a description like this could appear in a college catalogue—let alone the catalogue of one of America's top-ranked universities—underscores the uncontrolled corruption of academic curricula by radical ideologues bent on turning the classroom into a platform for political agendas. Begin with Professor Lal's contemptuous dismissal of Republican governor Arnold Schwarzenegger as an incompetent buffoon. In fact, as of this writing, Schwarzenegger has the highest approval ratings of any governor in the history of the state. Professor Lal's course description is a political argument that could not be more remote from any scholarly enterprise or pedagogical mission.

It is not surprising that the text assigned for Professor Lal's seminar is *Vietnam and Other American Fantasies* by H. Bruce Franklin, a radical who has edited a collection of writings by Joseph Stalin and provided a favorable introduction. In the Seventies, Franklin was head of a violent radical group called "Venceremos," whose activities led to his being fired by Stanford University—an act of academic wisdom which would probably not be repeated today. Professor Lal explains the importance of Franklin's text in this way: "Though many commentators have unthinkingly rehearsed the cliché that after 9/11 all is changed, our other principal text comes from one of the most respected scholars of American history"—though Franklin is in fact not a historian but a professor of English Literature—"whose relatively recent inquiry into the meaning of the Vietnam war in American life suggests that nothing has changed, insofar as the US remains on course in exercising its ruthless dominance over the rest of the world." There is not the slightest indication that this course will present students with alternative viewpoints to this anti-American perspective, or that it will open minds to the complex realities of American democracy. This is a course designed to draw one ideological conclusion, and indoctrinate students in an extreme left-wing point of view.

Given the pervasive left-wing bias in UC's academic hiring process, which has gone on for more than thirty years, this travesty of an academic seminar is neither surprising nor unique. The present UC administration tolerates such abuses; it has recently eliminated existing but unenforced safeguards of academic integrity from its policy guidelines, and has formally accepted the politicization of its teaching programs. The new guidelines leave the university's standards in this matter to the Academic Senate, and limit the criterion for what is acceptable in the classroom to academic "competence." This competence, however, is certified by the credentialing system before the professor enters a classroom. The revision of the guidelines for academic freedom in the UC system is a direct and explicit surrender of the academic curriculum to the political ideologues on the UC faculties. It is an announcement that UC administrators now sanction the political abuse of California's system of higher education by radical activists who have seized its faculties and who are bent on its exploiting its curriculum for the most extreme agendas of the radical left.

9

Democratic Abuse of the Academy

L ast week I spent a few days in Atlanta speaking at Emory University and meeting with its president, also meeting with the dean of Diversity at Georgia Tech and students there. I also met with the Georgia governor's education policy advisor to draw his attention to the matters I am about to discuss. One of the Georgia Tech students I met with was Ruth Malhotra, the president of its College Republicans and a public policy major who is at the center of a firestorm in the school.

Ruth had to withdraw from a required public policy course after being harassed by her professor for her political views. In the first week of classes, Ruth indiscreetly told her professor that she was going to Washington to attend the Conservative PAC conference (an event I spoke at). Her professor responded: "Then you will probably fail my class." On the first class test Ruth received an "F."

Ruth is an "A" student at Georgia Tech and is on the dean's list. Her professor frequently made abusive and derogatory remarks in class directed at conservatives and Christians. These incidents climaxed during a class discussion about George Bush's health-care policy. When Ruth defended the president's policy, her professor said, "You don't know what you're talking about. George

---

Originally published as "Democratic Abuse of the Academy," April 19, 2004, http://archive.frontpagemag.com/ReadArticle.aspx?ArtId=13362. These events are described in detail and through their conclusion in David Horowitz, *Reforming Our Universities: The Campaign for an Academic Bill of Rights*, op. cit., pp. 96–108

Bush isn't doing anything for you. He's too busy pimping for the Christian Coalition."

Ruth withdrew from the class. At present she is still being billed for the course and has a "W" (for "withdrawal") on her academic record. She is working to get both removed. While I was at Georgia Tech, Ruth and I met with the diversity dean, Stephanie Roy, who was cordial and agreed to speak to college officials about Ruth's case. I have now met with several diversity deans, all of whom have agreed that "intellectual diversity" should be part of the diversity programs, although nothing along these lines has been done.

The day I visited Georgia Tech, the School of Public Policy held a "Globalization Summit." The keynote speaker was former congresswoman Cynthia McKinney, who was driven out of Congress by her own party after suggesting that George Bush was behind 9/11, taking campaign funds from Muslim terrorists and failing to repudiate her father's anti-Semitic outburst during her campaign. McKinney did not appear at the globalization event as a deranged extremist but as a professor at Cornell, where she—along with former Attorney General Janet Reno and left-wing journalist John Pilger—are all visiting professors in Cornell's Bradley program. This is just one more illustration of how universities function as subsidiaries of the Democratic Party. McKinney's rehabilitation program (courtesy of Cornell, Georgia Tech and other schools) will succeed, and she will be returned to Congress this fall. The Ivan Allen School at Georgia Tech (named after a Democratic mayor) this year honored left-wing journalist Molly Ivins on its "Founder's Day." At this academic event Ivins ranted against George Bush and the war in Iraq. The abuse of universities does not lie just in the fact that only leftists are honored at these events, but that these events are themselves perverted into political rallies. If political figures must be invited, they should not only be reasonably diversified but should also drop their partisan masks and give addresses appropriate to an educational occasion.

My visit later to Emory was particularly satisfying. I met with President Wagner, who embraced the idea of "political diversity" (his term, not mine) and committed himself to fostering a dialogue at Emory that would include currently excluded voices from the other end of the political spectrum. The year before, I had spoken at Emory in the face of protests by a political left that then attempted to prevent my return. Intense pressure was applied to the College Council, a student body which provides speakers' funds. This pressure included a meeting at which five deans and administrators descended on the College Council and told them that my appearance would be "divisive" and would harm the Emory community. A college admissions officer was brought in to claim that "minority enrollment would decline" if I were allowed to speak. This was an absurd libel that illustrated the depths to which leftist college administrators would sink to get their way. In my speech I referred to these attacks and pointed out that when I spoke at Brown University, its president Ruth Simmons, who is black, was in the audience. It was only the second time in more than 250 college appearances I have made that a university president had deigned to honor me by being present.

Bias against conservative speakers by university faculties and administrations is virtually universal. Left-wing ideologues like Spike Lee and Cornel West command fees of $30,000 paid by student funds to come to universities to rant against George Bush and the war on terror, while conservatives have to raise their own honorariums and travel expenses from private sources, which is what the College Republicans at Emory had to do to bring me to their campus. This spring, while the Council denied College Republicans $5,000 to bring me to campus, they provided $7,500 to leftist groups to bring Jello Biafra, the lead singer of a failed punk band called "The Dead Kennedys."

Student funds are not the only monies available for leftist speakers that conservative speakers are denied. This year Emory's Ethics Center brought former Black Panther leader Elaine Brown to campus as the featured speaker for Martin Luther King Week. Brown was a particularly inappropriate choice for this occasion since she despised Martin Luther King, whom the Panthers referred to as "Martin Luther Coon" while they preached violence. The Ethics Center also brought Ralph Nader this spring and provided him with a $20,000 honorarium. For several years, commencement speakers at Emory have been former members of the Clinton and Carter administrations. This year the speaker will be UN official Mary Robinson, organizer of the Durban hate-fest against Jews and the United States, which was held 10 days before 9/11. The platform for this disgraceful UN event was drawn up in Teheran—where Jews, Americans and members of the Baha'i faith were banned by government edict from attending—and was so offensive that the United States delegation walked out of it.

Thanks to the grit of the Emory College Republicans, however, we were able to hold our event. It was attended by 500 students and gave the campus community something to think about.

10

A Victory in Colorado

In the early summer of 2003, we laid the groundwork for a campaign for academic freedom in the state of Colorado. I met with the President of Colorado University, the governor and a dozen state legislators to discuss the problem of intellectual intolerance on Colorado's public university campuses. We were concerned about the treatment of conservative students as second-class citizens and the abuse of the classroom by faculty who used their positions of authority as educators to pursue political agendas. We were concerned about the absence of intellectual diversity in the collegiate curriculum and by the practices of some professors who used their classrooms for political indoctrination.

The remedy we offered was the Academic Bill of Rights. When I met with Elizabeth Hoffman, the president of Colorado, she told me that she didn't think these were significant problems at her university and that existing protections for academic freedom already adopted by the university covered all the protections that might be contained in the Academic Bill of Rights. Public statements by other college administrators echoed these views, and all parties refused to take active steps to correct the situation. So we turned to legislators to remedy the stalemate.

From the moment I met with legislators, our efforts in Colorado were subjected to an all-out attack by the political left, whose partisans were entrenched in the faculty organizations, the

---

Originally published as "Victory!," September 13, 2004, http://archive. frontpagemag.com/ReadArticle.aspx?ArtId=11430

Colorado media and the Colorado Democratic Party. The head of the faculty senate at Denver's Metro State College called for an investigation of the "secret" meetings I allegedly had had with state legislators and the governor. The Democrats' Senate Minority Leader, Joan Fitz-Gerald, denounced the bill as "affirmative action for conservative Republicans, to get them into universities," and warned: "There is something chilling and troubling about a movement like this. They're going to create a climate of fear in our universities, fear of being the professor who says the wrong thing."[1]

In fact, the Academic Bill of Rights we were proposing did just the opposite. It explicitly forbade the hiring or firing of professors, conservative or liberal, on the basis of their political opinions. What it did not sanction was the abuse of classrooms and the use of grades to indoctrinate students in the political prejudices of their professors—something the American Association of University Professors has been on record as opposing for more than half a century.

A bitter political argument ensued. At the request of Colorado Senate President John Andrews, a legislative hearing was held in December 2003 on a proposed bill to incorporate provisions of the Academic Bill of Rights in a Senate resolution.[2] Many students and faculty members came forward to share their personal experiences of discrimination and harassment on campus because of their political or religious views. Among the evidence presented at this December hearing was testimony from a student at the University of Northern Colorado, who told legislators that a required essay topic on her criminology mid-term exam was: "Explain why George Bush is a war criminal." When she instead submitted an

---

[1]Peggy Lowe, "GOP College Proposal Called McCarthyism," September 9, 2003, *Rocky Mountain News*, http://www.studentsforacademicfreedom.org/news/1049/OldCoRMNGOPproposalmccarthyism090903.htm
[2]"Colorado Academic Showdown," *Students for Academic Freedom*, February 6, 2004, http://www.studentsforacademicfreedom.org/news/362/COhearingtranscripts020604.htm

essay explaining why Saddam Hussein was a war criminal, she was given an "F."

Another legislative hearing was held in the Colorado House in February to support similar legislation introduced by Representative Shawn Mitchell. At one point a student at Metro State testified that his teacher had thrown him out of the course he was taking, stating, "I don't want your right-wing views in my classroom." The student told legislators that he hoped that passage of the Academic Bill of Rights would put a "chill" on this type of abusive behavior. As the student stepped away from the microphone, he was confronted by a man who was subsequently identified as the head of the philosophy department at Metro State. In front of over 100 witnesses, the professor jabbed his finger at the student and said in a loud voice: "I got my Ph.D. at Harvard. I'll see your f–ing ass in court. Then we'll see a chilling effect."[3]

Representative Keith King, a member of the legislative committee who witnessed the nose-to-nose confrontation, called the professor out on his inappropriate behavior, declaring: "Sir, you are the very reason we need this bill." Representative Shawn Mitchell, the primary sponsor of the House resolution, observed, "If he behaves that way in a hearing room, in front of legislators and the press, imagine how powerful he feels in his own classroom." After the hearing, Shawn Mitchell's resolution, House Bill 04-1315, passed the Education Committee on a party-line vote of 6–5.

The hearings and impending legislation were sufficient to convince university administrators that they needed to do something. After the Education Committee vote was announced, and passage of the bill by the Colorado House appeared likely, Representative Mitchell was approached by Colorado University President Hoffman and the presidents of Colorado's other major public universities to see if he would be willing to withdraw the bill if they would voluntarily adopt those provisions of the Academic Bill of Rights their regulations did not already cover. Mitchell agreed. The result

---

[3]Ibid.

was a Memorandum of Understanding, signed in March 2004, in which the universities pledged to provide protections to students of all political viewpoints, emphasizing that "Colorado's institutions of higher education are committed to valuing and respecting diversity, including respect for diverse political viewpoints."[4] Subsequently, the Colorado legislature as a whole overwhelmingly adopted Senate Joint Resolution 04-033, commending the university presidents for their leadership and willingness to revise campus policies and procedures to provide these needed protections, and requesting that the administrators regularly report to the legislature on their progress.

To anyone familiar with the state of American college campuses today, where the suppression and harassment of conservative viewpoints is routine, this was a momentous victory—one that might well mark the beginning of a change in American higher education itself. All this was provisional, however, on whether the university presidents would put into practice what they had agreed to. Colorado legislators were determined to see that they would. Senate President John Andrews called the presidents of each of the major state universities before a joint legislative committee at the opening of the fall school term to see what had been accomplished. The results were impressive. President Elizabeth Hoffman of Colorado University reported that a task force of students, faculty, and administrators had been appointed to incorporate protections and support for political diversity into the codes and policies of the entire CU system.

Over the summer, the faculty senate of the Colorado University Law School adopted a new binding Rule on Political and Religious Non-Discrimination which, among other things, adopts this crucial provision of the Academic Bill of Rights: "Students shall be graded solely on the basis of their reasoned answers and appropriate

---

[4]"Memorandum of Understanding," *Students for Academic Freedom*, May 25, 2004, http://www.studentsforacademicfreedom.org/news/1891/COmemorandumofunderstanding.htm

knowledge of the subjects and disciplines they study, not on the basis of their political or religious beliefs." Law School Dean Lorenzo Trujillo further demonstrated his determination to enforce the new code by swiftly disciplining a property law professor who in the first week of class had told his students, "Everyone knows that the 'R' in Republican stands for 'racist,'" and called a student who challenged his statement a "Nazi." Dean Trujillo is also actively inviting conservative speakers to an upcoming conference on international law, something one might think would be taken for granted at an educational institution but unfortunately is not.

The president of Colorado State University reported that the Fort Collins and Pueblo campuses had revised their policies to protect students from "discrimination or harassment on the basis [of] religion, creed [or] political beliefs." In addition they had provided instructions to students on how to use campus grievance procedures in the event of a violation of the new policies. These guidelines have already been published in the 2004–2006 Course Catalogue, and have been incorporated into presentations given to each student during orientation. The Memorandum of Understanding and the Senate Joint Resolution have been published on the webpage of the president, along with a letter in which CSU President Penley emphasizes his personal "commitment to a campus environment that respects the rights of students and faculty to express diverse, and at times, unpopular opinions, [since] that is at the heart of what it means to be a great university."[5]

In terms of today's college campuses, this is a revolution in the making, and an idea whose time has come.[6]

---

[5]Colorado State University, Office of the President, September 3, 2004, http://www.president.colostate.edu/academic-freedom/letter_03sept04.aspx

[6]Unfortunately, this was not to be. In fall 2004 the Democrats won a majority in the legislature and since they had no genuine interest in remedying the campus situation which was beneficial to their political fortunes, they failed to ensure that the principles that had been endorsed were also enforced, which was the very problem to begin with.

The Orwellian Left

A semiotically confused website called Whiskey Bar—evidently the work of a historically challenged individual with the *nom de Net* of "Billmon"—has attempted a heavy-handed satire of the academic freedom movement, caricaturing it as an attempt to pull off a Maoist purge of left-wing academics and their doctrines on American university campuses. Other equally at-sea leftists have linked to the Billmon agitprop and spread it across the Net. Professor Michael Bérubé recommends it: "[Billmon's] brilliant analysis of the Contemporary Cultural Revolution is not only scholarly and erudite, but *illustrated*."[1] The artistically gifted but politically unhinged cartoonist Tommy Tomorrow concurs: "This is brilliant."[2]

Actually it's quite stupid. The Cultural Revolution that took place in China in the 1960s (when Tommy Tomorrow and Michael Bérubé were campus radicals supporting the Communists) was a massive political purge conducted by China's dictator, Mao Zedong, who had turned against the course his appointed heirs had taken. The purge was aimed at party and state officials and also intellectuals whom Mao regarded as following the wrong party line. He incited the infamous "Red Guards," which included many students, to attack the Party establishment. Officials and

Originally published as "The Orwellian Left," March 21, 2005, http://archive.frontpagemag.com/ReadArticle.aspx?ArtId=9206
[1]http://www.michaelberube.com/index.php/weblog
[2]http://thismodernworld.com/

professors were sacked from their positions, hauled out of their classrooms and offices, imprisoned, beaten to death, put before firing squads or simply "disappeared" for having politically incorrect ideas. In fact, it's from the writings of Mao that leftist professors like Michael Bérubé and his friends actually appropriated the term "political correctness."

Students for Academic Freedom, the target of Billmon's graphic jibe, is not even a poor candidate for a modern Communist Party. Organized along libertarian lines, this is a movement to introduce intellectual diversity into an intellectual monolith, not to remove politically incorrect individuals or ideas. It is a further irony that those who oppose this movement (and who love to caricature it) are themselves defenders of the monolith and the privileged elite that enforces it. Another irony Billmon's satire missed is that I actually designed a little red book to serve as a guide for the students in what was a calculated trope. There are 150 chapters of Students for Academic Freedom, and I have never met 90 percent of the students who are organizing these chapters, which are independent and not under my control. All I have asked of the student organizers is that they adhere to the guidelines laid down in the little red book.

This guide book is published for all to read on the Students for Academic Freedom website.[3] It describes the movement's themes and campaigns, and answers tactical questions that students might ask; Billmon could easily have looked at these questions and answers before launching his attack. For example: "Can a teacher express his or her personal opinions and political views in class?" Answer: "Yes." "Should professors be denied the right to give their opinions on controversial issues?" Answer: "No." But "they should treat all students with courtesy and not just those who agree with their political opinions."

The little guide book instructs students that "this is a campaign to promote reasoned intellectual pluralism, fairness, civility

---

[3]http://www.studentsforacademicfreedom.org/

and inclusion in higher education; to secure more representation for under-represented viewpoints; to end the tyranny of majority or minority viewpoints; and to create a positive learning environment for all students regardless of political or religious beliefs. It is a campaign to ensure that intellectual difference is fairly treated." That is the full text of the statement on what the campaign is about, and it concludes with this sentence: "The campaign is about Diversity, Fairness, Civility, Inclusion and Respect for Intellectual Difference."

Is this so difficult to understand? Apparently it isn't, which is why faculty ideologues are so eager to distort it. For who can oppose fairness, inclusion, diversity and civility? No one can. That's why the AAUP is instead attempting to label this movement "a grave threat to academic freedom," and why opponents like Bérubé and Billmon are trying to convince the public that we, not they, are the totalitarians.

An unscrupulous fellow like Billmon would have no difficulty distorting any campaign. Thus, his "Scenes From the Cultural Revolution" page begins with this epigraph: "The left has taken over academe. We want it back—Mike Rosen." Mike Rosen is not a member of Students for Academic Freedom. He is not a student, in fact, but a popular radio talk-show host on station KOA in Denver. I have been on Rosen's show many times and have actually debated this very point with him. Rosen is justly upset by the academic commissars who have purged conservatives and conservative viewpoints from the academy; who use university resources to fund the left and use their classrooms as political soapboxes. But Mike Rosen and I differ on how to correct an egregious situation and restore educational values to the university. My campaign is not about driving the left out of the university or taking faculties back through political purges. It is about fairness, inclusion, diversity and civility.

That's why I made the following proviso into the very first principle of the Academic Bill of Rights, which is the first goal of the campaign: "No faculty shall be hired or fired, or denied promotion or tenure on the basis of his or her political or religious beliefs." Mike Rosen has said in so many words that he wants "an affirmative action hiring program for conservatives," which this would forbid. In sum, the analogy to Mao's Cultural Revolution praised by Michael Bérubé and other members of the faculty left is a lie, and not a small one. Many other quotations are taken out of context by Billmon and presented in ways that distort or even reverse their meanings. For example, Billmon quotes an article about a student who put up a "Wanted" poster with the face of a leftist professor (who, it happens, had abused his position). But Billmon doesn't mention the part of the same article that quotes me deploring this action. This deviousness and disregard for the truth is to be expected from the actual heirs to the revolutionary aspiration of Mao Zedong. Radicals necessarily have little respect for institutions or principles except as a means to their own power and political ends.

Why does the left indulge in transparent shenanigans like this? Because it can't handle the fact that it is not the victim class or the voice of the oppressed in the university but the victimizer and the oppressor. So it makes a myth that hides this fact, like portraying me as a communist. The viciousness of left-wing academics intimidates non-radical academics and scholars from standing up for the principles of tolerance, inclusion and academic freedom. Comparing us to communists is designed to confuse authentically liberal professors and hide the threat to their values posed by tenured radicals, who are currently giving their profession a bad name. Ours is a campaign on behalf of students whose professors commit daily outrages by using their authority in the classroom and their control over grades to intimidate students into agreeing with them and to suppress sides of the argument that differ from their own. They are personally abusive to students who do not follow their party line, and they deny all students access to the full spectrum of scholarly ideas and opinions.

Our campaign, as I testified to the Ohio Senate, is not about liberals or conservatives, Republicans or Democrats, as the attacks on us maliciously claim.[4] We have defended left-wing students against abuses by conservative and Republican professors as well.[5] Our example of an exam in Colorado, which required students to explain why George Bush is a war criminal, was devised by an anti-war Republican (or someone who claims to be).[6] Such an assignment is as abusive and unprofessional from a Republican as it would be from a communist.

We are not calling for the dismissal of such professors. We are calling on university departments and university administrators to adopt policies that would correct such abuses and restore educational values to the classroom. Our mission is to undo the "cultural revolution" that has turned so many of our liberal arts colleges and professional schools into ideological training and recruitment centers, and return academia to its educational mission—its commitment to intellectual pluralism.

---

[4]"Why an Academic Bill of Rights Is Necessary," David Horowitz, *Students For Academic Freedom*, March 14, 2005, http://www.studentsfor academicfreedom.org/news/997/DHohiotestimony031505.htm

[5]"Intimidating College Liberals," Michael Wiesner, December 15, 2004, http://www.studentsforacademicfreedom.org/news/332/FoothillWiesner Art121504.htm

[6]"University of Northern Colorado," *Students For Academic Freedom*, http://www.studentsforacademicfreedom.org/news/?c=University-of-Northern-Colorado

12

Evil Spirits

J effrey Dubner is young man I have never met, but whom I spent an hour with on the telephone the other day in what I thought was an interview for an article he was writing. The article was for *The American Prospect*, a magazine funded by Bill Moyers and dedicated to moving the Democratic Party even further to the left than it already is. I've asked Dubner for his tape of the interview, but don't have high expectations of getting it. Dubner has written two malicious and error-filled articles—one for the print magazine and one for the online magazine—which collectively contain exactly one sentence from our conversation, while turning the meaning of the academic freedom campaign on its head.[1] A campaign to defend students from professorial abuse is presented as a witch-hunt to persecute the abusers. To do this Dubner ignores everything I told him, every document the campaign has produced, and every sentiment and value expressed in the Academic Bill of Rights. But no matter; Horowitz is a conservative, the wolf pack is already at his heels and anything goes.

Both articles reveal Dubner to be an unreflective mouthpiece for the American Association of University Professors and other unprincipled opponents of the academic freedom campaign.

Originally published as "The Power of Pablum," March 22, 2005, http://archive.frontpagemag.com/ReadArticle.aspx?ArtId=9183
[1] Jeffrey Dubner, "College Try," *The American Prospect*, March 20, 2005, http://prospect.org/article/college-try-0

Following their lead (and taking everything they told him at face value), Dubner alleges that in launching the academic freedom campaign I set out to conduct a political witch-hunt of radical professors and to target one professor, in particular: Oneida Meranto, a political scientist (so to speak) at Metro State College in Denver.

The truth in the matter of Oneida Meranto is exactly the opposite. To begin with, I had never heard of Oneida Meranto until she targeted *me*. Literally. In October 2003, I was invited by the student government at Metro State to speak on the subject of academic freedom. When I arrived at the school I had to pass by a gaggle of demonstrators who were protesting the very fact that I had been invited to speak.[2] My academic freedom campaign had barely begun, but the demonstrators were out to stigmatize me as someone so tainted that his very presence was an offense to the academic community. Among the leaders of the demonstration was the head of the Faculty Senate. Dubner is right that there is a witch-hunt on campus. But it is I who am target and it is professors like Meranto who are busily lighting the pyre.

Meranto's claims of persecution are a perfect example of the Lizzie Borden defense, so much admired by her fellow radicals. First you attack people and then, when they defend themselves, you appear in court as the victim of persecution. With politically sympathetic reporters like Dubner, it is a strategy that works. Meranto is actually more than a radical; she is a radical unhinged—as she demonstrated first in the wacky speech she gave during the Colorado University football scandal, and then when, in the middle of the controversy she created at Metro State, she invited an Indian shaman to smoke out the "evil spirits" unleashed by conservatives who were allegedly haunting her

---

[2]David Horowitz, "Horowitz Visits Colorado," *Students For Academic Freedom*, September 29, 2003, http://www.studentsforacademicfreedom.org/news/128/DHBlog093003.html

campus.[3] But Dubner is willing to credit her ravings since she is a radical who shares his political agendas.

After my appearance on the Metro State campus, an undergraduate named George Culpepper, who was taking Meranto's course, decided to form a chapter of College Republicans, an organization that had had no presence on the campus before. A few weeks later, Meranto expelled Culpepper and all the Republican students from the Political Science Association, for which she was the faculty advisor. The Association was an academic club that had been officially set up for all students, but Meranto claimed that the Republican students were conspiring with a local conservative think tank to get her fired from her job. Inspiring this paranoia were false reports that had appeared in *The Denver Post* and *Rocky Mountain News* that the Academic Bill of Rights was a plot by conservatives to fire liberal professors and hire conservatives in their place.[4] Since Meranto was the head of the Metro State Political Science Department, the anathema she pronounced on the College Republicans was quite serious, particularly as many of them were political science majors. Meranto's paranoid vendetta against the College Republicans, and her notice to them that they could not be members of the Political Science Association, were the cause of everything that followed, and the substance of the complaints that the students raised in public hearings about my Academic Bill of Rights months later.

Expanding on Meranto's paranoid accusations, Dubner claims I not only spoke at Metro State in October 2003 but spent the months of September and October in Colorado training students to attack her. This is absurd. I spoke at Metro State in October and

---

[3]Tom Elia, "Oneida Meranto's Racist Speech," *Students For Academic Freedom*, February 29, 2004, http://www.studentsforacademicfreedom. org/news/524/Merantoracistspeech030104.htm; Jim Spencer, "Two Wrongs Don't Make a Bill of Rights," *Denver Post*, February 5, 2004, http://www.studentsforacademicfreedom.org/news/376/DPcleansingceremony020504.htm
[4]"Horowitz Visits Colorado," op. cit.

was gone the next day. I didn't meet with any students following my lunch address at Metro State, and didn't meet George Culpepper or any others who filed the complaint until more than six months later, when I had dinner with students from several Colorado schools including Culpepper. I had been totally unaware of the incident itself until Culpepper wrote an article for *FrontPage* about the event two months after it occurred.[5]

Culpepper testified at the Colorado Senate hearings (at which I was not present) that Meranto's vendetta had prompted him to drop her class for fear of reprisal. On the day of the hearings, Meranto told *The Denver Post* that Culpepper had testified about these events and withdrawn from her class because he was failing. This was demonstrably false, and a naked intimidation of other students who might come forward with similar complaints. It also broke federal law protecting students' privacy, which caused Meranto to be formally disciplined by her school administration. Dubner writes about this without acknowledging that Meranto lied about the grade, while describing Meranto's violation of Culpepper's privacy as his contention rather than a proven fact. Dubner then acknowledges that others regarded it as an invasion of privacy but elides the serious nature of what she did and suppresses the information that after an administrative inquiry she was formally disciplined for breaking the law. Dubner refers to it merely as being "criticized for the privacy violation."

In his article for *The American Prospect*, Dubner makes a big deal out of a tape that Meranto made of her class to refute claims that yet another student, William Pierce, filed against her, implying that our organization put Pierce up to these complaints (which we didn't) and that we should have something to say about them. We don't because we have never been supplied the Meranto tape, which Pierce claims Meranto edited to protect herself. We never

---

[5]George Gordon Culpepper Jr., "How a Leftist Professor Violated My Rights," *Students For Academic Freedom*, January 5, 2004, http://www.studentsforacademicfreedom.org/news/434/Culpepperaccount010604.htm

lodged a formal complaint on Pierce's behalf and I explicitly told Dubner, in the interview he ignored, that we do not support the validity of all student claims; we merely want students to get a fair hearing. I published Pierce's article about Meranto's class in *Front-Page* so that he would get a hearing.[6] The idea that professors who behave like Meranto are being targeted for persecution, as Dubner argues, is without merit. Has Meranto received death threats, as she claims? So have I. That's the territory for public figures these days, and I certainly did not make the decision that Meranto should have a public life. As already noted, she was accusing me of leading a campaign to get her fired before I even knew who she was.

Meranto is not without allies in her aggressions against conservative students who have been put in her charge. Meranto's ejection and defamation of her Republican students were regarded as acceptable by the Metro State administrators who denied their complaints. Meranto is the poster child for the Teachers Union and the Faculty Senate at Metro State. She got a kid glove treatment in a writeup in *The Chronicle of Higher Education* in which she was also portrayed as a martyr by its reporter.[7] The only real persecutors in this saga are Meranto and the educational establishment, and it is a sign of how far the leftists at *The American Prospect* have strayed from their own professed values that they should have forgotten who holds the power in American universities and who does not. Instead they produce articles like this Dubner attack to prevent students from getting an Academic Bill of

---

[6]Dubner also invoked the case of the student who was given a failing grade on an exam for not describing President Bush as a "war criminal" as an example of my persecution of innocent professors. I have set the record straight on this case in *Reforming Our Universities: The Story of the Campaign for an Academic Bill of Rights*, op. cit. pp. 81–91

[7]Sara Dogan, "Setting the Record Straight," *Students For Academic Freedom*, December 7, 2004, http://www.studentsforacademicfreedom. org/news/320/ChronicleResponseonMerantoSaraDogan120804.htm

Rights based on time-honored precepts of academic freedom that are presently honored in the breach rather than in the observance.

13

Bowling Green Barbarians

On March 30 I spoke at Bowling Green State University, a
state school in a blue-collar area about thirty miles outside Toledo, whose 20,000 students each pay $15,000-a-
year tuition to attend. On election eve 2004, the university put on
a showing of *Fahrenheit 9/11*, Michael Moore's propaganda film
against George Bush and the American liberation of Iraq. This was
a fairly typical violation of federal codes by universities like Bowling Green, which as state institutions are barred from using their
funds and facilities for partisan political activities. But as is generally the case, there seem to be no adults around at universities to
enforce the rules. The most depressing aspect of my campus visits,
however, is not observing how politically partisan these institutions have become; it is glimpsing the abusive activities of faculty
bullies who use their enormous power over students to ridicule
and abuse those whose conservative views they despise. By converting their classroom lecterns into political soapboxes, they also
deprive their liberal students of a decent education.

These days the principal theme of my visits to university campuses is to explain to the audiences who have come to hear me the
difference between education and indoctrination, a distinction
that seems to have been lost on the current academic generation.
The abuses I have encountered are not even subtle, though no resident official or faculty committee seems concerned to stop them.

Originally published as "Bowling Green Barbarians," April 4, 2005,
http://archive.frontpagemag.com/ReadArticle.aspx?ArtId=9040

There is something pathetic in adults who cannot restrain the urge to vent their political frustrations on a captive and youthful audience who would risk ridicule and, worse, punitive grades that can negatively affect careers for opposing them.

At Bowling Green, I was informed by students that a Spanish language professor reserves a ritual ten minutes or 20 percent of his class time in every class for what he calls a "political parenthesis." This is a class segment in which he indulges in tirades against Republicans, George Bush, the war in Iraq, and conservatives generally. In fact, such a practice is forbidden by the Bowling Green Faculty Handbook under the section describing "Ethical Responsibilities" of professors: "3) The responsibility to state clearly the objectives of the courses taught, to direct the instruction toward the fulfillment of these objectives, and to avoid the persistent intrusion of material irrelevant to the established course definition or apart from the faculty member's area of scholarly competence." George Bush's policies and the war in Iraq are obviously not part of a Spanish language professor's "area of scholarly competence."

As indefensible and offensive as the "political parenthesis" may be, it is only the tip of the iceberg. At every school I have visited over the last 15 years—more than 300 in all—there are entire departments in the Liberal Arts divisions exclusively devoted to non-academic activities and dedicated in particular to indoctrinating students in the perspectives of tenured radicals. These courses are generally interdisciplinary and are ideological in their very conception (and often in their self-description), bearing little relation to other parts of the same university—the hard sciences and professional schools on which its prestige is almost entirely based. There is nothing academic about curricula that insist on one ideological perspective, and regard their mission as indoctrinating students in politically correct views.[1] The text for a basic Ethnic

---

[1]To this subject I have devoted an entire book, co-authored with Jacob Laksin, titled *One-Party Classroom*, Crown Forum, 2009.

Studies course at Bowling Green, for example, is Howard Zinn's communist cartoon, *A People's History of the United States.*[2] Students are taught that American history reflects the agendas of a racist, sexist, imperialistic mentality and governance by a ruling class. As at other schools, undergraduates at Bowling Green cannot avoid these indoctrination courses, because undergraduates are compelled to take a sampling of them in order to fulfill their "multicultural" requirement.

When I arrived on the Bowling Green campus, I was forewarned that the atmosphere was not going to be hospitable by an editorial in the school paper about my speech that evening. Introducing me as a former leftist whose views are now "staunchly right-wing," the editorial continued: "Despite objections to Horowitz and his ideologies, *The BG News* feels it to be important to hear this man speak. Noam Chomsky once said of a pro-Nazi professor, 'I don't support the things he says, but I support his right to say them.' It is with this attitude that we encourage students to attend Horowitz's lecture." So before opening my mouth, I was put in the category of Nazis, without a chance of responding in a way that would reach the vast majority on the campus who would not be attending my speech.

I had already been alerted by my student hosts that there was a demonstration planned for my arrival. As I approached the entrance to Olscamp Hall, where the event was scheduled to take place, I saw a crowd of about twenty members of the Revolutionary Communist Party chanting, "George Bush and David Horowitz Get Out of the Way, Christian, Fascist, USA." Despite the protest, the hall filled up with more than 200 people among whom I would guess 50—including half a dozen Bowling Green professors—shared the enthusiasms of the Revolutionary Communists, cheering the name "Ward Churchill" when it came up, and

---

[2]Dan Flynn, "Master of Deceit," *FrontPageMag.com*, June 3, 2003, http://archive.frontpagemag.com/readArticle.aspx?ARTID=17914

signaling in other ways that they were there to protest rather than listen to my speech.

I began my remarks by saying I hoped they enjoyed the chanting, and that I regarded it as their First Amendment right to embarrass themselves in public. I was not about to play passive victim and probably contributed to the fireworks that erupted periodically during the evening. The Spanish language professor with the political parentheses was there and visibly flinched when I mentioned his ritual, but said nothing. An American Studies professor shouted from the audience something to the effect that I made too much money. "If you had my talents, maybe you might earn as much," I retorted to the obvious pleasure of the conservative students who had invited me and who were the real targets of the attacks on my presence.

The writer D. H. Lawrence once remarked that the intellectual life was "rooted in envy, envy and spite," and I had given the tenured radicals present plenty of cause to be upset. I reminded them that schools had once been the ladders of opportunity for the poor. My own grandfather had come to this country with nothing and earned $3 a week as a tailor, remaining poor his entire life. But the family had sent my father to public school and on to City College, a free school as well, and he had become a teacher enabling our family to enter the middle class.

All that had changed. The tuition at Bowling Green—$15,000 a year—was an obstacle for working-class youngsters in the Toledo area in their efforts to get a shot at the American dream. "Eighty percent of the school budget consists of salaries," I said. "You make between $60,000 and $100,000 a year. You teach on average two courses and spend six hours a week in class. You work eight months out of the year and have four months' paid vacation. And every seven years you get ten months' paid vacation. If you are really as concerned about the working class as you pretend, why don't you volunteer to teach four courses and twelve hours a week and lower the tuition costs for these kids?"

When my talk was over I took questions and listened to rants for about an hour. Many of the Revolutionary Communists came to the microphone to amuse those present whose sanity was still intact. A man claiming to be a documentary filmmaker and Howard Zinn's hagiographer came up to defend his reputation against my charge that he was a "Stalinist." According to this man, Zinn had written articles critical of Stalin. Well, yes, now that Stalin is dead. Actually Zinn's preposterous "history" book, which was required reading at Bowling Green, still maintains that Stalin's well-documented aggression in Korea was actually an American aggression, just as the Communists had maintained fifty years ago. At one point the Zinn fan claimed that the United States was 41st in the world in infant mortality rates. "Should we be happy about that?" Then he began chanting: "We're 41! We're 41!"

The antics continued into the book signing and one-on-one encounters afterwards, as the larger crowd began filing out. A distraught woman who said she was a bio-ethics professor got in my face as I was making my way to the door, claiming I was maligning her and her professor husband by saying that they only worked eight months out of the year and had a four-month paid vacation at her students' expense.

"Well," I replied, "what do you do between the middle of May when finals are over and the end of September when school re-opens?"

"I write my research papers," she said in a tone belligerent and richly indignant.

"Oh," I said, "in other words you use the time to work for yourself at the students' expense."

PART IV

The Campaign for an Academic Bill of Rights II

An Ill-Bred Professor
and a Bad Situation

T he story I am about to relate took place on a visit to the Honolulu campus of the University of Hawaii. I have decided to write about it because it is indicative of the behavior of too many professors on our college campuses. This particular case concerns Professor Jonathan Goldberg-Hiller, chairman of the Political Science Department at the Manoa campus in Honolulu.[1] I was invited to campus by a political science major I will call "Jamie" who acted on behalf of the College Republicans. In anticipation of my visit, Jamie asked Professor Hiller if his department would sponsor my talk and host a reception for me. Professor Hiller said yes to both requests.

A possible reason that Professor Hiller consented to the requests was that Ward Churchill had spoken at the university weeks before to a very bad national press. The same concern probably lay behind the decision of the university to put up a modest honorarium for my speech. It would be a display of fairness and diversity. Before Churchill's arrival, professors in political science and other departments vied with each other for the honor of introducing him. When he arrived they attended his speech in droves, and encouraged their students to do likewise.

Originally published April 25, 2005, as "An Ill-Bred Professor, and a Bad Situation," http://archive.frontpagemag.com/ReadArticle.aspx?ArtId= 8826
[1] "2003 Regents' Medal for Excellence in Teaching," University of Hawaii, http://www.hawaii.edu/offices/bor/medals.php?medal=hiller

No professors showed up for my speech. Instead there were about 40 protesters inside the hall holding up signs that said, "No academic freedom for fascists" and similar sentiments. The protesters were vocal and I could not begin my speech for twenty minutes because of the din of their demonstration. Security provided by the university was present, but I had trouble persuading their chief to establish order so I could speak. Finally, a vice president of the university appeared and gave the security chief the authority he needed to quiet the crowd. When order was finally restored, I delivered my speech which went tolerably well. Throughout my remarks there was a wall of hostile posters facing me from the rear of the audience; but aside from a few catcalls there were no significant interruptions. At the end, I was even presented with a floral lei.

The talk was in the evening, so the reception at the Political Science Department had been scheduled for earlier in the afternoon. At the appointed time, Jamie, a soft-spoken, well-mannered young man, brought me to the department offices where faculty members were supposed to meet me. The first thing I noticed was that the chairman's office door was adorned with a large anti-Iraq War poster. I have conducted a personal campaign against such political statements on professorial offices, where students go for counseling. Such partisan statements create a wall between professors and the students whom it is their professional responsibility to help. Such incitements serve no purpose but to vent the spleen of tenured adults who apparently lack the self-discipline to control their emotions and meet their professional obligations. I asked Jamie, who is a senior and whose father served in the military, if he had ever taken a course with Professor Goldberg-Hiller. When he said no, I asked him why. He pointed to the sign.

While I was standing in the reception area with Jamie, I noted a man looking nervously at me. His expression was conflicted, as though he had a duty that he absolutely did not want to perform. I knew immediately it was the department chair, Professor Goldberg-Hiller. I went up to him, gave him a reasonably warm smile and said, "I'm David Horowitz," and was about to put out my hand when he retorted, "I'm one of the liberals on your list."

What he meant was my so-called "McCarthy blacklist." This was the by-now-tedious accusation of the left, which at first had been nonplussed at having to oppose a campaign for academic freedom. It recovered itself by putting on its accustomed mantle of victimhood and claiming that the attempt to defend students from political harassment by professors is actually a witch-hunt against the professors' political views. If one thought about it, this was a not very persuasive line of attack, since the Academic Bill of Rights begins with a defense of professors' rights to express their political views without reprisal. But no one was thinking in the emotionally charged atmosphere that pervaded university campuses. According to Jamie, there was but a single conservative in Professor Goldberg-Hiller's department; yet I was the one at whom the department chairman was pointing the finger, calling me a blacklister.

Professor Hiller is anything but the "liberal" he claims to be. On his faculty website, he boasts that his inspiration is Antonio Gramsci, an Italian Communist who worshipped the mass murderer Joseph Stalin, a fact I refrained from mentioning.[2] But my tone did immediately change in response to his insult. I said, "Well, since you've dropped the hammer, how is it that you put political propaganda on your office door where students come to you for counsel? What would you think if I were a professor in this department and put up a sign on my office door calling peace protesters traitors?"

"You're not a professor in my department," he said testily.

"Of course not," I replied, "and I couldn't be one, since liberals like you have instituted a blacklist against conservatives like me."

That was the end of our conversation.

Jamie and I left the reception area and walked about 20 feet to where the Political Science Department had reserved the room in

---

[2]Ibid.

which professors were to meet with me. On the wall outside the room. just to the left of the entry door, was a poster which had a picture of me next to Joseph McCarthy. Very subtle. I need hardly add that the only professor who showed up for the reception was the lone conservative in the department whom I already had met, and who as a woman and a minority had slipped through the hiring screen.

This incident depressed me more than any pie in the face or raucous protest could. The insult, which had been carefully planned by this chairman and his department, was not hurtful to me—since I get insults every day from university faculty—but to Jamie, and to all the conservative students at the University of Hawaii who would be there when I was gone; who would spend their four years in college as second-class citizens, tainted by their association with conservative ideas and conservative personalities like me.

What kind of teacher would do a thing like this to his students? Who could be so petty, so deficient in human grace, as to inflict such an injury on a youngster who had come to learn, and for so trivial a triumph, if you could even call it that? At bottom, this is really what my academic-freedom campaign is about. It is about professorial bullies, so pathetically lacking in self-esteem that they carry on a daily war against students 20, 30 or 40 years younger. To behave like this, they have to abandon the most basic ethical principles of their calling. But of course in their minds they do it for a higher purpose. They see themselves as social redeemers, busily indoctrinating the next generation of Gramscians and Churchillian haters of their country. This is the real mission that drives them, not the academic filler. It is why the intellectual level of the humanities is at an all-time low, and why the academic environment has never been less free.

2

Dishonest Opponents

E ver since I launched the campaign for an Academic Bill of Rights some eighteen months ago, the most salient feature of the battle against it has been the dishonesty of its opponents. They have gone so far as to compare my campaign for intellectual diversity on college campuses to Mao Zedong's purges during the "cultural revolution," surely an unintended reflection on the critics themselves. William E. Scheuerman, chair of the American Federation of Teachers' higher education division, has called the Academic Bill of Rights "crazy," "Orwellian," and "McCarthyite." Scheuerman has said that the provisions requiring equal representation of views on controversial issues would require courses on the Holocaust to change so that "on Monday we would hear that the Holocaust was bad, on Wednesday that it was good, and on Friday that it never happened."[1] There is no such lunacy either present or implied in the Academic Bill of Rights.

I planned the campaign for this bill to repair a broken academic process, and hoped that it would be a non-partisan effort. In launching the campaign I hoped to restore the educational practices that had been in place when I was an undergraduate at Columbia University in the 1950s. These practices had protected me as a student with left-wing views in the McCarthy era. My

---

Originally published April 29, 2005, as "The Strange Dishonest Campaign Against Academic Freedom," http://archive.frontpagemag.com/Read Article.aspx?ArtId=8764
[1]Scott Jaschik, "Playing Defense and Offense," *InsideHigherEd*, April 18, 2005, http://www.insidehighered.com/news/2005/04/18/aft

parents were both Communists, teachers who had lost their jobs during the loyalty investigations of that time. While I was then a budding "New Leftist," my views reflected my Marxist upbringing. Yet in all the years I was at Columbia, my professors never singled me out for my political leanings but treated me instead like any other student. The papers I wrote were examined for the way I handled the evidence and constructed my arguments, never for the political conclusions or judgments I made.

I am grateful to my Columbia professors for their professionalism, for the fairness with which they treated me as a student and for their faithfulness to the educational concept. They did not regard the classroom as a place for airing their political prejudices, and did not expect students to adopt opinions they regarded as politically correct. The educational environment I experienced at Columbia in the 1950s was the gold standard for what I wanted to achieve.

It is my view, based on thirty years of experience around college campuses, that American universities are less intellectually free today than they were in the McCarthy era. The difference is that then the commissars of political correctness were political figures outside the university, whom the university community regarded with hostility as well as fear. Today the commissars of political correctness are an integral part of the university community itself. They are professors and administrators who think it is the university's place to train students in "progressive" attitudes and ideas, and enlist them in the armies of "social change." But the university is not—and should not be—a political party.

In devising the Academic Bill of Rights, I was careful to make it viewpoint-neutral, since it was my intention to protect *all* students—not just conservative ones—from McCarthy-like attacks on their political affiliations and beliefs. For the same reason, I believed—however mistakenly—that I could marshal support for my reforms from members of the academic community, even if they came from the left side of the political spectrum. Of course I realized that the existing situation worked against my non-partisan intent and would make such a broad-based coalition diffi-cult. Over the last thirty years there has been a general intellectual cleansing of conservatives from the faculties of American univer-sities, so that by now libertarians, conservatives and religious Christians are a dwindling remnant in any university department. Consequently, left-wing professors commit most of the abuses against academic freedom, while most of those on the receiving end are conservative students. Moreover, the university has become increasingly politicized, so that many professors no longer think it improper to introduce their political agendas into their academic classrooms; in fact, they regard it as their right.

I did not delude myself into imagining that it was possible to correct the glaring exclusion of conservatives from university fac-ulties by administrative or legislative fiat. To attempt such a "cul-tural revolution" would destroy the university itself. Therefore I concentrated my efforts on the problem of professorial behavior, specifically the unwarranted intrusion of political agendas into the classroom to the detriment of the educational process. Thus the Academic Bill of Rights can be seen as a modest attempt to restore academic *manners* to the classroom, to ensure the decorum appro-priate to the task of education and the enterprise of learning. I also realized that since tenured radicals had come to see the university as their political base, and to regard their captive audiences as potential recruits to political causes, there would be a reaction from some radical faculty quarters once I got started. This reaction was likely to be magnified by the fact that I am a conservative intellectual, and therefore not the best messenger for a non-parti-san campaign. On the other hand, these problems have been fester-ing for nearly twenty years in the university, and there was no other candidate volunteering to address them or to lead a cam-paign for institutional reform.

To make my proposed reforms as unassailable as possible in these imperfect circumstances, I took several precautionary meas-ures. In particular, in drafting the Academic Bill of Rights I based the text as closely as possible on the academic-freedom principles that had been established by the American Association of University Professors. These principles were first articulated in the *1915 General Report on Academic Freedom and Tenure*, which was written for the AAUP by the celebrated philosophers John Dewey and Arthur Lovejoy, and is generally regarded as the canonical document of academic freedom. When I completed drafting the bill, I sent for comments to three prominent left-wing academics—Stanley Fish, Todd Gitlin and Michael Bérubé—and asked them to review and criticize it. When their reviews were in, I removed everything from the draft to which they objected, without exception.

I have made this point publicly before now, with little impact. Indeed, the only result of my reviewing these facts has been to inspire an attack on my integrity by the American Association of University Professors, the chief opponent of the bill, through a spokesman named Graham Larkin, who is a faculty member at Stanford. Larkin contacted the three left-wing professors I had consulted and, in an article titled, "More Than a Stretch: David Horowitz's Imagined Supporters Speak Out," accused me of misrepresenting the facts.[2] He later escalated the insult in a defamatory rant published by *InsideHigherEd.com*, an online education site whose agendas seem indistinguishable from those of Larkin and the AAUP.[3] In that article, Larkin referred to me as a "liar extraordinaire" for repeating the claim about the three academics on a PBS show we had appeared on together. Larkin's claim that the professors' support for the bill was imaginary is based on his deliberate confusion of the original bill, which was designed for university administrations, with the resolutions that some legislators based on it. Consequently, when Larkin emailed the three

---

[2]Graham Larkin, "More Than a Stretch: David Horowitz's Imagined Supporters Speak Out," *American Association of University Professors*, February 22, 2005

[3]Graham Larkin, "David Horowitz's War on Rational Discourse," *InsiderHigherEd*, April 25, 2005, http://www.insidehighered.com/views/2005/04/25/larkin

professors and asked them if they had endorsed legislation, they said they had not—which I could have told Larkin myself, as I had never claimed they had.

There were other deceptions as well. One of the three professors, Michael Bérubé, wrote Larkin: "It's more than a stretch for David to suggest now that I endorsed the final Academic Bill of Rights." Bérubé, who became one of my chief and most unscrupulous opponents, claimed he had objected "because it would lead to all manner of absurd conclusions, under the seemingly benign banner of 'diversity.' We should ask David if he really wants, for example, the al-Qaeda perspective on the Middle East more widely taught in American universities, because right now it is severely underrepresented."

But Bérubé's interpretation of the bill is faulty, and his memory of what he said at the time is false. The word "diversity" only appears once in the text of the Academic Bill of Rights—in point 4, which Bérubé actually said he especially liked in his original comment to me: "Academic disciplines should welcome a diversity of approaches to unsettled questions." It's more than a stretch for Bérubé to suggest now (as he did not in his original email to me) that this sentence would lead to a requirement to include al-Qaeda's perspective on the Middle East in an *academic* curriculum. Al-Qaeda does not represent part of the "significant spectrum of scholarly viewpoints," which is how the Academic Bill of Rights describes the diverse viewpoints about which students should be made aware.

Here is Bérubé's original email to me:

From: Michael Bérubé [mailto:mfb12@psu.edu]
Sent: Wednesday, September 17, 2003 7:39 AM
To: David Horowitz
Subject: Re:

Hi David—
    The academic bill of rights looks fine to me in every respect
but one: the taping of all tenure, search, and hiring committee

deliberations. It's a poison-pill clause, for one thing; completely unenforceable, for another; and last but not least, it would lead to all manner of ugly unintended consequences, none of which would necessarily have to do with anyone's political or religious beliefs.... *Otherwise, everything else looks fine.* I especially like point 4, since I regard all questions in the humanities as unsettled, and have often complained about the academic mode in which people write, "as Foucault has shown...." After all, this ain't mathematics, and we don't deal in proofs. "As Foucault has argued" is a better way to proceed, followed by "Foucault's critics, however, contend...." (emphasis added.)
Michael

I removed the clause about taping tenure, search and hiring committee deliberations, directly responding to his and Professor Todd Gitlin's objections at the time.

The new objection Gitlin has voiced to Larkin is, by Gitlin's own account, not an objection to the *text* of the bill but to the idea of legislating it: "I did and do, object to interventions by such higher authorities, as is envisioned in his current campaigns directed at state legislatures," Gitlin wrote. "But the issue didn't come up in our correspondence [over the actual text of the Academic Bill of Rights]. So far as I understood matters then, it was Horowitz's intention to campaign for university resolutions, not legislative interventions." And so it was.[4]

In sum, I have never claimed that Stanley Fish or Todd Gitlin or Michael Bérubé approved *legislation* in behalf of the Academic Bill of Rights, which admittedly introduces a new dimension of possible concerns. On the other hand, Gitlin is a professor at a private university, Columbia, which the proposed legislation exempts from its provisions. Yet neither Gitlin, nor any group of professors anywhere, has come forward to propose that their own

---

[4]The course which led me to seek legislative *resolutions* supporting the bill is described in *Reforming Our Universities: The Story of the Campaign for an Academic Bill of Rights,* op. cit., pp. 21 et seq.

universities adopt an Academic Bill of Rights. It is for this reason that I turned to legislatures.

In my efforts to persuade university officials to adopt these principles, I soon discovered that administrators live in fear of their radical faculties—a fear well founded, as Harvard president Lawrence Summers recently discovered. Early in my campaign, I became aware that no university administrator would adopt the Academic Bill of Rights I had written, even when they agreed with it, unless it was proposed by the faculties themselves. But I already knew that this was not going to happen.

3

How to Get an "A"

L ast week I visited Wheaton, an elite private college in New England that requires a combined 1250 SAT score for entry and $40,000 a year in tuition fees to attend. I was there to debate a liberal, and before the event I met with the conservative members of the student club that had invited me. The vice president of the club, a political science major and a junior at the school, told me the following story. In a political science course he had just taken, he wrote a paper on the Iraq War, which his professor was outspokenly against. In my mind, this was problematic to begin with. Why is the Iraq War—a current event, about which passions are so high—the subject of an undergraduate academic course? When I went to Columbia in the 1950s, any event that wasn't 25 years in the past was considered too recent for academic inquiry, particularly at the undergraduate level. It was regarded as too open to what was then called "present-mindedness," which was considered an obstacle to reflective academic thinking. That a current war around which passions were inflamed would be the subject of an academic assignment reflected the fact that far too many of today's tenured faculty are political activists rather than teachers.

When the student's paper was returned by the professor, it had been graded "F." A previous paper he had written for the course had received a "C–", despite the fact he was an "A" student. He

Originally published May 11, 2005, as "How to Get an 'A' at One Elite School," http://archive.frontpagemag.com/ReadArticle.aspx?ArtId=8652

didn't think he deserved such a low grade, but accepted it grudg-
ingly because he couldn't believe his professor was grading him for
his political views rather than for his academic performance. But
the "F" was patently ridiculous. No student at this elite college,
which required high SAT scores for admission, received "F's" on
their papers unless they failed to hand them in. The student went
to his professor and complained. Affected by his passion in defending his paper, the professor conceded that maybe he had graded it
unfairly. "I'll give you a chance to rewrite it," he said, "but you
need to use the sources more." Since the sources the professor had
recommended were without exception hostile to the war in Iraq,
the cue was unmistakable. The student went back and, instead of
rewriting the paper, simply changed every statement that represented his own point view on the war to its opposite to reflect his
professor's views. Where he had argued the conflict in Iraq was
central to the War on Terror, he changed the relevant sentence to
say that it was a "distraction" from the War on Terror, and so on.
The entire structure of the paper, however, remained the same.
Only the conclusions had changed. He resubmitted the paper and
this time the grade was an "A." From that moment on, he lied on
the papers he wrote for this professor, feeding him the left-wing
conclusions he wanted to hear, and received "A's" on all of them.

Repellent as this story is, there was worse to come. Because I
was debating a liberal, the reception before the event attracted several professors who were not conservative, and I introduced myself
to one of them. He was a somewhat rotund, white-haired individual whose eyes squinted in a cheerful way that invited a certain
informality and trust. I was still upset by what the student had told
me; since this professor was also a member of the Political Science
Department and seemed approachable, I relayed the story to him
without mentioning the student's name. I was sure he would find
what I told him disturbing. My intention was to ask him how this
might be brought up to his colleague so that he would reconsider
his approach to his conservative students. But when I finished my
interlocutor said, "I don't believe it." And that was all he said.

"You don't believe it!" I said in exasperation. "Are you calling this student a liar? Don't you have any interest in finding out what's going on in your own department?" Instead of answering, he repeated what he had said: "I don't believe it." I was floored by his lack of concern for the student, and his readiness to conclude that he was lying.

He had informed me earlier that he was a Democrat. I told him that his response was typical of an arrogant leftist. "Fuck you," he said.

Even I, who am used to such heated exchanges, was taken aback by this vulgarity. After all, he was a professor and we were at an academic reception in the drawing room of a 200-year-old New England college. It hardly seemed the place or time. On the other hand, since today's professors dress like truck drivers rather than professionals, I should not have been surprised to hear them talk that way as well. His outburst triggered my concern that there might be repercussions for the student, who was standing within earshot of the conversation. I certainly did not want to cause him trouble at his own school. But the student now stepped boldly forward and took ownership of the story. He assured the political science professor that he was telling the truth and that it had happened to him at the hands of one of his political science department colleagues. At the same time he turned to me, pointed to my antagonist and said, "This professor is fair."

Attempting to pull back from the previous eruption, I thanked the professor for having earned this testimony from his student. My words calmed the moment and we shook hands. Then, encouraged by all this, I took another step. "Why wouldn't you believe this student? You can see that this student is perfectly capable of distinguishing between your fairness and your colleague's unfairness. Why don't you let him tell you what happened?"

His expression turned sour. "I don't want to hear it," he said, and walked away.

4

The Multiple Lies
of Clinton Liberals

I was surfing the blogosphere the other day and came across an eye-catching sentence on a blog called "Folkbum's Rambles and Rants," which describes itself as being "A Small Squeaky Cog in the Vast Left-Wing Conspiracy."[1] Actually it was two sentences quoted from another site that caught my eye, and they went like this: "Do we also have to start rounding up the college professors and putting them in camps? David Horowitz is *this close* to being that explicit."[2]

In the course of my campaign for academic freedom on college campuses, I've grown used to malicious, mendacious and unprincipled attacks from leftists generally, and Democrats in particular—people who generally like to preen themselves as liberals but haven't had a tolerant impulse towards people who disagree with them in years. For proposing an Academic Bill of Rights that would defend intellectual diversity, I have been called a Maoist, a Stalinist, a McCarthyite, an Orwellian, a thought-controller, a

Originally published May 12, 2005, as "The Multiple Lies of John Podesta and Friends," http://archive.frontpagemag.com/ReadArticle.aspx?ArtId=8614

[1] Jay Bullock, "Evolution v. Creationism," *Folkbum's Rambles and Rants*, April 17, 2005, http://folkbum.blogspot.com/2005/04/evolution-v-creationism.html

[2] "David Horowitz, Champion of Open Debate," *ThinkProgress*, January 16, 2005, http://thinkprogress.org/politics/2005/02/16/254/david-horowitz-champion-of-open-debate/?mobile=nc

witch-hunter and a fascist. I have also been called a liar on more occasions than I wish to recall.

The reason is not difficult to discern. If I draw attention to the fact that students are being graded politically and forced to parrot left-wing clichés to satisfy their professors, the academic left's first defense is to deny the reality. There's no evidence, except Horowitz's word. He made it up. On the other hand, if I or some legislator sponsoring my bill puts out a call for student testimonies of professorial abuses to support our claims, the left jumps into the op-ed pages of the principal metropolitan newspaper in the area (always wide open to them) to cry "witch-hunt!"[3] All across the country we've been attacked by irate professors claiming that we're turning students into *informers*. I don't hear these people decrying the Enron corporation employees who came forward to describe the abuses of *their* superiors as "informers."

But Folkbum's suggestion that I am close to recommending that left-wing professors be put into camps certainly raises the bar a bit. I believe this is the first time that my modest proposal to hold academics to their own academic-freedom guidelines has been called "Nazi." Where could *this* idea have come from? As it happens, the link leads to a site created by John Podesta, former chief of staff for President Clinton, and current head of the Center for American Progress. Podesta's site, *Think Progress*, is one of many that he has launched from his tax-exempt foundation. The link on Folkbum takes the reader to a page on the Podesta site which is part of its regularly featured "Radical Right-Wing Agenda."[4] Ponder this little piece of information for a moment. An Academic Bill of Rights, whose principles are drawn entirely from the academic-freedom principles articulated by John Dewey and

---

[3]Eric Ostermeier, "McCarthyism Charge First Levied at Bachmann in 2005," *University of Minnesota—Humphrey School of Public Affairs*, July 24, 2012, http://blog.lib.umn.edu/cspg/smartpolitics/2012/07/mccarthyism_charge_first_levie.php

[4]"Stories Tagged with 'David Horowitz'," *ThinkProgress*, http://thinkprogress.org/tag/david-horowitz/

Arthur O. Lovejoy for the American Association of University Professors, is characterized by Podesta and his hirelings as a "Radical Right-Wing Agenda."

Under Podesta's "Radical Right-Wing Agenda" you will find this explanation of why my academic campaign is included: "Conservatives in the Ohio State Senate are considering a bill that would prohibit public and private college professors from introducing 'controversial matter' into the classroom and shift oversight of college course content to state governments and courts." These are both blatant lies. In fact the Ohio Bill would *not* prohibit teachers from introducing controversial matter into the classroom, *nor* would it shift oversight of curriculum to legislatures. The Podesta team's source for this misinformation is the website of the Ohio chapter of the American Civil Liberties Union. The Ohio ACLU is one of the chief opponents of the Ohio legislation along with the American Association of University Professors, which has simply turned its back on its own academic-freedom tradition. A third prominent opponent is the Ohio office of the Council on American Islamic Relations (CAIR), an organization with multiple links to terrorist groups including its parent organization, the Muslim Brotherhood.

In point of fact the Ohio Bill says this: "Faculty and instructors shall not infringe the academic freedom and quality of education of their students by persistently introducing controversial matter into the classroom or coursework *that has no relation to their subject of study and that serves no legitimate pedagogical purpose.*"[5] [emphasis added] These words from the bill are actually taken verbatim from the American Association of University Professors' famous *1940 Statement on the Principles of Tenure and Academic Freedom.* It is also, word for word, one of the principles of

---

[5]"Ohio Senate Bill 24," *Students for Academic Freedom,* http://www.studentsforacademicfreedom.org/news/?c=Ohio. [Emphasis added.]; David Horowitz, "Why an Academic Bill of Rights is Necessary," *Students for Academic Freedom,* March 14, 2005, http://www.studentsforacademicfreedom.org/news/997/DHohiotestimony031505.htm

academic freedom included in the *Faculty Handbook* of Ohio State University, Bowling Green University and other Ohio state schools.[6] The point of the Ohio Senate bill is to hold university administrators to principles they *already claim to embrace,* and also to take what are now listed as "faculty responsibilities" and make them *student rights.* If a professor is obligated to behave professionally, students have the right to expect them to behave professionally.

This is what has leftist professors and politicians aroused: the fact that someone wants to take existing academic-freedom rights seriously and extend them to protect students. There is absolutely no language in the Ohio Bill or any of the academic-freedom bills that would give the legislature "oversight" of course content, as the Podesta site maliciously claims. Moreover, every university is free right now to enforce the existing academic-freedom provisions and protect their students, which would obviate the need for legislation.

The Podesta lies continue: "The language of the bill comes from right-wing activist David Horowitz's 'Academic Bill of Rights', which recommends states adopt rules to restrict what university professors could say in their classrooms and halt liberal 'pollution' on campus."[7] The words "restrict what university professors could say in their classrooms" and halt liberal "pollution" on campus come directly from a Democratic Party website. They cannot be found anywhere in the Ohio Senate bill or in the Academic Bill of Rights, or in the tens of thousands of words written by myself or by other spokesmen for the academic freedom movement. They are pure inventions of the left, along with the main claim that the academic freedom movement is targeting liberals and hopes to "halt liberal" ideas. The Academic Bill of Rights explicitly protects liberals, leftists and communists from persecution for their ideas.

---

[6]Ibid.
[7]"Ohio Democratic Party," http://ohiodems.org/

Having lied not only about the substance of the Academic Bill of Rights but also about its details, Podesta's site proceeds directly to character assassination: "Horowitz, who is the driving force behind the movement for 'Academic Freedom' in Ohio and other states, has a distinguished history of intellectual defamation, historical inaccuracy and political bullying." Epistemologically speaking, the line between criticism and defamation can be in the eye the beholder. Are John Podesta and his friends liars? Or have I defamed *them?* I'm sure their view will be very different from mine. I have never been sued for defamation, let alone convicted, as has, for example, Democratic presidential aspirant and Podesta friend Al Sharpton. So to accuse me of having "a distinguished history of intellectual defamation" is simply a lie.

I also have no record of "historical inaccuracy," except according to my political enemies who are prone to confusing differences of opinion with factual inaccuracies.[8] Like everyone who has written as much or made as many public speeches as I have, I have sometimes erred or misspoken. But these instances have been few and far between, do not touch on important matters, and have always been corrected by me when pointed out. The same has not been true of my critics—as the Podesta site's repetition of previously refuted falsehoods makes clear.

The Podesta site gives the following absurd examples of defamations and inaccuracies attributed to me:

1. "He has freely compared American liberals to Islamic terrorists."[9]

In fact, I have never compared actual liberals to Islamic terrorists. The reference provided by the Podesta site is to the Amazon

---

[8]And not only *my* enemies. There were fifty books on the "lies" of George Bush published by progressives during the 2004 presidential contest, for example.

[9]David Horowitz, *Unholy Alliance: Radical Islam and the American Left,* Regnery, 2004; http://www.amazon.com/exec/obidos/ASIN/089526076X/qid=1108503551/sr=2-1/ref=pd_ka_b_2_1/102-0136851-7758552

site where my book *Unholy Alliance: Radical Islam and the American Left* is sold. The title gives the game away. It's about radical Islam and the American *left*, not American liberals. The gravamen of my book is that the American left has formed a *de facto* alliance with Islamic radicals and that, through its influence in the Democratic Party, it was able to dramatically affect the last election, in particular by turning supporters of the Iraq War like John Kerry into opponents. My book specifically praises American liberals and Democrats Bill Clinton, Joe Lieberman and Dick Gephardt for resisting the pressures of the left and supporting a noble and necessary war.

2. "Slandered the Democratic Party and John Kerry for criticizing the war in Iraq."[10]

The source for this charge is a column decorously titled, "Is David Horowitz a Lunatic?" (no defamation here apparently) by David Corn, the Washington bureau chief of *The Nation* magazine—a publication that supported Stalin, Mao, Ho, Castro, Alger Hiss and the Rosenberg spies, and has sympathized with every American enemy in the last fifty years, while also supporting every Democratic candidate for president, especially including John Kerry.[11] Like so many leftists, Corn labels as "slander" the criticism of "progressives" like Kerry for their hypocrisy in opposing a war they had previously supported, in order to win a presidential primary. Liberals like Lieberman and Gephardt might think otherwise.

3. "and made a habit out of accusing his detractors of racism."

The Podesta site's source for this charge is MediaMatters, a site created and run by the self-confessed liar, Soros protégé and

---

[10]David Horowitz, "How Credible Is David Corn?," *FrontPageMag.com*, April 14, 2005, http://archive.frontpagemag.com/readArticle.aspx?ARTID=8982

[11]I have responded to and refuted the claims made in this *Nation* column here: "How Credible Is David Corn?," op. cit.

Podesta ally David Brock.[12] MediaMatters is entirely dedicated to smearing Republicans and conservatives and has no other evident purpose. The Media Matters list of instances in which I am alleged to have called detractors of mine "racists" begins with Al Franken and includes six other individuals and organizations including the Democratic Party. Five of these have never been my detractors as such, so it is yet another lie to suggest that I use "racist" as term with which to smear my detractors. I use the term to describe racists. In the case of Al Franken, he referred to me casually in a book as a "racist" without a shred of evidence provided. I called him a racist in return to show him how it feels. I made it publicly explicit that in calling him a "racist" I was doing just that.[13] For the record, I described the Democratic Party as racist for supporting race-preference laws and running corrupt and failing school systems in America's inner cities whose trapped students are mainly Hispanic and black.

The Podesta site portrait is barely 200 words long but it contains several more lies, which I will not bother going into since it takes multiple times the space to set the record straight. Unfortunately, this is what the political argument has become and what the campaign against the Academic Bill of Rights is about.

---

[12]"MediaMatters for America," http://mediamatters.org/
[13]David Horowitz, "Al Franken: Racist," *FrontPageMag.com*, November 30, 2004, http://archive.frontpagemag.com/readArticle.aspx?ARTID=10397

5

A High School Indoctrination

Just before the Memorial Day Weekend, I was able through a chain of unforeseen circumstances to invite myself to a propaganda offensive against the Iraq War conducted by the anti-American left at Pacific Palisades High School. It was an experience that revealed more than I was happy to know about the state of our public school classrooms. The in-school event was a production of the Pali High English Department, whose plan was to corral 300 students for an hour-and-forty-five minute lecture by an antiwar speaker from "U.S. Tour of Duty," a group that works with Medea Benjamin's Code Pink leftists to engage in active obstruction of America's war effort. The outside organizer was a former member of the Pali High English Department named Marcy Winograd, who is now president of an organization called "Progressive Democrats" and also a member of Palisadians for Peace, an organization composed of retired Communist Party members and like-minded activists.

The event was held during school hours, between 10 a.m. and noon, and my presence was the result of sheer happenstance. I had been contacted a week earlier by the organizer for U.S. Tour of Duty, Jeff Norman, who wanted to know if I would debate a former CIA analyst named Ray McGovern, who had apparently gone over to the other side. The venue Norman suggested—a Venice church—did not appeal to me, since I knew the audience would be composed of left-

Originally published June 6, 2005, as "Indoctrination in High School," http://archive.frontpagemag.com/ReadArticle.aspx?ArtId=8372

wing activists whom I also have reason to know are intolerant, nasty and sometimes violent when gathered in a public setting. I asked him to find another more hospitable venue. McGovern resides in Virginia and was only in California to visit his son, so there was little flexibility in his schedule to work with. It came down to one or two dates, and Norman was having trouble securing a new venue on such short notice. Then I received an e-mail that Marcy Winograd had sent to McGovern, copying me, whether inadvertently or not I do not know. The e-mail referred to an event she had set up for McGovern at Palisades High School for a captive audience of teenagers.

I knew just what they had in mind, and didn't like it at all. Here I was crusading nationally to take politics out of college classrooms and these leftists were planning an indoctrination session for 14- to 18-year-olds in high school. I sent an e-mail to McGovern suggesting that the high school would be an acceptable venue from my point of view if he wanted to hold our debate on that occasion. McGovern agreed, and even suggested that our encounter should be framed as a friendly discussion rather than a debate, to which I agreed. I suggested that the topic should be, "How should we look at the war in Iraq?" But before I heard back from him, I received an email from Marcy Winograd saying she wanted the topic to be: "The U.S. government should rapidly terminate its occupation of Iraq. Agree. Disagree. Qualify."

This email told me that there was a precise political agenda to the event, which was confirmed the following week when Marcy Winograd and Progressive Democrats and Palisadians for Peace organized two actions. The first was to descend on the offices of Democratic Representative Jane Harman and hector her for not signing a resolution to withdraw immediately from Iraq. The second was a campaign to descend on Hispanic high schools in East L.A. to dissuade students from volunteering to serve in the military. The Hispanic community is one that has already provided many of the heroes of the Iraq War, including its only Congressional Medal of Honor winner, and as a community takes great pride in the military service of its young men and women.

When I arrived at Pali High, the auditorium was filling up. I introduced myself to more than a dozen of the teenagers present and asked them if they knew why they were there. Only about four did. All of them said they were there because their teachers had brought them there. One of the students said the same group had been shown an antiwar film by the same English Department teachers a few days earlier. One of the teachers present was wearing a T-shirt with a picture of John Brown on the front and a political slogan advocating the use of force and violence to overthrow governments that were unjust. When I visited this teacher's classroom some days later, I was treated to an array of radical posters including one of Che Guevara and another the socialist labor organizer Mother Jones, along with a sign that said, "Iraq is Arabic for Vietnam."

Had I not intruded myself into the Pali High proceedings, these schoolchildren would have been subjected to the unchallenged views of Ray McGovern who, during our presentation, described the war in Iraq as a "war for oil." "We're running out of oil," he claimed, along with saying that the War on Terror was caused by "America's support for Israel." He told the students that 100,000 innocent Iraqis had been killed by America (repeating a false story the left was spreading) and that President Bush's war policy was really the policy of Israel's prime minister, Ariel Sharon—a not-very-subtle insinuation that the Jews controlled American foreign policy. McGovern told the students that America should get out of Iraq at once, even if it meant a bloodbath at the hands of the terrorists, because staying in would be much worse since we were spreading terror and killing innocents by being there in the first place. The only way to fight the War on Terror, he summed up, was to "deal with the grievances of those who hate us," which in his view were principally our policies in support of Israel.

When it was my turn to speak, I pointed out that the war in Iraq was defined by its results, primary among which was the vote of 70 percent of the Iraqi people for freedom and against terror on January 31. These were the two agendas and achievements of the Bush administration's war. It was not the Jews who had caused the

Muslim hatred of the United States or the conflict in the Middle East. That conflict was caused by Muslim hatred of Jews and intolerance for the tiny Jewish state, which had been built on the ruins of a 400-year-old empire that was not Palestinian or Arab but Turkish. The War on Terror was a result of the determination of radical Muslims to establish Islamic law globally and to kill all infidels—Christians, Jews and non-believers—in their path.

But even though I felt my arguments had prevailed, receiving vocal support from half the students present, I was deeply troubled by the event itself, and by the ongoing program of indoctrination that the left was obviously conducting in this and many other K–12 schools. Why were high school teachers staging political events during school hours, let alone events featuring such extreme views? What educational purpose was served by exposing students to extreme-leftist political propaganda, which is unanchored in any professional expertise let alone simple acquaintance with the facts (e.g., the world is not running out of oil and the Jews do not control American foreign policy). Students I spoke with afterwards volunteered that the school was "very political" and that their teachers were very left-wing. One student told me he had been thrown out of a class by his teacher for claiming that Saddam Hussein had used chemical weapons against his own people, a view which the teacher rejected but which happened to be true. Other students told me their leftist teachers constantly harangue them on controversial issues. A conservative teacher whom I talked to told me he was afraid to speak up because of inevitable reprisals from the faculty's left-wing majority.

I confronted several of the teachers present over these abuses of students in their charge. Using students as a captive audience on whom to inflict one's political prejudices was entirely unprofessional, I said, and a violation of their academic freedom. Students are in school to be educated. They have a universally recognized right, at least in American schools, not to be indoctrinated. None of the teachers present so much as acknowledged the possibility that the outrageous scene that had just taken place was not perfectly reasonable. When I asked the English teacher with the John Brown T-shirt why she was wearing a political slogan, and whether she didn't agree it was abusive to inflict her political opinions on her students, she deflected the question by accusing me of being insensitive to the Muslim students present in my remarks about the War on Terror. Of course she had no words of concern for the Jewish students present, whose community had been blamed for the war and the death of innocents; nor for the half a dozen Hispanic and black students who were the only students who raised their hands when asked if anyone present had a brother or sister in Iraq. Apparently it was fine to bring in a former CIA agent to tell them that their brothers and sisters were risking their lives for oil companies and the Jews, and that their principal purpose in Iraq was to kill innocent Iraqis and spread terrorism.

I told the teacher that she was a disgrace to her profession. This was over the line for her. "You are on this campus illegally," she said, "and I am going to have you removed." "Go ahead," I said, knowing that I had been invited and that the regulation about uninvited visitors was to keep drug dealers from accessing the teenagers. It occurred to me that what the school really needed was a regulation barring people like her from dealing political intoxicants. Leaving the crowd that had gathered for our little dust-up, I found myself walking alongside Marcy Winograd.

"Don't you think it's abusive to inflict your political agendas on school children who are here for an education?" I asked. "But the media are all on the other side," she whined. "Even if your claim were correct," I said, "and it is not, this is not the media. This is a school. Can't you appreciate the difference?" "The media are on the other side" she repeated, apparently unable to think up a second argument. I could see the whole issue was above her mental ceiling and gave up.[1]

---

[1]Winograd subsequently launched a primary challenge to Representative Jane Harman and won 40 percent of the Democratic vote.

6

An Academic Freedom Bill
I Won't Support

The Arizona legislature is now considering a Republican amendment to its higher education statutes which I will oppose. The amendment—SB 1331—is called "Alternative Coursework and Materials" and would guarantee students "an alternative course, alternative coursework, alternative learning materials or alternative activity" if the students are personally offended by the academic matter with which they are presented.[1] They would have the right to such alternatives "without financial or academic penalty" if they objected "on the basis that [the material] "conflicts with the student's beliefs or practices in sex, morality or religion."

At first glance this legislation might appear to be authored by the academic freedom movement with which I am associated, and which I have launched in the name of intellectual diversity. Lending credibility to this impression would be the fact that the bill's sponsors are conservative and Republican. But this impression would be wrong. In fact, I oppose the bill on grounds that it is anti-intellectual and attacks the very core of what a liberal—or democratic—education should be about, which is to challenge students' habitual modes of thinking and teach them to think for them-

---

Originally published February 13, 2006, as "An Academic Freedom Bill I Won't Support," http://archive.frontpagemag.com/Printable.aspx?ArtId= 5574
[1] "Alternative Coursework and Materials," *Arizona State Legislature,* 2006, http://www.azleg.gov//FormatDocument.asp?inDoc=/legtext/ 47leg/2r/bills/sb1331p.htm&Session_ID=83

selves. The core mission of education in a democracy is to train a citizenry that thinks for itself. But under the proposed bill, SB 1331, students could avoid being challenged at all. This is not education. It is a form of self-indoctrination. It is a perverse form of what my campaign for academic freedom is designed to oppose.

The Academic Bill of Rights is a challenge to the current imposition of intellectual orthodoxies by professors who have abandoned academic professionalism for academic activism. The politicization of the classroom, which is routine today—extending to the ridicule and harassment of students who are religious, who are white, and who have traditionalist beliefs—was undoubtedly an inspiration for the misguided Arizona legislation. But its sponsors have not taken their cue from my Academic Bill of Rights, which preserves the appropriate relationship between teacher and student. Instead they have been influenced by the very activists who have made universities the most intellectually repressive institutions in American life. After all, the idea that students should avoid discomforting moments in their educational endeavors is the precise philosophical assumption of left-wing diversity movements. What is "political correctness," and what are "speech codes," but attempts to impose a political and ideological orthodoxy on members of the academic community by claiming that unorthodox ideas are offensive?

What we have here is another expression of the historic clash between equality and liberty. The academic left acts in the name of equality—using minorities, whose sensibilities they claim are injured by the presence of non-leftist ideas, as a trump card to prevent such views from being expressed. It is these abusive attempts by activist academics to impose their orthodoxies on the classroom that have created the climate in which bills like SB 1331 appear. It is a case of the chickens coming home to roost.

The role of a teacher is to challenge students to break out of the habitual thought patterns with which they have been comfortable and begin to think for themselves. To this end, students have to trust their professors to lead them into discomfort. The basis of trust is the professionalism of the teacher. It is a trust that the teacher is not there to seduce them into accepting his or her prejudices and opinions as proven facts. The teacher is there to share his or her expertise, not to use the authority of the classroom to compel the student to accept conclusions on matters that are and will remain controversial. When professors violate this trust by introducing their political agendas into the classroom—e.g., by railing against the war in Iraq—they betray their professional calling. The task of a teacher is to teach students *how* to think, not tell them *what* to think. The Academic Bill of Rights is an attempt to restore professionalism to the classroom. By contrast, SB 1331 is an attempt to allow students to avoid the unprofessional classroom. But in providing students with the right to avoid the unprofessional classroom, SB 1331 also encourages them to avoid the discomfort of learning. That is why it is anti-intellectual and why I oppose it.

7

"A Fight I Want"

lthough I have been in many political battles in my life, I
have never encountered an opposition as personally
vicious and reflexively dishonest as the opposition to the
campaign for academic freedom, and specifically to the campaign
for an Academic Bill of Rights, which would make professors
accountable for adhering to a professional standard of behavior in
the classroom. This opposition is composed of radical professors
who want to enforce political correctness on vulnerable students;
of the teacher unions who represent them and their agents in the
Democratic Party; and of their political allies in the news and editorial rooms of national and local media. These political forces
have been unrelenting in their misrepresentation of the Academic
Bill of Rights, and in their readiness to slander its supporters no
matter what facts they have to disregard or invert.

Here is how a representative editorial describes a local legislator who had the temerity to sponsor hearings on academic freedom: "Rep. Gibson Armstrong, R-Lancaster, isn't exactly engaged
in a witch-hunt.... Actually what Rep. Armstrong has in mind
amounts to crueler punishment than the usual means of torture.
We're talking about being sued, the modern equivalent of being
hanged, drawn and quartered."[1] Every statement in this editorial,

Originally published March 28, 2006, as "Leading the Fight for Academic
Freedom," http://archive.frontpagemag.com/Printable.aspx?ArtId=5068
[1]An account of the Pennsylvania legislation and hearings can be found in
*Reforming Our Universities: The Story of the Campaign for an Aca-
demic Bill of Rights*, op. cit. pp.145–182

which appeared in Pennsylvania's *Patriot News,* is a lie. There is no law in Pennsylvania that would allow anyone to sue professors for ideological abuse of the classroom; and Representative Armstrong, a veteran of Mogadishu, has proposed no such law. The hearings he has sponsored have asked only one question: Are *existing* academic-freedom protections in Pennsylvania's public universities being enforced? Period. The rules established by the Republican majority on the committee in fact *prevent* any individual's name from being mentioned—*even* if that individual is violating current academic-freedom policies at Pennsylvania colleges. The reason for the rule is that the Republican sponsors of the committee believe the identification of such abuses should be left to the universities themselves.

In other words, the hearings are the exact opposite of what the editorial claims. The only Pennsylvania witch-hunt is the slanderous assault by the teacher unions and the press against the committee and its supporters. Every protection has been taken by the committee to prevent the hearings from damaging the reputation of any professor, including those who are violating the academic freedoms of their students. The hearings themselves, which have been proceeding for months, have been restricted to the existing policies of universities and to the question of whether they are being enforced—though the public would never know this from reading the local and national press. Instead, working from the talking points of the teacher unions, editorial writers and journalists in the education media have reported the academic freedom movement as exactly the opposite of what it is, which is an attempt to take political agendas out of the classrooms and to enforce existing academic-freedom guidelines. Teachers should teach, not preach.

Yet despite these unscrupulous attacks the movement presses on. Legislation endorsing the principles of the Academic Bill of Rights is now being brought to the floor of Congress. This is the work of three members whose courage under ferocious political fire should not go unnoticed: Representative Jack Kingston of

Georgia, Representative Howard "Buck" McKeon of California, and House Majority Leader John Boehner of Ohio. This week Boehner issued a statement to the press which announced the legislation and included a generous acknowledgement of my own efforts, despite the fact that I have been demonized by the opposition: "Last year, I met with Mr. Horowitz to discuss his Academic Bill of Rights. At the time I was Chairman of the House Education & the Workforce Committee. I expressed to Mr. Horowitz that the committee shared his concern ... and we agreed that students should be protected against discrimination based on their political or ideological views."[2]

After that meeting Boehner worked with McKeon, who was then chairman of the Subcommittee on Higher Education, and with Jack Kingston, who is the House sponsor of the academic freedom bill, to fashion an amendment to the Higher Education Authorization Act (HR 609) that would incorporate those ideas. As Boehner put it, the amendment "would strengthen current student speech and association rights" and was "rooted in the spirit of both Rep. Kingston's bill and Mr. Horowitz's Academic Bill of Rights."

In contrast to the malicious characterization of the Academic Bill of Rights in attacks by the left-wing education lobby, its agenda was summarized by Boehner in these terms: "The goal is not to tell an institution what to teach and how to teach it. The goal of the Academic Bill of Rights is to protect students against discrimination, and to encourage student speech and expression. That's our goal as well. In HR 609, we think we've found the right balance between protecting student speech and association rights and avoiding any federal intrusion into institutional autonomy. We want to ensure students are not discriminated against based on their viewpoints—whether that viewpoint is conservative, liberal,

---

[2]John Boehner, "Defending Academic Freedom on Campus," August 24, 2007, https://johnboehner.house.gov/defending-academic-freedom-on-campus/

or any other. Doing so is crucial if we expect students to receive a full and rigorous education."

The Academic Bill of Rights is a liberal document in the traditional sense of that term. Its left-wing opponents have not presented a single clause as evidence that the bill would restrict free speech or target left-wing professors. Nor could they, since the bill is strictly viewpoint-neutral. But it is also a bill that would encourage "intellectual diversity"—and this strikes at the heart of their agenda to use educational classrooms for political indoctrination. In attacking the bill so savagely, the left-wing professoriate and teacher union leaders are in effect conceding that this is exactly their intention. But they are confident they can count on a complicit media to cover for them and join in their defamatory attacks on anyone who has the effrontery to stand in their way.

I remember well my visit to Boehner's office almost a year ago. In particular, I remember my feelings as we sat in his inner chambers and listened to his staff report on the status of the bill, and the angry opposition to it. I was conscious that the attacks Boehner's aide was reporting were different from those I had endured. I was merely a private citizen, and any consequences for me were mainly personal. Unlike Boehner, I was not responsible for legislation that included other mandates which would affect millions of American lives. Nor was I an elected official who had to face a referendum on myself in a community where the local media would be savage and untruthful in reporting the issue.

At our meeting, Boehner's legislative aide described how the polarized atmosphere in Congress, because of the war in Iraq, was making it difficult to get any legislation through. This was in itself a problem for Republicans seeking re-election as a House majority. Then I heard her say that, among the myriad items in the hundreds of pages which made up the re-authorization bill, there were just four that the Democrats and their education lobby backers had refused to negotiate at all. One of them was mine. They wanted it out.

When she finished, it was my turn to speak. I felt my resolve melting even before the words came out. I was trying to imagine the real-world implications of what I was asking for. I was thinking of the war in Iraq, and how it would be gravely affected if Republicans lost the House. I was thinking of the enormous ramifications unknown to me if the authorization bill failed because of the provision I had requested. I knew that the principles we were proposing to put in the bill without enforcement mechanisms were merely a gesture—important, but still a gesture. I tried to visualize the kind of burden our request had put on the shoulders of the man to whom I had come with this request for help.

I decided to give Boehner an out, if he wanted one. Not that he would need permission from me if he decided to withdraw our clause. I just wanted him to know that I would understand and would continue to support him if he did. I could move the agenda of academic freedom in other ways, even if it were dropped from his legislation.

I said to him: "If in the current political circumstances this provision is an obstacle to passage of your legislation, I would understand if you took it out."

Boehner looked at me and said: "This is a fight I want."

I could have hugged him right there. This was the spirit I saw in the other brave sponsors of the Academic Bill of Rights, Gib Armstrong, Jack Kingston and Buck McKeon. They understand that the battle for academic freedom is a battle for the American future.

8

Intellectual Thuggery

Michael Bérubé is a professor of literature at Penn State University who won't take no for an answer. Like many other opponents of the academic freedom campaign, Bérubé is in the habit of repeating falsehoods about the campaign. I have taken the time to refute not once but many times. His falsehoods have also been refuted by others on his own website at michaelberube.com. Distortion of the goals of the academic freedom campaign is the principal weapon of its opponents like Bérubé, who is a leader of the American Association of University Professors.

Bérubé has now launched another familiar attack: "David Horowitz says he's campaigning for 'academic freedom.' In reality, he's campaigning for direct legislative oversight of professors, reading lists, and entire fields of research. He wants state legislators to insure that public universities have a certain quantum of 'intellectual diversity,' and because he complains so strenuously about the preponderance of registered Democrats on the faculty, it would seem that by 'diversity' he means 'more Republican professors.' Lately, he has even begun to speak of 'anti-Christian bias' on college campuses, with such fervor that my colleagues in the sciences have begun to wonder whether they, too, will be arraigned for 'liberal bias' against creationist theories."[1]

Originally published April 12, 2006, as "Intellectual Thuggery," http://archive.frontpagemag.com/ReadArticle.aspx?ArtId=4872
[1]http://www.centredaily.com/mld/centredaily/news/opinion/14299369.htm [no longer online]

Bérubé cites no actual statements from me to back up these accusations because all of them are false. I am not campaigning against "liberal bias." In fact, I have never employed the term "liberal bias" except to disown the phrase itself.[2] Far from planning to arraign scientists "for 'liberal bias' against creationist theories," I have publicly said that creationism and intelligent design are not scientific theories and have no place in a scientific curriculum.[3] Yes, I have singled out Rhode Island professor Michael Vocino for harassing a Christian student in class.[4] But I would have complained about Vocino if he had harassed a student who was Jewish or Muslim or an atheist as well. Harassing a student for his or her religious beliefs has no place in a classroom.

I am not campaigning for direct legislative oversight, as Bérubé claims, and have said this on many occasions.[5] Nor would my Academic Bill of Rights require "direct legislative oversight of professors, reading lists, and entire fields of research." The legislative measures I have supported are resolutions, not laws, and they merely urge universities to implement the principles they officially claim to embrace. Again, I have said and repeated this on many public occasions, evidently to no avail as opponents of the academic freedom campaign are concerned.[6]

I have not complained about the presence of Democrats on faculties but about the exclusion of conservatives, and have never called for "balance" of any kind. The Academic Bill of Rights specifically forbids the hiring of professors on the basis of their political views, a fact that Bérubé acknowledges only in order to dismiss it: "The 'Academic Bill of Rights' forbids the hiring or firing of faculty on the basis of their political or religious beliefs— and in that respect it is simply unnecessary, since the American

---

[2]*The Professors*, p. xxvi
[3]"Replies to Critics," *Students For Academic Freedom,* http://studentsforacademicfreedom.org/reports/RepliestoCritics.htm
[4]*The Professors*, pp. 345 et seq.
[5]"Replies to Critics," op. cit.
[6]Ibid.

Association of University Professors already forbids this." Bérubé is right about this. Since it is a protection for faculty, the AAUP will actively support it, something they will not do for students. I included it in the Academic Bill of Rights for two reasons. First was to forestall malicious slanders like Bérubé's, since I anticipated that the first line of attack against the bill would be to accuse me of conspiring to fire liberals and hire conservatives. What I didn't anticipate was that this malicious charge would be the first line of attack despite its inclusion.

The second reason was that the famous AAUP statements written nearly forty years ago, which forbid hiring on the basis of political beliefs, are only being selectively honored by the AAUP. Surveys show that faculty with conservative views are a rapidly diminishing presence on university campuses.[7] Why has the AAUP not conducted an inquiry to see if a litmus test is being applied in the hiring process? Why is Bérubé, as an AAUP leader, not concerned about this? The question is not whether the AAUP has the guidelines in place but whether it is prepared to see that they are implemented, and implemented fairly. An equally important question is whether, as a faculty guild, it is prepared to defend the academic freedoms of *students* as well as professors. Our academic freedom campaign was launched because we believe the answer is *no* to both questions.

---

[7]Daniel Klein, Andrew Western, "Voter Registration of Berkeley and Stanford Faculty," *Academic Questions*, March 2005, Volume 18, Issue 1, pp. 53–65, http://link.springer.com/article/10.1007/s12129-004-1032-3; Daniel Klein, Charlotta Stern, "How Politically Diverse Are the Social Sciences and Humanities? Survey Evidence from Six Fields," 2004, http://ratio.se/publikationer/working-paper-53-politically-diverse-social-sciences-humanities-survey-evidence-six-fields/; Daniel Klein, Andrew Western, "How Many Democrats per Republican at UC-Berkeley and Stanford? Voter Registration Data Across 23 Academic Departments," 2004, http://ratio.se/publikationer/working-paper-54-many-democrats-per-republican-uc-berkeley-stanford-voter-registration-data-across-23-academic-departments/; For other surveys of faculty disparities see: "Studies on Faculty and Campus Diversity," *Students For Academic Freedom*, July 4, 2006, http://studentsforacademicfreedom.org/reports/FacultyStudies.htm

From false and alarmist assertions about the Academic Bill of Rights, Bérubé adds further speculations ungrounded in any facts. Since the Academic Bill of Rights seeks to encourage "intellectual diversity," Bérubé suggests this would open the academic door to Holocaust deniers, astrologists and gay-bashers. In the first place, there already are Holocaust deniers on university faculties who are apparently welcome under present academic rules, and whom the AAUP has taken no steps to remove. Professor Norman Finkelstein at DePaul University in Detroit is but one example, but since anti-Semitic and anti-Israel attitudes have become fashionable in "liberal" academia, his crackpot views are actually defended rather than deplored. Bérubé himself has written that the notorious article by professors Mearsheimer and Walt, which blames the Jews for the war on terror and the Jewish lobby for controlling American foreign policy and the American media—a sort of contemporary version of the Protocols of the Elders of Zion—"has many virtues."[8]

The Academic Bill of Rights would not increase the number of Holocaust deniers, nor would it encourage the hiring of creationists and intelligent designers—charges that I have already dealt with many times.[9] The Academic Bill of Rights says quite clearly and explicitly that intellectual diversity consists in making students aware of the spectrum of "significant scholarly viewpoints," not crackpot or bigoted opinions. But Bérubé is not deterred by facts or attempts to apprise him of the facts. "For two years [Horowitz] claimed that a student was flunked for refusing to write an essay on why George Bush is a war criminal, until the claim was debunked—partly by the Republican professor who taught the course." In fact, the student who went into this final test with an "A" was told that she had flunked the exam; and the professor admitted he had given her a low final grade which she

---

[8]Scott Jaschik, "War of Words Over Paper on Israel," *InsideHigherEd*, March 27, 2006, http://insidehighered.com/news/2006/03/27/israel
[9]"Replies to Critics," op. cit.

was able to raise to a "B" after a successful university appeal process. In violation of university regulations, the professor destroyed the original and controversial exam. He was forced to reconstruct it for the appeals procedure.[10] It was this reconstructed exam that the university released to the public.

The section of the exam in dispute consisted of four questions, each one requiring students to explain core concepts of left-wing social analysis (e.g., feminist doctrines and power theory). There were two required essay topics and two optional "questions" from which the students had to choose one: 1) make the case for gay marriage; or 2) make the case for why the United States' "invasion" of Iraq was criminal. These were obviously not exam questions but instructions. This professor did suggest to one reporter that he was a Republican or had voted Republican; my office called the local Republican Party and checked the voter rolls, but found no record to prove that his claim was true, not that it would matter to anyone but Bérubé. All this information was available to Bérubé, since it was not only published on our website but also on his, by a professor who challenged him when he made the same claim about this case on his blog.[11] Up to that point, the fact that he was making these discredited claims could be construed as intellectual laziness. That he continues to make these claims after they have been refuted on his own blog can only be construed as dishonesty.

"More recently, [Horowitz] has insisted that a Penn State biology professor showed Michael Moore's *Fahrenheit 9/11* to his class just before the 2004 election; that claim, too, fell apart. Did Horowitz apologize for the 'mistake,' or retract his claim? On the

[10]All these facts are available here: "University of Northern Colorado," *Students For Academic Freedom*, http://studentsforacademicfreedom. org/reports/UNCcasefile.htm; and here: David Horowitz, "The Case of the Colorado Exam," *Students For Academic Freedom*, April 20, 2005, http://studentsforacademicfreedom.org/archive/2005/April2005/DHCas eofColoradoExam042105.htm

[11]Michael Bérubé, "It's a Gas Gas Gas," February 10, 2006, http://www.michaelberube.com/index.php/weblog/comments/852/

contrary: he tried to stay on offense even though he'd dropped the ball. 'These are nit picking, irrelevant attacks,' he said." In fact—as I have written in posts available on several easily accessible websites—the claim did not originate with me but with a staffer of the Pennsylvania legislature. I publicized the claim among many other similar anecdotes that Bérubé fails to mention, but ceased doing so the minute the claim was challenged and the source was unable to confirm it. When asked about this during my testimony at the Temple hearings on academic freedom, I conceded that the claim was mistaken despite Bérubé's statement that I did not. I said making an issue of it was "nit-picking" because I had presented evidence about virtually identical abuses that the Democrat on the committee, who was questioning me, ignored.

These facts are easily checked, since *Inside HigherEd.com* ran a lead story after interviewing me about the testimony I gave at Temple.[12] " I wrote a post responding to this article, which I also posted on my blog.[13] Bérubé knows this but chooses to ignore the facts in pursuit of his goal of discrediting me by pretending that all I do is make these abuses up.[14] Like Bérubé's accusations, the *InsideHigherEd* article was part of an agenda, focusing on this trivial correction while ignoring the actual testimony I gave.[15] At the hearings I testified about academic freedom abuses at Temple University for an hour and a half, never once referring to the alleged showing of *Fahrenheit 9/11;* nor did any other witness in the nine hours of testimony before the committee at Temple, or in the pre-

---

[12]Scott Jaschik, "Retractions From David Horowitz," *InsideHigherEd*, January 11, 2006, http://insidehighered.com/news/2006/01/11/retract
[13]Ibid. I also posted my response in my blog.
[14]Michael Bérubé, "On Civility," February 14, 2006, http://www.michael-berube.com/index.php/weblog/2006/02/P8/
[15]It was also unfair in referring to its own misreporting of the Colorado exam story as a case where a claim I made had been "debunked." It had not. My Temple testimony is available here: David Horowitz, "What I Told Pennsylvania's Academic Freedom Hearings," *FrontPageMag.com*, January 11, 2006, http://www.frontpagemag.com/Articles/ReadArticle.asp?ID=20855

vious three days of testimony at the University of Pittsburgh and in Harrisburg. It was only at the end of that question period that a Democratic member of the committee, who was hostile to the very idea of the hearings, asked me if I could substantiate the claim, even though it was not a claim I had made before the committee and was of no significance to the claims I was making about academic freedom in Pennsylvania.

To me this was just a reflection of what has become a national campaign to attack my credibility and destroy my witness about academic abuses.[16] It is a campaign orchestrated and financed by the teacher unions, who have created a national organization called the Coalition for the Free Exchange of Ideas, with paid operatives and a website wholly dedicated to this agenda. The Democrat who interrogated me at the hearings was a keynote speaker at two union-sponsored protests against the committee of which he is a co-chair, accusing it of "McCarthyism"—even though the hearings have addressed only policy issues and a committee rule bars the use of faculty names in testimony.

Professor Bérubé certainly does not lack gall in accusing me of disregard for the facts: "But few newsmakers are as sloppy and careless as Horowitz." His evidence? "In [Horowitz's] recent book, *The Professors,* he attributes to Eric Foner, a professor of history at Columbia University, a long passage that was actually written by someone else. When Foner called him on the error, Horowitz, true to form, attacked Foner's 'honesty,' and insisted, 'the error in my book is an inconsequential one' and 'it was my intention to cite the authentic quote.'"

As in the other cases, I have already answered this charge.[17] The passage in question is actually fairly short (four sentences to

---

[16]"Teachers Unions Defend Campus Free Speech," *The Professors,* March 26, 2006, http://www.studentsforacademicfreedom.org/dangprofs//2006/03/attack-teachers-unions-defend-campus.html

[17]David Horowitz, "Reply to Critic: Not as Serious as a Heart Attack," *The Professors,* February 27, 2006, http://www.studentsforacademicfreedom.org/dangprofs//2006/02/reply-to-critic-not-as-serious-as.html

be precise), and I have not denied that it was erroneously tran-scribed from a symposium on 9/11 in the *London Review of Books* to which both Foner and the other writer contributed. The Foner statement that should have been quoted was, in fact, one that I had used previously in my book *Unholy Alliance,* so I was very aware of what he had said in the passage when describing it in my new text. As I have already pointed out in my response to this charge, the wrongly attributed quote does not really differ from Foner's own statement that there was probably more to fear in America's response to the 9/11 attack than in the attack itself. In *The Professors* I wrote: "Professor Foner focused not on the atroc-ity itself but on what he perceived to be the threat of an American response." What Foner actually said (and what I failed to quote) was this: "I'm not sure which is more frightening: the horror that engulfed New York City or the apocalyptic rhetoric emanating daily from the White House." So this is a distinction without a dif-ference, which is why I called the error "inconsequential." All this information—including the two contributions to the symposium as they appeared on the page—was posted on my website and read-ily available to Bérubé. In fact he read my response and simply chose to ignore the substance of what I said, so he could pursue his agenda of discrediting me.[18]

Bérubé concludes his attack with a final false claim: "Fortu-nately, Penn State already has a strong policy on academic freedom (HR 64), defending the rights of both professors and students. And we have a chapter of the AAUP, dedicated to maintaining profes-sional standards in and out of the classroom."[19]

Despite Bérubé's unsubstantiated claim, the AAUP is not in the business of defending students and, for example, did not defend the Christian student whom Professor Michael Vocino

---

[18]Michael Bérubé, "Discover the Matrix Reloaded," February 28, 2006, http://www.michaelberube.com/index.php/weblog/2006/02/
[19]In 2010 the Faculty Senate at Penn State eviscerated HR 64 with no protests from Bérubé or the AAUP. On the contrary, the campaign against HR 64 was led by AAUP president Cary Nelson.

singled out for attack in his class. Nor has the AAUP shown any concern about fact that Vocino is not qualified to be a full professor or that he lacks the credentials to teach a course in political science, a field in which he has no academic expertise.[20] If the AAUP is concerned about maintaining professional standards, it is certainly doing a poor job.

In the second place, only a handful of faculty and probably no students would even be aware of Pennsylvania's policy HR 64 if my academic freedom campaign had not begun making them and the general public aware of it more than two years ago. It was a centerpiece of my testimony to the Pennsylvania legislature in 2005 and my testimony to the Ohio legislature the year before, both available on my website.[21] It was featured in a pamphlet published by my organization called *The Campaign for Academic Freedom*, also available on my website. In the testimony I gave to the Pennsylvania subcommittee on Academic Freedom in Higher Education (also available on my website) Bérubé would know it is my contention—and that of our campaign—not that the academic freedom policy HR 64 does not exist, but that the academic freedom policy HR 64 *is not enforced*. In fact he does know this.[22]

Persuading administrators to enforce existing academic-freedom policies of their universities is the centerpiece of our campaign in Pennsylvania. The campaign is not about liberal bias, and is not an attempt to have the legislature impose requirements on

[20]David Horowitz, "Attack of an Academic Zero," *FrontPageMag.com*, March 21, 2006, http://www.frontpagemag.com/articles/ReadArticle. asp?ID=21734

[21]David Horowitz, "What I Told Pennsylvania's Academic Freedom Hearings," *FrontPageMag.com*, January 11, 2006, http://www.frontpagemag.com/Articles/ReadArticle.asp?ID=20855; David Horowitz, "Why an Academic Bill of Rights Is Necessary," *Students For Academic Freedom*, March 14, 2005, http://studentsforacademicfreedom.org/archive/2005/March2005/DHohiotestimony031505.htm

[22]David Horowitz, "Pennsylvania's Academic Freedom Reforms," *Students For Academic Freedom*, December 1, 2006, http://studentsfor academicfreedom.org/actions(boxattop)/Pennsylvaniapage/PennHearing s. htm

universities; nor is it an attempt to get conservatives hired. It is an effort to pressure the administrations of Pennsylvania universities to enforce existing academic-freedom policies like HR 64 and—equally important—to make students aware of their rights in regard to these policies. This is the campaign Michael Bérubé and the American Association of University Professors fear so much that they are willing to distort its agendas and make up lies about its spokesman in order to avoid confronting the issue it is attempting to raise: the dereliction of university authorities and themselves.

9

What's Not Liberal
About the Liberal Arts

O pponents of efforts to end political discrimination and classroom indoctrination on college campuses follow a predictable game plan:

- Deny these problems exist.
- Question the veracity of anyone who claims they do.
- Misrepresent the supporters of academic freedom as the witch-hunters they are trying to thwart.

Michael Bérubé's new book, *What's Liberal About The Liberal Arts?: Classroom Politics and 'Bias' in Higher Education*, is a case study in these techniques.[1] Bérubé is a professor of English Literature at Penn State and a member of the National Council of the American Association of University Professors, which has cast itself as the chief antagonist of the movement for academic reform.

Bérubé's attack on the academic freedom movement is made up of two parts. The first consists of chapters that describe his class-

---

Originally published October 20, 2006, as "What's Not Liberal about the Liberal Arts," http://archive.frontpagemag.com/ReadArticle.aspx?ArtId= 1989

[1]"What's Liberal About the Liberal Arts?: Classroom Politics and 'Bias' in Higher Education," Michael Bérubé, W.W. Norton, 2006, http://www. amazon.com/Whats-Liberal-About-Arts-Education/dp/0393060373/sr=1- 1/qid=1161310147/ref=pd_bbs_sr_1/104-3074636-5323134?ie=UTF8&s= books

room teaching practices and are designed to show how academic, fair, and ultimately innocuous these sessions are. In other words, it is only the ignorance of conservatives concerning what a university class is actually about, along with their visceral prejudice against liberals, that makes classroom indoctrination and political harassment issues at all. The second part of the book is an "analysis" of the activities of conservative reformers like myself. In this section, Bérubé describes us as dishonest, censorious and driven by Machiavellian agendas. In his telling, the conservative critique of academia is not about unfair practices or politically corrupted intellectual standards, as we have claimed. Instead, ours is a sinister campaign to purge the universities of liberal ideas. Our motive in doing so is that "conservatives control all three branches of government and a good deal of the mass media," and want to close down the last bastion of resistance to their rule (p. 21).

This falsehood is typical of the attacks on the academic freedom campaign. Yet none of the serious critics of the academic status quo—Stephen Balch, Mark Bauerlein, Anne Neal, Alan Kors, or myself—have ever called for the firing of a single academic for political views. In my book, *The Professors*, a text that Bérubé has criticized on more than one occasion, I have stated my view of professorial bias quite clearly: "[*The Professors*] does not propose that a left-wing perspective on academic faculties is a problem in itself. Every individual, whether conservative or liberal, has a perspective and therefore a bias. Professors have every right to interpret the subjects they teach according to their individual points of view. That is the essence of academic freedom." (p. xxvi)

tx:In order to stigmatize me as a leader of "the fringe right wing" and my campaign as "no more consequential than the extreme right's past campaigns against the fluoridation of drinking water and the introduction of zip codes," (pp. 28–29) Bérubé has to disregard every statement I have made to the opposite effect.[2] The

---

[2]"Academic Bill of Rights," *Students for Academic Freedom*, http://www.studentsforacademicfreedom.org/documents/1925/abor.html

basis for Bérubé's caricature rests on statements not by me but by two legislators who have sponsored versions of the Academic Bill of Rights. The legislators made statements in favor of Intelligent Design theory. The implication drawn by Bérubé is that the Academic Bill of Rights would require the inclusion of Intelligent Design theory in biology courses. In fact, the Academic Bill of Rights legislation *requires* nothing. The bills Bérubé refers to are merely resolutions without enforcement powers, and they explicitly limit the diversity they would encourage to "the spectrum of significant scholarly opinion"—a spectrum that is defined by the academic community. Under the Academic Bill of Rights, Intelligent Design theory would still be excluded from biology classes.

I have publicly stated—and more than once—that Intelligent Design is not a scientific theory and has no place in a biology curriculum. I have explained to both the legislators cited by Bérubé that my Academic Bill of Rights will do nothing to further their agendas in regard to Intelligent Design, nor should it. Yet without reference to the actual text of any resolution I have supported or to any statement I have made, Bérubé asserts that my campaign would impose non-academic agendas, like Intelligent Design, on the academic curriculum.[3]

Bérubé's consistent theme is that I am promoting a witch-hunt of liberal professors and liberal ideas. He attempts to establish this lie by referring to a bulletin board on my academic freedom website which is called the "Student Abuse Center."[4] He describes this as a forum "to allow conservative students to report on the doings and teachings of liberal professors—or, more accurately, professors who offend conservatives' political sensibilities in one way or another."

---

[3]Bérubé also draws on a hostile newspaper account of the Florida legislation to suggest that the Academic Bill of Rights would provide a basis for students to sue their professors. No such basis could be provided by a resolution without statutory teeth—and all the legislation regarding an Academic Bill of Rights thus far has been of this nature.

[4]*Students for Academic Freedom*, http://www.studentsforacademicfreedom.org

This description of what we have called the "Student Abuse Center" is false in more ways than one. The idea that there is something wrong with "allowing" students to voice complaints is itself odd, coming from a man who is busy warning others about the danger of suppressing ideas. The "Student Abuse Center" is not, as Bérubé claims, a site designed for conservative students to complain about liberal professors, but for students of any political persuasion to comment on faculty behavior they find abusive. This includes complaints from liberal students about abuses by conservative professors—and we have posted entire articles representing such complaints.[5] The "Student Abuse Center" features this disclaimer: "These are examples of student complaints. Students for Academic Freedom has not investigated these complaints and does not endorse them. It is providing this bulletin board to illustrate the kinds of complaints that students have." We also invite professors to respond to the complaints. Moreover, the "Student Abuse Center" is explicitly *not* for students to complain about professorial views that offend them. It instructs students as to what kind of complaints are appropriate. These are listed on the form provided for postings:

- Required readings or texts covering only one side of issues.
- Gratuitous singling out of political or religious beliefs for ridicule.
- Introduction of controversial material that has no relation to the subject.
- Forcing students to express a certain point of view in assignments.
- Mocking national, political or religious figures.
- Conducting political activities in class (e.g. recruiting for demonstrations).

---

[5]E.g., Michael Wiesner, "Collegiate Intimidation," *Frontpagemag.com*, December 15, 2004, http://archive.frontpagemag.com/readArticle.aspx? ARTID=10231. See below.

- Allowing students' political or religious beliefs to influence grading.
- Use of university funds to hold one-sided partisan teach-ins or conferences.

It is obvious from these instructions that whether a professor's views are liberal or radical is not a cause for complaint. In his book, Bérubé discusses particular complaints he has found on this site, but he never mentions these instructions or lets his readers know that they exist. If he did, he could not cite the "Student Abuse Center" as evidence of a witch-hunt.

In setting up the argument of his book, Bérubé describes his position as follows: "I believe that the liberal ideal consists in engaging my most stringent interlocutors, so long as we share a commitment to open-ended rational debate." But rational debate is hardly possible with someone who deliberately misrepresents his opponents, who engages in gratuitous name-calling, and whose only purpose is to taint opponents sufficiently to remove them from the debate.

It is hard to take Bérubé seriously when he claims to regard "some forms of conservatism [as] absolutely essential to my conception of liberalism." Bérubé explains that this is because he is committed to a form of inquiry "whose outcomes cannot be known in advance." (p. 21) Consequently, he explains that as a process liberal, "I do not have and cannot seek unanimity in political and cultural matters." (p. 22)

Anyone familiar with the Academic Bill of Rights—a document which Bérubé has derided and condemned—would instantly recognize in these very words the bill's philosophical basis, and also the philosophical basis of the campaign I have organized. Here is the relevant passage from the Academic Bill of Rights:

> 3. Curricula and reading lists in the humanities and social sciences should reflect the uncertainty and unsettled character of all human knowledge in these areas by providing students with dissenting sources and viewpoints where appropriate. While teach-

ers are and should be free to pursue their own findings and perspectives in presenting their views, they should consider and make their students aware of other viewpoints. Academic disciplines should welcome a diversity of approaches to unsettled questions.

Is this not precisely the liberal ideal that Bérubé is touting? Of course it is! Which is why, when I submitted the text of the Academic Bill of Rights for Bérubé's own approval—and did so before publishing it—he sent me the following email:

Hi David—

The Academic Bill of Rights looks fine to me in every respect but one: the taping of all tenure, search, and hiring committee deliberations. . . .[6]

The reference about taping is to a clause in the original version I sent him that would have required the recording of all tenure and hiring committee proceedings. I removed this clause from the final text precisely because Bérubé objected. Everything else was left exactly as he had approved it. I did this because I wanted a document that both liberals and conservatives could support. How liberal of me. How worthy of Bérubé's dialogue between liberals like him and conservatives like me. But of course there is no mention of this fact in Michael Bérubé's book, let alone any effort to conduct a serious intellectual argument.

Instead, Bérubé attacks me as belonging to a group of conservatives he calls "radicals" who are unworthy of serious argument. According to Bérubé, conservative radicals "attack" the university "not simply on the substance of liberalism but on procedural liberalism itself, on the idea that no one political faction should control every facet of a society." In other words, it is not liberal academics but conservatives who seek to enforce an ideological monopoly in their institutions. This is as a neat a case of projection as one might expect to encounter.

---

[6]Bérubé's email was sent September 17, 2003.

In addition to misrepresenting my clearly stated agendas, moreover, Bérubé's statement reveals an attitude that is hardly that of a procedural liberal. By pairing Republican control of political institutions like the White House with liberal control of the university, Bérubé betrays an attitude that assumes the university should be a political institution as well.

According to Bérubé, the Republicans who control the House of Representatives are conservatives of the radical kind—essentially totalitarians—because they have allegedly "rewritten the rules of the chamber so that Democrats cannot offer amendments, propose legislation, or challenge committee chairs." (p. 21) Bérubé seems unaware that this result did not require rewriting the rules, and that Democrats actually ran the House according to these rules when Republicans were the impotent minority for 35 years. If Bérubé misunderstands the actual politics of the democracy in which he lives (and therefore the nature of the Republican politics he despises), it is hardly surprising that he should also misunderstand the legislation regarding the Academic Bill of Rights.

Bérubé opens the chapter of his book titled "Conservative Complaints" with a frontal attack on this bill, which he portrays as a radical conservative bid to purge campuses of liberal thought. To justify this assessment, he focuses on a piece of legislation that briefly became Senate Bill 24 in the state of Ohio. I have published thousands of words about the legislation in Ohio, including my own testimony before the Senate Education Committee in behalf of the bill. All of these statements are readily available on my website. Bérubé refers to none of them. Instead, he quotes—at length—an article that appeared in *The Columbus Dispatch*, which focused on one sentence in the Senate Bill: "Faculty and instructors shall not infringe the academic freedom and quality of education of their students by persistently introducing controversial matter into the classroom or coursework that has no relation to their subject of study and that serves no legitimate pedagogical purpose." (pp.26–7)

The reporter for the *Columbus Dispatch* asked Senator Larry Mumper, the bill's sponsor, what the term "controversial" meant.

Senator Mumper replied, "Religion and politics, those are the main things." Bérubé comments: "If Senate Bill 24 were to pass in Ohio, in other words, there would be at least one state senator who understood it as a license to challenge college courses that dealt 'persistently' with religion or politics. Bad news for political science, history, philosophy, sociology, and religion departments, but good news for people who would prefer universities devoted largely to sports and weather." In other words, it was good news for yahoos like Senator Mumper and his rural Ohioan constituents.

But this is an inexcusable misreading of the sentence in question. The text clearly refers to controversial matter "that has no relation to their subject of study and that serves no legitimate pedagogical purpose." In other words, college courses can indeed refer to controversial matters, but within the range of the subject matter; i.e., English professors should not give lectures on the war in Iraq. Bérubé's willful failure to understand the legislation is more egregious still. The sentence in Senate Bill 24 which Bérubé finds so problematic is actually quoted from a famous clause in the "Declaration on the Principles of Academic Freedom and Academic Tenure." This statement was issued in 1940 and amended in 1970 by the American Association of University Professors, to whose National Council Bérubé has recently been elected. I have repeatedly and publicly pointed this out in statements readily accessible to Professor Bérubé.[7]

Bérubé's misrepresentation of these matters gets worse. He neglects to report the fate of the Ohio bill, which refutes his claims about the intentions of its authors. Before the bill came to

---

[7]American Association of University Professors, *DiscoverTheNetworks. org*, http://www.discoverthenetworks.org/groupProfile.asp?grpid=6526; David Horowitz, "Why an Academic Bill of Rights is Necessary," *Students For Academic Freedom*, March 14, 2005, http://www.studentsfora-cademicfreedom.org/news/997/DHohiotestimony031505.htm.   The phrase "and that serves no legitimate pedagogical purpose" was actually added to the AAUP statement to make it less open to objection.

a vote, Senator Mumper was approached by the Inter-University Council of Ohio, representing 17 of its largest and most prestigious public and private universities. They asked Mumper if he would withdraw his bill if the IUC would embrace the recent recommendations of the American Council on Education regarding academic freedom. The ACE is a liberal umbrella group, representing 2,000 American colleges and universities. On June 23, 2005, responding to the Academic Bill of Rights, the ACE issued its own statement on academic freedom, which asserted: "Intellectual pluralism and academic freedom are central principles of American higher education."[8] It also frowned on political discrimination against students and professors, and called for the creation of a grievance machinery to handle student complaints. The American Association of University Professors was one of the signers of the Council Statement.

Senator Mumper, whom Bérubé portrays as a legislative Torquemada, readily embraced this compromise, which I also welcomed publicly as a victory for our academic freedom campaign.[9] These developments shred Bérubé's repeated claims that ours is a vigilante campaign against liberal academics, and that our goal is legislative control over university curricula. Although accounts of these events are readily available on the web, Bérubé ignores them. This is the abysmal level on which Bérubé proposes to conduct a "rational debate."

Not content with misrepresenting the nature and purpose of the academic freedom campaign, Bérubé also attacks the credibility of those who claim there is a problem that needs to be addressed. He does this by defaming students who have complained about professorial abuses, along with those of us who have

---

[8] American Council of Trustees and Alumni, "Academia's Failing Grade," *Students For Academic Freedom,* December 13, 2005, http://www.studentsforacademicfreedom.org/news/?c=ACE-Statement-and-Responses

[9] "Agreement on Academic Freedom Reached in Ohio," *Students For Academic Freedom,* September 15, 2005, http://www.studentsforacademicfreedom.org/news/1230/OhioSB24AgreementPressRelease091505.htm

attempted to publicize these complaints. "Most people outside academe," Bérubé writes, "are thoroughly unaware of how well-organized the anti-academic right is, and how successful the Horowitz machine has been in getting its version of campus controversies represented in national media—regardless of the actual realities of the events they describe." (p. 29)

Bérubé analyzes three cases to illustrate his claim. I will deal with the two that refer to me directly.

"The first involved a student at an unnamed Colorado college who was allegedly compelled to write an essay on why George Bush is a war criminal, and who allegedly received an F when she turned in an essay on why Saddam Hussein is a war criminal instead. Horowitz wrote about this case in his online magazine *Frontpagemag.com* on December 5, 2003.... [In Horowitz's telling] it is a cautionary tale about academic liberal bias so virulent as to punish innocent students for failing to impugn their President during a time of war. The only problem with the story is that it is false; no such essay was required, the professor in question was a registered Republican, and the student did not receive an F." Bérubé then quotes at length an article that appeared in *InsideHigherEd.com* making these (unsubstantiated) claims.

The problem is that all Bérubé's "corrections" are themselves either false or repeat unsubstantiated assertions by the professor who gave the exam. The *InsideHigherEd.com* article appeared at the beginning of the controversy, before all the facts were known. Bérubé gives no indication to his readers that other information came to light which undermines or challenges the *InsideHigherEd* account. The college in question was the University of Northern Colorado, a fact that was known from the outset because both the incident and the formal appeal of the exam were referred to by the president of the college in a legislative hearing on the Academic Bill of Rights.

The question of whether the professor was a Republican is irrelevant. The issue is whether the so-called question was appropriate for a final exam in a criminology class. Contrary to Bérubé's claim, the student probably did get an F on the final exam, as she has maintained throughout, but had her class grade raised to a B after filing a grievance over what she considered to be an unfair grade. The actual grade on the exam has been kept confidential by the university—only the final class grade has been released. However, if the student did not get an F on the final exam as she claimed—or some comparably low grade—why would she have gone through the ordeal of an appeal?

The student did claim that the question on the exam was to explain why George Bush was a war criminal, but no outsider—including Bérubé—knows what the question actually was, because the professor destroyed the exam papers prior to the student's appeal, in clear violation of university rules. In order to respond to the student's appeal, the professor then reconstructed the exam question. After the *InsideHigherEd.com* article containing the professor's denial appeared, we asked university officials to make the (reconstructed) exam question public, which they did. The full text of the question has been posted many times on my websites and is printed verbatim in my book *The Professors*, with which Bérubé is familiar.[10]

The crucial final sentence of the question in the final exam reconstructed by the professor reads: "Make the argument that the military action of the U.S. attacking Iraq was criminal." This is equivalent to requiring the student to make the case that George Bush is a war criminal, since as commander-in-chief he would be legally responsible for American actions in Iraq. Moreover, even as reconstructed by the professor, the exam question confirms the very charge I made in all my statements, which was not that it showed "liberal bias" but that it was not really a question; it was an instruction to students—with the grade hanging over their heads—to take one side of a controversial issue. It was therefore

---

[10]*The Professors*, 2005, pp. 130-131; a full account of this controversy can be found in David Horowitz, *Reforming Our Universities: The Story of the Campaign for an Academic Bill of Rights*, 2010, op. cit. pp. 81-91.

inappropriate for a final exam and illustrated precisely what I meant by indoctrination.

It would equally have been indoctrination if it had required the student to explain why the Iraq War was morally right. The point of view is not the issue; the failure to allow students to make up their own minds on matters that are and will remain controversial is the issue. Evidently the grievance committee at the University of Northern Colorado agreed when they raised the student's grade to a B. All of this information, which refutes the claims made in Bérubé's book, was aired on Bérubé's own website in a correspondence between Bérubé and Professor Art Eckstein of the University of Maryland. Bérubé simply ignored the evidence presented to him, and fails to mention it to readers of his new book.[11]

Bérubé's next example of a false student claim is described by him as "still worse" than the case of the Colorado exam. This one involved a Kuwaiti immigrant named Ahmad al-Qloushi who, according to Bérubé, "claimed that he received a failing grade on a term paper about the U.S. Constitution because it was 'pro-American.'" Al-Qloushi appeared on several national media outlets, and "Horowitz flogged this case as well." (pp. 30–31) According to Bérubé, the case died when the term paper was published on the Web, because it showed that al-Qloushi deserved his failing grade. The essay, Bérubé says, is "shoddy" and "terribly written" and "not a college-level essay." (p. 33) He quotes several paragraphs of the student's paper in his book as evidence.

Since conservatives made the treatment of al-Qloushi an issue, the episode has great significance in Bérubé's view, undermining their claims that abuses exist: "For any teacher who has ever encountered an incompetent essay of any kind, the elevation of al-Qloushi to the status of conservative Hero is a profound testimony to the intellectual vacuity of the anti-academic right—and the intellectual bankruptcy of the right-wing media apparatus for

---

[11]Michael Bérubé, "Horowitz Agonistes," February 11, 2006, http://www.michaelberube.com/index.php/weblog/comments/853/

which such tales of atrocity and oppression are now a stock in trade." (p. 34) Once again, conservatives are presented as ignoramuses who don't know what they're talking about.

There is something distasteful but instructive in this intemperate attack by a professor on the writing ability of a 17-year-old immigrant from Kuwait, who had been in the United States all of three months when he was given the assignment in question by his junior college professor. Moreover, without comparing al-Qloushi's paper to that of other students at Foothill Junior College, how can Bérubé be so certain that this was not in fact a college-level essay for the students attending this school? Would Bérubé exhibit the same callousness towards an immigrant student from Mexico who was attempting to explain her dissatisfaction with, say, American immigration policy? But what makes Bérubé's comments unforgivable is that a failing grade was not actually al-Qloushi's complaint.

In an article posted at *FrontPageMag.com*—of which there is no mention in Bérubé's text—al-Qloushi explained what his actual concerns were: "Professor Woolcock didn't grade my essay. Instead he told me to come to see him in his office the following morning. I was surprised the next morning when instead of giving me a grade, Professor Woolcock verbally attacked me and my essay. He told me, 'Your views are irrational.' He called me naïve for believing in the greatness of this country, and told me, 'America is not God's gift to the world.' Then he upped the stakes and said, 'You need regular psychotherapy. Apparently, if you are an Arab Muslim who loves America, you must be deranged.' Professor Woolcock went as far as to threaten me by stating that he would visit the Dean of International Admissions (who has the power to take away student visas) to make sure I received regular psychological treatment."[12]

---

[12]Ahmad Al-Qloushi, "Dissident Arab Gets the Treatment," *Frontpagemag.com*, January 6, 2005, http://archive.frontpagemag.com/read Article.aspx?ARTID=10008

In other words, al-Qloushi's complaint was that Professor Woolcock took exception to his *views*, not his writing style, and
attempted to bully him into retracting them; that the professor
made it clear that he regarded disagreement with his own negative
views of America as a form of mental disorder; and that he then
made an implicit threat to an immigrant student about his resident
status. These are pretty serious charges and hardly demonstrate the
intellectual bankruptcy of those who gave al-Qloushi support.

But why should we believe al-Qloushi? Maybe he made all this
up to serve his right-wing views. In fact, *FrontPageMag.com* had
previously published another story about the incident by another
Foothill College student—a *liberal* student named Michael
Wiesner:

> "My name is Michael Wiesner and I am a former student at
> Foothill College in Los Altos Hills, California. I am writing this
> article in the wake of an incident in which a teacher at the col-
> lege recommended psychological therapy to an Arab student who
> had praised the U.S. Constitution. On December 1st, a professor
> named Joseph Woolcock suggested a Kuwaiti Arab Muslim stu-
> dent named Ahmad al-Qloushi should seek therapy after the stu-
> dent submitted a paper arguing that the U.S. Constitution was a
> step forward for America and the world.[13] The Foothill College
> Republicans reported Dr. Woolcock's behavior to the media, and
> Dr. Woolcock lodged a grievance in a further attempt to silence
> the student. The college is treating the matter as if it is an iso-
> lated incident. They are doing everything they can to distance
> themselves from the matter. But in truth, teacher intimidation
> goes to the very heart of the Foothill College bureaucracy. It has
> become commonplace for the school to silence students with
> ideas or opinions contrary to those of their professors."[14]

---

[13] "Ahmad's Essay," *Students For Academic Freedom*, December 9, 2004,
http://www.studentsforacademicfreedom.org/news/314/Ahmad%27ses-
say121004.htm

[14] Michael Wiesner, "Collegiate Intimidation," *Frontpagemag.com*,
December 15, 2004, http://archive.frontpagemag.com/readArticle.aspx?
ARTID=10231

Wiesner went on:

> "Foothill College is not only a place where conservative stu-
> dents like Ahmad are low-tracked by liberal teachers. It is also a
> place where conservative professors feel free to bust down liberal
> students like me. The problem goes beyond politics. Foothill
> College is a place where teachers are free to target students they
> dislike, out of pique, race, religion, or sexual orientation, with
> inappropriate comments during class, intimidation, and grade
> manipulation. I am writing this article because it happened to
> me, and I have been intimidated into silence about my ordeal for
> three years. It is Ahmad al-Qloushi's courage in this matter that
> brings me to speak about my experience. Ahmad and I are speak-
> ing out as two students at the opposite ends of the political
> spectrum."

To this, Wiesner added:

> "I find most of David Horowitz's right-wing views to be offen-
> sive. I led an antiwar rally at Foothill College, and I voted against
> George W. Bush both times. That having been said, intellectual
> pluralism is not a political issue. We must treat intellectual plu-
> ralism as an issue of intellectual freedom. Both liberal students
> and conservative students ought to be free to express their ideas
> in the classroom."

Wiesner then went on to explain his abuse at the hands of a
conservative professor, a cause in which our academic freedom
campaign supported him. I have quoted his comments at length
because they refute the entire case Bérubé has made against my
campaign for academic freedom. It is not about right-wing agendas, or defending only conservative students, or holding only liberal professors to account; it is not based on non-existent facts or
unsubstantiated student claims; it is not an attempt to challenge
the authority of professors over the curriculum. It is (as Michael
Wiesner observed) about intellectual pluralism, about respect for
students who dissent, and about protecting their right to draw
their own conclusions on controversial matters.

I recognize that more honest critics of my campaign than Michael Bérubé may hold legitimate concerns about the legislation regarding an Academic Bill of Rights I have promoted. I have explained many times that my purpose in seeking these legislative resolutions—and they are only resolutions—was to wake up university administrators, so that they would begin to enforce the academic-freedom provisions that are already on their books and promote respect for intellectual diversity in the same way they now promote respect for other kinds of diversity.

My purpose in seeking legislation has now been served. In three years, we have been able to put the issue of intellectual diversity on the national radar. On every campus in the country, intellectual diversity is now a matter for discussion and debate. A large part of the credit must go to our legislative resolutions— none of which has been actually enacted. It is these proposed actions by legislatures that have produced the lion's share of the attention. However, in the course of the campaign I have discovered another way to advance the cause of academic freedom that does not have the drawback of confusing people about our legislative intentions, as resolutions in behalf of an Academic Bill of Rights may do. This is to hold legislative hearings on the academic freedom policies of universities and their implementation on the campuses of state universities.

This summer, as result of such legislative hearings in Pennsylvania, Temple University became the first university to adopt a student bill of rights—or, more accurately, to incorporate student rights into existing regulations about academic freedom. Until now, almost all academic-freedom regulations have applied exclusively to the responsibilities and rights of faculty, and faculty alone.

Penn State University, for example, has a particularly admirable academic-freedom policy, which reads in part: "It is not the function of a faculty member in a democracy to indoctrinate his/her students with ready-made conclusions on controversial subjects." (Policy HR 64) But this policy is found in the Penn State

Policy Manual, which applies only to Penn State *employees*. Consequently the 40,000 Penn State students are likely to be unaware of its existence and are not covered by its provisions: "This policy applies to members of the faculty who have official teaching or research responsibilities at the University."[15] And: "Appeals: If a faculty member feels that his or her academic freedom rights have been violated, the procedure listed in the policy entitled 'Faculty Rights and Responsibilities,' HR 76 may be used."

The adoption by the Temple trustees of its policy on "Faculty and Student Rights and Responsibilities" has shown how this state of affairs can be changed, and it is precisely along these lines that I intend to proceed in the future. I will focus on promoting academic freedom hearings and then actions by university boards on adopting policies similar to Temple's. It is time for the academic freedom campaign to recognize its success and move on to new tactics. I invite my opponents to change their own tactics as well—to take this opportunity to step forward and look at the grievances of students like Michael Wiesner and Ahmad al-Qloushi, and join me in the effort to rectify these abuses.

---

[15]Ibid.

10

The Professor Unions' Battle

From September 2005 to June 2006, a Select Committee of the Pennsylvania legislature held hearings on the condition of academic freedom at the state's seventeen public university campuses. A ferocious opposition to the hearings was organized by the American Association of University Professors, the American Federation of Teachers, and the National Education Association.[1] These efforts were part of a two-year-long battle to discredit the Academic Bill of Rights and its supporters as promoting "a solution in search of problem," and as surreptitiously attempting to insinuate right-wing agendas into the academic curriculum.[2]

On the first day of the hearings, Democrats on the committee—who had opposed its formation—denounced its proceedings as "a colossal waste of time." Its Democratic co-chair, Lawrence Curry, keynoted two union-sponsored rallies at which his own

Originally published November 7, 2006, as "The Professor Unions' Botched Battle," http://archive.frontpagemag.com/ReadArticle.aspx? ArtId=1692
[1] American Association of University Professors, *DiscoverTheNetworks. org*, http://www.discoverthenetworks.org/groupProfile.asp?grpid=6526; The hearings were inspired by the Academic Bill of Rights. I was an advisor to Gib Armstrong whose bill created the committee. The evolution of the committee and the nature of the opposition are recounted in Horowitz, *Reforming Our Universities: The Story of the Campaign for an Academic Bill of Rights*, op. cit. Ch. 9, *The Pennsylvania Hearings*, pp. 145–182.
[2] "Academic Bill of Rights," *Students For Academic Freedom*, http://www.studentsforacademicfreedom.org/documents/1925/abor.html

committee was condemned as a McCarthy witch-hunt. Testifying before the committee for the American Association of University Professors, Joan Wallach Scott compared the Academic Bill of Rights to the practices of regimes in fascist Germany and Communist Russia and referred to its supporters as "the pro-Sharon lobby," a reference to the Israeli prime minister despised by the left.[3] The local press in Pennsylvania provided a sympathetic sounding board for these attacks. The *Centre Daily Times*, which serves the Penn State community, even titled an editorial on the hearings "Good Night and Good Luck" after the George Clooney film about the McCarthy era.

But despite the overwhelming preponderance of these antagonistic voices in the public arena, and the weakness of the Republicans who failed to raise an eyebrow over the sabotage efforts of their committee colleagues, no sooner were hearings over than they had already produced a positive result. The administration at Bloomsburg University modified its student code to include a provision expressly forbidding the grading of students on the basis of their "political or religious opinions." And on July 19, the trustees of Temple University adopted a new academic policy which met most of the criteria for an academic bill of rights that sponsors of the hearings like myself had asked for.

Under the heading "Faculty and Students Rights and Responsibilities," the new Temple policy created rights for students that had not existed before. The existing academic freedom policy, like the policies at virtually all of Pennsylvania's public universities, referred only to "faculty responsibilities." There were no provisions for student rights. The new Temple policy recognizes these rights and also creates a grievance machinery that specifically addresses academic-freedom issues (which the previously existing grievance procedures did not). Finally, the new Temple policy creates an unprecedented reporting system to inform trustees of aca-

---

[3]David Horowitz, "Betraying Academic Freedom," *FrontPageMag.com*, January 20, 2006, http://archive.frontpagemag.com/readArticle.aspx?ARTID=6000

demic-freedom abuses, which is a crucial provision because of the intimidation students feel when confronting faculty members who have power over their grades. The likelihood is quite high that Temple's example will be followed by the other universities in the state (and beyond).[4]

The AAUP's Michael Bérubé summed up the hearings in these grossly misleading terms: "In one way, the very formation of the committee was a triumph for conservative culture warriors—in particular, the conservative culture warrior David Horowitz, who has spent the past three years promoting his 'Academic Bill of Rights,' which seeks to protect students from 'biased' courses and lecturers. But the committee also dealt a blow to Horowitz's campaign." Bérubé adduced as evidence the fact that a representative of the Penn State administration "revealed that it had received all of 13 student complaints about political 'bias' over the past five years—on a campus with a student population of 40,000."[5]

Bérubé's example is illuminating, but not in the way he intends. Penn State's academic freedom policy HR 64 is laid out only in its faculty handbook. Consequently, the 40,000 Penn State students are unlikely to be aware of its existence. Moreover, should they actually read the policy, they would find that it does not apply to them: "This policy applies to *members of the faculty* who have official teaching or research responsibilities at the University."[6] (emphasis added) And: "Appeals: If a *faculty* member feels that his or her academic freedoms have been violated, the procedure listed in the policy entitled 'Faculty Rights and Responsibilities,' HR 76 may be used." In other words, there is no provision for students to appeal should they feel that their rights are being abused.

---

[4] This proved to be a false hope, thanks to the opposition of the AAUP and the teacher unions.

[5] Michael Bérubé, "The Academic Blues," *The New York Times*, September 17, 2006, http://www.nytimes.com/2006/09/17/magazine/17wwln_lede.html?_r=3&ei=5090&en=10fed6edad38dc04&ex=1316145600&adxnnl=1&partner=rssuserland&emc=rss&adxnnlx=1162825245-jAj2M4ZipMBBZcHxzudqww&

[6] Ibid.

In other words, it's surprising that even 13 students went out of their way to try to appeal violations of what they believed to be their academic-freedom rights. Put in context, even this figure may not seem so insignificant. The McCarthy era lasted nine years, nearly twice the five covered by the Penn State figures. A study by historian Lionel Lewis of academic persecutions during that era turned up only 126 cases at 58 institutions nationally in which a professor's appointment was threatened because of his beliefs.[7] These cases led to 69 terminations, of which 31 were at a single institution (the University of California), the result of a loyalty oath. Yet, small as this number may appear among the thousands of universities and hundreds of thousands of professors, the author concludes that "the chilling effect on the expression of all ideas by both faculty and students was significant, although in fact there is no way to measure adequately their full impact."[8]

My academic freedom campaign is not designed, as Bérubé claims, "to protect students from 'biased' courses and lecturers." In fact, I have said exactly the opposite and in so many words: "Professors have every right to interpret the subjects they teach according to their individual points of view. That is the essence of academic freedom." This is a quote from my book *The Professors*, with which Bérubé claims to be familiar. My concern is not professorial bias but academic *professionalism*. Professors are entitled to their bias, but they are not entitled to force students to adopt their bias. That is the issue.

Do professors cross this line? Consider the following course description from the catalogue of the University of Colorado: "This seminar is designed to give students the ability to apply Marx's theoretical and methodological insights to the study of

---

[7] Lionel Lewis, *Cold War On Campus: A Study of the Politics of Organizational Control*, Transaction, 1987, supra note 122 at p. 12; cited in Neil Hamilton, *Zealotry and Academic Freedom*, Transaction, 1995, p. 27. Hamilton is Trustee Professor of Legal Studies at William Mitchell College of Law.
[8] Ibid.

current topics of theoretical and political importance." (Sociology 5055) Marxism is not a science, yet this entire course is about how to apply Marxism as though it *were* a science. The course does not examine whether Marxism is in fact a thoroughly obsolete doctrine, as historical events have shown. This approach to Marxism is not scholarly; it takes away from students the option to regard Marxism as anything but a body of proven truths.

This is not a small problem in the academy. Course descriptions provided by Women's Studies departments in universities across the country similarly presume that some form of radical feminism is an established truth. The Department of Women's Studies at UC Santa Cruz has actually been renamed the Department of Feminist Studies. Feminism as taught at Santa Cruz is an ideology.[9] What would be the academic reaction if there were a Department of Conservative Studies?

Bérubé and other opponents of academic freedom have resorted to such a heavy-handed and implausible campaign to discredit the Academic Bill of Rights because what they are really defending is not liberal "bias" in the classroom—with which I have no problem—but the teaching of radical ideology as an academic discipline, with which I do. Like it or not, this is a clear form of indoctrination that is widespread in the post-contemporary academy which violates time-honored academic standards. The attempt to deny this problem by grossly misrepresenting the aims of the academic freedom campaign has not worked until now. It is unlikely to work in the future.[10]

---

[9] Horowitz and Laksin, *One-Party Classroom*, op. cit. pp. 28–284.

[10] Again, an overly optimistic view; the misrepresentation campaign backed by the teacher unions, the education media and the Democratic Party was ultimately effective from stifling these reforms.

What We're Up Against

The *Pittsburgh Post Gazette* weighed in today with an editorial reflecting the view of the teacher unions, denouncing the Pennsylvania academic freedom hearings as a "big waste of time."[1] The editorial is based on the final report of the committee, which was itself the result of an 11th-hour *coup* by Republican Lynn Herman who joined the Democratic minority to convert it into a majority. Herman represents the Penn State district and is a willing accomplice of the teacher unions and university administrators. At the time the *Post-Gazette* story was written, Herman's changes weren't even voted on; the editorial appeared at midnight, while the vote was scheduled for 9 A.M.. This shows how the teacher unions, the university administrations and members of the Pennsylvania House like Lynn Herman work hand in glove to deny Pennsylvania students their rights.

The key finding of the original report was that there are *no* academic freedom provisions for students in the state of Pennsylvania. That is because all the existing academic-freedom provisions apply only to professors, not to students. A colossal disinformation campaign is underway in Pennsylvania to prevent the public from learning about this finding.

Originally published November 21, 2006, as "What We're Up Against—The Lying Pennsylvania Press," http://archive.frontpagemag.com/Read Article.aspx?ArtId=1415

[1]Maryclaire Dale, "Temple to Tout Grievance Process after Academic Freedom Lawsuit," *Pittsburgh Post-Gazette*, July 25, 2006, http://www.post-gazette.com/stories/news/education/temple-to-tout-grievance-process-after-academic-freedom-lawsuit-443470/

Here is how the *Pittsburgh Post-Gazette* sums up the findings and recommendations that were put in its hands by Lynn Herman before the committee had even voted on them. "The verdict: It turns out that political bias is rare at Pennsylvania's public colleges and universities. The committee concluded that a statewide policy governing college students' academic freedom is unnecessary, the Associated Press reported. Credit the committee with having the intellectual honesty not to go beyond the evidence. In its report, the committee also had some reasonable recommendations to protect against possible abuses. For example, it said public colleges should review existing academic-freedom policies to ensure that students understand their rights and the grievance procedures. But, really, you don't have to have a college education to understand that this was a big waste of time."

In fact there are no academic-freedom rights for students in the state of Pennsylvania, and there are no grievance procedures for academic rights that relate to students. Before its findings were rewritten at the last hour, the committee had found that students in Pennsylvania have no academic-freedom protections and recommended that Pennsylvania universities review their existing academic-freedom policies and change them so that they protect students as well. The *Post-Gazette* and the teacher unions are engaged in a massive cover-up of this fact in a desperate effort to deny Pennsylvania students of the right not to be indoctrinated by their activist professors. Here is what the original report said before it was gutted by Lynn Herman and the Democrats:

Temple University

At the time of these hearings, the Temple policy did not specify students or offer student protections. It was in faculty-related sections of the handbook and therefore not likely to be accessed by students. Additionally, it was not associated with any grievance policy specific to its provisions.

Pennsylvania State University

The Penn State policy HR 64 on academic freedom is especially admirable in making clear the distinction between First

Amendment rights and the professional responsibilities of the classroom teacher to respect the academic freedom rights of students. No other policy of a Pennsylvania school approaches the Penn State policy for clarity and concreteness in defining the professional responsibilities of faculty in regard to students' academic freedom.

As at most other Pennsylvania schools, the Penn State policy is expressed as a "faculty responsibility," not a student right. Consequently, while the policy specifies behavior that professors should avoid in the classroom, it offers no protections for students when they are confronted by such behavior and makes no provision for the student's right to be free from political indoctrination by faculty. While describing inappropriate faculty behavior, it offers no basis for student complaints about such inappropriate behavior. However, according to the policy, "[i]f a faculty member feels that his or her academic freedom rights have been violated, the procedure listed in the policy entitled 'Faculty Rights and Responsibilities,' HR 76 may be used."

University of Pittsburgh

The University of Pittsburgh Faculty Handbook contains a "Policy on Academic Integrity," which states:

"It is the direct responsibility of faculty to encourage free inquiry and expression and to provide an academic environment in their classrooms and in their contact with students that reflects a high standard of integrity and is conducive to learning."

Thus, like the policy at Penn State, the Pitt "Policy on Academic Integrity" is addressed to faculty, not students, and is formulated as a faculty responsibility, not a student right. Its placement under faculty responsibilities in the handbook is appropriate to this conception, but it is unlikely that a student looking for a list of his/her rights would be aware of this policy. Its formulation as a policy on academic integrity would not lead a student to connect it with issues of academic freedom. In testimony before the committee, the university's provost, Dr. James Maher, conceded that "most of the academic integrity cases that come up involve accusation of cheating in exams and that is not really the focus of this Committee or today's discussion."

The Pennsylvania State System of Higher Education

The 14 schools of the Pennsylvania State System of Higher Education (PASSHE), almost without exception proclaim their commitment to academic freedom on their official websites. But these websites, so far as the Committee has been able to discern, without exception, provide no definitions of "academic freedom," nor do they specify any protections associated with academic freedom.

A system-wide provision for academic freedom does exist for PASSHE schools. This is the AAUP "Statement on the Principles of Academic Freedom and Academic Tenure." But, this Statement and its provisions are part of the faculty-union contract, and thus do not specifically apply to students. Nor would they be accessible to students who did not have a reason to research the faculty union contract.

The President of Millersville University, Dr. Francine McNairy, testified on March 23, 2006 at the public hearing held on the Millersville campus. Comments from this testimony have been included below.

Dr. McNairy: As a capital university, meaning all 14 universities in the same system having the same collective bargaining agreement, Millersville has been diligent in developing policies to protect students' academic freedom. And these are listed in the "Students' Bill of Rights and Responsibilities" which is published on our website and in the Student Handbook and also our governance manual.

The Select Committee commends Dr. McNairy and her administration for specifying the rights that Millersville students have and informing them of their rights in a Student Handbook. The Committee notes however, that the policy leaves significant gaps where academic freedom issues are concerned. Thus, in its very first article defining "freedom" there is no mention of students' rights not to be discriminated against because of their political affiliation or ideas.

Article I. Discrimination

FREEDOM: Every aspect of university life should be free from discrimination because of race, religion, color, ancestry, national origin, sex or sexual preference. Student housing organizations, athletics, classes and community facilities should be open to all who desire to participate.

In her testimony Dr. McNairy drew attention to Article XI, which is the only article in the "Student's Bill of Rights and Responsibilities" that specifically discusses student academic freedom rights in the classroom:

> *Dr. McNairy:* In particular, Article XI of the "Student's Bill of Rights and Responsibilities" in the section entitled "In the Classroom" addresses the issue of academic freedom as follows: "Students should be free to express their thoughts and positions on all issues pertaining to curricular material being presented in the classroom."
>
> This is an admirable policy, but the document does not contain the grievance process to be used if a student feels such rights have been violated. For this reason, it may be necessary to include a statement directing students to the location of a grievance process that can be used to file an academic freedom complaint if such rights are violated.

Does indoctrination occur? The following sentence appears in the course description of a Millersville University sociology course, available on the university website: "Given these premises, this course is dedicated not to whether or not these theorists and participants in social movements are right or wrong in some kind of objective sense, but instead is dedicated to understanding the importance of changing the American social structure to bring about new forms of social justice, and to understanding the relationship between social theory and social praxis."

The instructor's dismissal of objectivity, and the commitment of his course to a political agenda of radical social change, is hardly in keeping with academic-freedom principles such as Penn State's admonition: "In giving instruction upon controversial matters the faculty member is expected to be of a fair and judicial mind, and to set forth justly, without supersession or innuendo, the divergent opinions of other investigators."

Nor is it compatible with this classic statement of Robert Gordon Sproul, longtime president of the University of California: "The function of the university is to seek and to transmit knowledge and to train students in the process whereby truth is to be made known. To convert or to make converts is alien and hostile to this dispassionate duty. Where it becomes social, or sectarian movements, they are dissected and examined, not taught, and the conclusion left, with no tipping of the scales, to the logic of the facts...."

Iraq Vets Under Fire

In his hatchet job on the results of our academic freedom campaign in Pennsylvania, *InsideHigherEd* editor Scott Jaschik misreports an incident that took place at Bloomsburg University this fall in another attempt to discredit me and the students whom I met there, two of whom happened to have been Iraq War vets.[1]

I spoke at Bloomsburg this fall and met with about eight College Republicans for dinner. One of the students, John Boyer, told me that he had been given a final exam in political science by Professor Diane Zoelle which included a required essay on the topic: "Explain Why the War in Iraq Is Morally Wrong." For the record, I haven't seen the exam and have only the testimony of the students to go on. Upset by the assignment, John instead wrote why going to war was morally right. For his efforts he received a "D." John is an Iraq War veteran. Naturally I was outraged by the treatment he had received. When I spoke that evening to 600 students, I referred to the professor who, students told me, regularly indoctrinates her classes, presents only one side of controversial issues, and grades students down if they disagree with her. I said this was a disgrace

---

Originally published November 22, 2006, as "Who Would You Believe—an Iraq War Vet or a Professor?," http://archive.frontpagemag.com/read-Blog.aspx?BLOGID=732
[1]Scott Jaschik, "From Bad to Worse for David Horowitz," *InsideHigherEd*, November 22, 2006, http://www.insidehighered.com/news/2006/11/22/tabor

and unacceptable. The president of the university was on the platform with me when I said this.

The local press reported my remarks and the Political Science
Department was flooded with calls. In response, faculty members
summoned the students to discuss their "breach of academic
integrity." Apparently exercising your First Amendment right to
discuss an exam question at dinner is regarded as an unacceptable
transgression by some faculty at Bloomsburg. When another member of the group, also an Iraq War vet, named Jason Walters called
me for advice, I told them not to go to the faculty meeting. "It's a
hanging party," I said. But these were Iraq War vets, and they went.

The meeting had an unexpected and welcome result. A philosophy professor named Kurt Smith, who wanted the students
hauled on the carpet, was himself reprimanded. Professor Zoelle
apologized for her exam question. The students were released from
the threat.

In *InsideHigherEd.com* Scott Jaschik tells a small piece of this
story and quotes me as saying I could not confirm the entire
episode. That is because I am in California and I have to rely on
what I was told about the end of this sequence of events by students who were there. I also did not see the exam. I knew Jaschik
was gunning for me, so I asked him if he thought all these students
were lying. I gave him the students' names, expecting that if he
wrote about the story he would get their view of what happened.
But the only person he called was Professor Diane Zoelle.

Jaschik could have called the university president, who knew
this story because I told it to her personally before I re-told it from
the stage. He could have called the professors who were present at
the meeting and, I was told, supported the students. He could have
called the students. But Scott Jaschik was not interested in the
truth. He was interested only in serving his left-wing friends in the
teacher unions and discrediting me. Even though I have been the
target of vicious and unprincipled attacks like this ever since I
started the academic freedom campaign three years ago, I never
cease to be amazed by the level of mendacity and vindictiveness,

and the lack of concern for students who bear the brunt of these abuses from academics like Diane Zoelle and their union supporters. And I never cease to be shocked when journalists like Scott Jaschik don't have the simple decency or professionalism to do their jobs.

13

Intellectual Muggings

George Orwell began one of the most famous essays in the English language with this observation: "In Moulmein, in Burma, I was hated by large numbers of people. It was the only time in my life that I have been important enough for this to happen to me." As a result of my efforts to remove political agendas from academic classrooms, I have come to appreciate this Orwell comment.

Recently, I traveled to Bloomsburg University in Pennsylvania to debate the Academic Bill of Rights and the legislative hearings on academic freedom which the bill had inspired.[1] My opponent was Bloomsburg philosophy professor Kurt Smith, who had been a hostile witness at the hearings. In his testimony, Smith compared the proceedings to Socrates's execution for "corrupting the youth," to Hitler's imposition of loyalty oaths on German professors, to Mao's cultural revolution which "killed or removed [professors] to labor camps," and to Woodrow Wilson's Committee on Public Information, an eccentric choice but also a favorite target of MIT radical Noam Chomsky.[2]

Originally published February 19, 2007, as "Intellectual Muggings," http://archive.frontpagemag.com/ReadArticle.aspx?ArtId=90

[1] A transcript of the debate can be found here: "Does the Academic Bill of Rights Protect or Threaten Academic Freedom? A Debate between David Horowitz and Kurt Smith," *FrontPageMag.com*, September 19, 2006, http://archive.frontpagemag.com/readStatic.aspx?area=Debate_between _David_Horowitz_and_Kurt_Smith

[2] Select Committee on Academic Freedom in Higher Education, Hearings at Millersville University, March 23, 2006, Official Transcripts, p. 123

The Bloomsburg debate was held on September 19, 2006 and moderated by the university's president, Jessica Kozloff, whom I had met earlier in the day. She informed me that, in response to my reform efforts, the university had already amended its existing academic grievance policies. She gave me a copy of the new regulation, which stipulated that students should not be penalized in their grades for their political views.

The hostility Professor Smith displayed towards me in our debate that evening turned out to be mild in comparison to what followed. Two months after my Bloomsburg visit, I mentioned the episode in a speech I gave at the Restoration Weekend, which was posted at *Frontpagemag.com*.[3] This prompted Smith to launch an intemperate attack in two articles he posted on *FreeExchangeOnCampus.org*, a website created by the American Federation of Teachers for the express purpose of attacking me and my campaign.[4]

According to Smith, virtually everything I had reported about my appearance at Bloomsburg was false: "With the exception of his physically being at Bloomsburg and having dinner, [Horowitz] gets almost every other 'fact' wrong." Among the items I allegedly got wrong, according to Smith, was the simple fact that I had come to Bloomsburg "to speak." "For starters," Smith corrected me, "Horowitz did not come to Bloomsburg to speak. As your readers know, he came to debate the future of academic freedom."

This hair-splitting was extreme even for a philosophy professor, but a small dose of what was in store. Smith described me as "a sophistical bully who bends and stretches the 'truth' (or just plain lies) to further his own ends." One of these ends, apparently, was to get rid of professors like himself: "Horowitz's fascist

---

[3]David Horowitz, "Restoration Weekend 2006: Storming the Universities," *FrontPageMag.com*, November 20, 2006, http://archive.frontpagemag.com/readArticle.aspx?ARTID=1446

[4]Jacob Laksin, "Truth-Free Exchange On Campus," *FrontPageMag.com*, April 14, 2006, http://archive.frontpagemag.com/readArticle.aspx?ARTID=4852

ideology ... casts ordinary, politically centrist Americans like me as leftists and enemies of the state."[5]

I have never used the phrase "enemy of the state" to refer to anyone. On the contrary, I have publicly stated in my book *The Professors,* and elsewhere, that far from being "enemies of the state" academics with left-wing views must be an integral component of a university education worthy of the name. Smith knows this because I said as much that evening at Bloomsburg. The label "fascist" Smith sought to pin on me was particularly bizarre, given the fact that I came to Bloomsburg as the founder of a campaign for academic freedom that was based entirely on liberal principles devised by the American Association of University Professors; and further, that I have never called for the firing of a single academic for his or her political views. Slanders like this are hardly the hallmark of a political "centrist," as Smith presents himself.

The union site that featured Smith's article contains a section called "Horowitz Fact Checker,"[6] which is part of a national campaign to discredit evidence of the faculty infringements of academic freedom that I have brought to light. The malice displayed on sites such as Free Exchange and by professors such as Smith tends to focus on me personally, but it is really directed at the students who risk faculty reprisals if they report abuses and who therefore are in need of advocates to draw attention to these issues. The agenda of this campaign is to create in advance the

---

[5]"What Really Happened at Bloomsburg University," *FreeExchangeOn-Campus,* November 27, 2006. Smith has posted his own remarks in the debate but has withheld the document which contains my remarks as well. I have posted the transcript here: "Does the Academic Bill of Rights Protect or Threaten Academic Freedom? A Debate between David Horowitz and Kurt Smith," *FrontPageMag.com,* September 19, 2006, http://archive.frontpagemag.com/readStatic.aspx?area=Debate_between _David_Horowitz_and_Kurt_Smith

[6]"Horowitz Fact Checker," *Free Exchange On Campus,* May 16, 2006, https://web.archive.org/web/20060516033128/http://www.freeex-changeoncampus.org/index.php?option=com_content&task=blogcate-gory&id=7&Itemid=34 [Note: The *Free Exchange On Campus* website no longer exists.]

supposition that if students seek my help in publicizing their political harassment at the hands of their professors, either they are lying or I am.

The events at Bloomsburg are a prime example of how these tactics are used by faculty members to silence students who feel their academic freedoms have been violated.[7] During my visit, I dined with a group of about seven College Republicans. Three of them were Iraq War veterans who voiced some disturbing complaints about a political science professor named Diana Zoelle. One of the complaints concerned an exam Zoelle had given. According to the student, it contained a question asking him to explain why the Iraq War was morally wrong. The exam was given in 2003 when the student was about to be shipped to the field of battle. He wrote an essay supporting the war and according to him received a "D."

A second student declared that Zoelle had refused to allow him to make up assignments he missed while fulfilling his military obligations in the Army Reserve. These required him to travel to Maryland for training. Despite his appeals, Zoelle insisted on giving him zeros for the assignments he missed, which adversely affected his grade. These views were supported by a third student at the table, a veteran of the war in Iraq, who had also taken a course with Zoelle and agreed about her in-class behavior.

Zoelle's anti-war views are part of her academic record. She has been a visiting professor at the left-wing Joan Kroc Institute for

---

[7]David Horowitz, "The Professors' Orwellian Case," *FrontPageMag.com*, December 5, 2003, http://archive.frontpagemag.com/Printable.aspx?ArtId=15136; Details of the events at Bloomsburg are based on my interviews with four students, Professors James Tomlinson, Neil Strine, and James Brown (who is also assistant dean of the College of Liberal Arts). These interviews are supplemented by my own observations when I was there. Not all parties agreed on all details, but there was unanimity on what transpired at the dinner and a consensus shared by the students and Dean Brown on what transpired at the Political Science Department meeting described below.

Peace Studies at Notre Dame.[8] What she believes as a private citizen is her business. All three students, however, felt that she regularly brought her politics into class. A remark that bothered one of the Iraq veterans was this: "When Republicans are in office, people are forced to scrub toilets or go into the military." A comment that rattled another was her answer to a question about the decline in gas prices just before the 2006 election: "The Republicans always lower the gas prices so they can be re-elected." Constant remarks of a similar nature caused this student to "turn her off." If these students are correct, this is neither a professional way to run a class nor a pedagogically productive one.

Because three students had testified to the in-class bias of Professor Zoelle, and because the exam question given to a student on his way to Iraq seemed particularly abusive, I decided to mention it during my debate with Smith that evening. Almost as soon as I left the campus after the debate, Professors Zoelle and Smith went into action against the students whom I had met. They called all the College Republicans with whom I'd had dinner—including the three veterans who had been her students—to a meeting in the Political Science Department. I was told about the meeting the evening before it was scheduled, when one of the students phoned to ask my advice. It was clear to me that this was an act of intimidation, which showed exactly why a student bill of rights was necessary at Bloomsburg. I advised the students not to attend the meeting but to go directly to President Kozloff and tell her what had happened. At the same time I sent my own emails to President Kozloff, to the chairman of the Political Science Department, and to Dr. George Agbango, the Dean of the College of Liberal Arts, protesting the summons.

The students disregarded my advice and went to the meeting. When they arrived, Professor Smith was in charge. He told them

---

[8]This academic program made national headlines by inviting Tariq Ramadan to its faculty despite the fact that the State Department had refused him a visa because of his links to al-Qaeda operatives and other terrorist organizations.

they were there to discuss what had been said at dinner and "possibly to have charges filed against them for violations of academic integrity."[9] They noted that Smith had brought a tape recorder, which further impressed them with the seriousness of the proceedings.[10] Several of the students involved were political science majors. "Violations of academic integrity" is a threatening phrase. Evidently both professors regarded the discussion of a past exam question, even one three years old, as off-limits—the First Amendment notwithstanding.

In his Free Exchange article, Smith describes the meeting as though it had been called as a fact-finding mission whose purpose was to see whether I had put words in the students' mouths: "Subsequently, we asked a co-advisor of the College Republicans who had arranged the dinner between Horowitz and members of the club to ask the students if they would be up for filling us in on what was in fact said at dinner—our initial suspicion being that Horowitz (and not the students) was at the bottom of the tale. But we wouldn't know until we asked the students." In this rose-colored account, Smith reveals his patronizing attitude towards the students, whom he regards as my puppets, retailing charges I had incited or invented. Worse, he presents a false version of what happened.

In his Free Exchange article, for example, Smith quotes my accurate account of the dinner and then spins it to create the impression that I am lying. In my account I referred to the student who objected to the exam as Jason Boyer. In fact his name is John. Smith writes: "There is no Jason Boyer here. Rather, there is a Jason Walter, as Horowitz will say below, but he isn't the one who claims to have taken the exam. It is another student, X (as I will call him), who claims this."[11]

---

[9]Interviews with two of the students present
[10]Ibid.
[11]Smith, op. cit.

Why does Smith refer to "another student, X" rather than naming him as John Boyer? Confidentiality is not the issue, since Smith doesn't feel an obligation to protect the identity of Jason Walter. In fact, Smith refers to the student as "X" simply to create the impression that my testimony is not credible. Smith knew the student I had referred to was John Boyer, since the three of us were standing within five feet of each other discussing Boyer's exam following the debate at Bloomberg. Smith also presided over the Star Chamber proceeding in the Political Science Department to which John Boyer, Jason Walter and Joel Breting, the third Iraq War veteran, were summoned. In other words, Smith's subterfuge in referring to a "Student X" was a malicious attempt to portray me as an unreliable reporter.

Smith also knows that the exam question did, in fact, disturb Boyer. He reveals as much, albeit inadvertently, in the article he wrote for Free Exchange, where he gives this version of events: "As an aside, I showed X the exam and asked him if this is what he was referring to when talking with Horowitz. Now that three years have passed, the student said that he now doesn't find the question inappropriate.... To be sure, he remembers being offended when taking the exam three years ago."

In other words, John Boyer did take an exam prior to being shipped to Iraq, which contained a question which he believed related to the war and which offended him at the time, and this was the question which he brought up at the dinner with me. It was immediately clear to Smith and Zoelle which exam Boyer was referring to; and it was immediately clear to Smith and Boyer, when they looked at the exam, which question on the exam was problematic.

Because John Boyer has refused to discuss these matters, I asked his roommate, Jason Walter, about Smith's rosy version of these events. Walter told me that even after being shown the exam by Smith, Boyer still felt the question was inappropriate. He backed off from his claim only under the pressure of the meeting in the Political Science Department. According to Jason Walter,

Boyer felt intimidated by the professors and did not want to confront them. All the students I interviewed still feel this worried that they might suffer reprisals for speaking up.

Fortunately, the students did not merely go like sheep to the meeting Zoelle and Smith had organized. Before the meeting, Jason Walter went to Dean George Agbango to discuss their summons. Dean Agbango said that he could not attend the meeting because he was a member of the Political Science Department and this might be a conflict of interest. He sent his assistant dean, Professor James S. Brown, who was a professor of literature, to go in his place. Soon after the meeting began, Dean Brown intervened and said, "Why is this meeting even taking place?"

Dean Brown's intervention changed the tone and tenor of the proceedings. The students regarded his action as "coming to their defense." Under his guidance it was agreed that the exam question they had been summoned to discuss was a "departmental matter" and this was an "inappropriate" meeting and setting in which to discuss it. After the meeting had gone on for a little longer, Dean Agbango appeared and said, "This meeting is over." Two days later, Dr. Agbango asked the three students—John Boyer, Joel Breting and Jason Walter—to stay after his class for a few minutes, during which time he apologized to them on behalf of the university, saying they should never have been summoned to the meeting in the first place.[12]

If there were any honesty on the other side of the academic-freedom debate, this little incident—and the fact that the dean and assistant dean of the College felt it necessary to terminate it and to apologize to the students—would in and of itself have settled the question as to whether there were problematic interactions between faculty members and students who disagreed with them politically. In his Free Exchange article, Smith defends the action he and Zoelle took against the students as perfectly in order. But

---

[12]Interviews with Joel Breting, Jason Walter and Dean James S. Brown

obviously that is not how the dean and the assistant dean of the College saw matters.

The resolution of this matter by the thoughtful intervention of Deans Agbango and Brown served to confirm my opinion that there is still a widespread university consensus on what is fair and on what constitutes appropriate academic behavior. Nevertheless, it took the authority of two deans to rein in the unprofessional behavior of Zoelle and Smith. This, again, underscores the importance of creating a formal policy on students' academic freedom rights and a grievance machinery to support them.

While I did not name Professor Zoelle during the Bloomsburg debate, a stringent critic might object to my mentioning the exam issue at all, since I hadn't seen the exam or the question myself. I decided to mention it because, in my view, the fact deserved attention that a young man who had risked his life to defend his country felt that his reasons for service had been disrespected by his teacher.

I did identify Zoelle in a conversation with President Kozloff, when we had a moment backstage before the debate.[13] During our conversation I told Kozloff that it was not my intention to polarize her campus or put her professors on the spot. My goal was to persuade her to institute a more comprehensive academic freedom policy than presently existed, and to see that it had provisions which provided protection for students. In my view, the problem was that there was not strong enough institutional support inside the academy for insisting on professional behavior by faculty. I also made my position on this issue clear to Smith, both during the debate and when we met afterwards. But he chose to ignore all these facts in order to portray me as a bully out to persecute "enemies of the state." Of course this did not prevent Smith himself from bullying the students who talked to me.

---

[13]In his article Smith calls my reference to this meeting "screwy" because he presumes it is the same meeting I had earlier in the day, which it was not.

Smith's deceptive account of these events has been uncritically taken up by his political allies and used to expand the attack on my character and to further divert attention from the problems students encounter at schools like Bloomsburg. On the well-trafficked website of Brad Leiter, a law professor at the University of Texas, for example, one can find the following headline: "Philosopher Kurt Smith v. Pathological Liar David Horowitz." This was actually the second Leiter post on the subject, the first being "Philosopher Kurt Smith Pulverizes Pathological Liar David Horowitz," which reproduced Smith's fanciful account of what transpired in our debate.[14] Professor Leiter had no interest in ascertaining the facts of the Bloomsburg student cases or of the Bloomsburg debate; his post merely referred readers to Smith's defamatory comments and to a leftist account on the far-left website *CounterPunch.org*.[15]

These events illustrate the strategy that has been adopted by opponents of academic freedom: deny that a problem exists at all, and then discredit anyone who says that it does. This explains the zeal displayed in the Bloomsburg case to dismiss and thereby suppress the complaints of the students; and it explains Smith's determination to discredit me as their advocate.

Denial that a problem exists is the central thesis of Michael Bérubé's *What's Liberal About the Liberal Arts?* the first book-length text to oppose the academic freedom campaign.[16] It was the principal argument in the testimony of union witnesses at the Pennsylvania hearings. It was the position taken by Democratic legislators on the panel, who spent their off-time demonstrating at

---

[14]Brian Leiter, "Philosopher Kurt Smith Pulverizes Pathological Liar Horowitz," *Leiter Reports*, September 27, 2006, http://leiterreports.typepad.com/blog/2006/09/philosopher_kur_1.html

[15]Dave Lindorff, "This Mouth for Hire," *CounterPunch.org*, September 25, 2006, http://www.counterpunch.org/2006/09/25/horowitz-on-campus/

[16]Bérubé is a well-known academic leftist and member of the national council of the American Association of University Professors.

union rallies against their own committee and who denigrated the hearings as "a hunt for BigFoot." Both Democrats and union leaders also denounced the hearings as a "witch-hunt" and an exercise in "McCarthyism," even though the committee operated under a self-imposed rule that no individuals could be named in testimony and that the committee would concern itself with policy alone.[17]

Such dishonest attacks would never have gained traction without the willing complicity of the education media covering these events. Prominent among them were *InsideHigherEd.com* and its editor Scott Jaschik, whose partisanship shaped their reporting of both the Pennsylvania hearings and the Bloomsburg case.

The Internet journal *InsideHigherEd.com* reaches a wide academic audience and has featured many articles on the academic freedom campaign, mostly written by Jaschik himself. Scott Jaschik is a hard-working editor and reporter. Our personal relations have been reasonably good. I invited him to moderate a panel at an academic freedom conference I hosted, and he conducted himself admirably, without bias or favor. He has expressed to me a will to be fair, and he has occasionally published articles I have written. As a reporter, he has called me regularly for comments on issues that concern the academic freedom campaign.

On the other hand, the articles he has written and the bulk of the commentary he has run have consistently reflected the political message of the teacher unions and other radical opponents of my efforts. Because his Internet journal presents itself as a provider of education news, these biased accounts have provided powerful support to the opponents of academic freedom and the vilification campaign directed against me. By the time Jaschik came to focus his attention on the Bloomsburg episode, he had already written several inflammatory features which misrepresented events in which I was involved and lent authority to the claim that abuses I had correctly reported were made up.

---

[17]David Horowitz, *Indoctrination U.: The Left's War Against Academic Freedom*, Encounter, 2007. This book contains an account of the attacks.

The most famous of these articles concerned a student's complaint about a final exam that had been given at the University of Northern Colorado and that had obvious parallels to the Bloomsburg case. The student's complaint had become a target of attack after I mentioned it briefly in an article in which I defended the Academic Bill of Rights against an official denunciation of the bill that been issued by the American Association of University Professors. The AAUP described my bill as "Orwellian" and said it was "a grave threat to academic freedom." In my response I pointed out that it was actually based on the AAUP's own academic-freedom principles, and lamented the fact that "when student rights have been widely infringed by faculty and university administrations, the AAUP has tended to overlook the infringements and even defend them."[18]

The Colorado case was one of five incidents I mentioned in the article to demonstrate that a problem existed. In other words, in and of itself the Colorado exam was but one of many incidents that revealed a general problem. Space permitting, I could have described many more. My opponents, however, had no interest in the actual point of my argument, namely that a problem did exist on American campuses. In all the attacks that subsequently appeared, not one of my opponents has ever bothered to mention, or refute, the other four examples I gave. Their strategy has been to focus their attention on discrediting one case in an effort to discredit all the rest without giving them a hearing. In other words, the case of the Colorado exam has been treated by the left as a symbol for all the rest.

The complete reference to the Colorado exam, as it appeared in my article in the *Chronicle of Higher Education*, is this: "Nor are the problems of professorial excess absent today. This year, for example, a criminology class at a Colorado university was given an assignment to write a paper on 'Why George Bush Is a War

---

[18]"The Professors' Orwellian Case" op. cit.

Criminal.' Bad enough. But a student who chose to submit a paper on 'Why Saddam Hussein Is a War Criminal' received a failing grade."[19]

The student who attended the University of Northern Colorado had filed a formal complaint about the exam with the university's grievance committee, which had then favorably adjusted her grade. The case had been mentioned by the university president during a public hearing on academic freedom which was held by the education committee of the Colorado legislature. Yet the opening attack on my claim denied the very existence of the student, the professor and the exam.

This attack came from Mano Singham, a professor in Ohio, where a version of my Academic Bill of Rights was being considered by the state legislature. Singham's comments appeared as a column in the *Cleveland Plain Dealer* under the headline, "That Liberal Fiend Can't Be Found."[20]

"That Liberal Fiend" referred to the professor who gave the exam. As with Kurt Smith's false claim that I regarded him as an "enemy of the state," the "liberal fiend" in Singham's column was his own invention. I had not identified the professor's politics at all, since this was not relevant to the case or to my campaign, which is not about liberal bias but about professional behavior in the classroom. It wouldn't have mattered to me if the professor who gave the exam had been a Republican. The student's complaint was that her professor had provided an exam question on a controversial matter to which she was allowed only one correct answer. This was a violation of the student's academic freedom, regardless of whether the answer was one preferred by the political right or the political left.

As in the Bloomsburg case, the issue—academic freedom—was of no interest to my detractors. Their goal was to suppress the issue

---

[19]Ibid.
[20]Mano Singham, "That Liberal Fiend Can't Be Found," *Students For Academic Freedom*, March 2, 2005, http://www.studentsforacademicfreedom.org/news/1062/PlainDealerliberalfiendcantbefound030305.htm

by creating doubt that the incident had occurred at all. Thus Singham claimed in his column that he had called the University of Northern Colorado, questioned its faculty, and could find no one to verify the incident. The faculty members he talked to had apparently never heard of such a professor or exam. He also claimed that he could not locate a student who had lodged a complaint.

While Singham's charges were spreading rapidly across the Web, the university refused to release information that would settle the matter. At the same time, frightened of possible reprisals from her teachers, the student would not identify herself or appear for interviews. Thus my hands were tied in responding to Singham's irresponsible and baseless charges as they were repeated on multiple venues, including *MediaMatters.org* and other widely read partisan attack sites.

An additional problem—mentioned by none of my critics—was the fact that the professor had destroyed the original exam, violating university regulations in the process. The fact that the professor destroyed the evidence never became a subject of interest to the academic media. Yet the copy of the exam which he eventually provided to the university grievance committee—eventually released by the university administration and taken at face value by the education press—was, in fact, only his reconstruction of the original exam, not the exam itself.

In the midst of this controversy, Scott Jaschik chose to write a summary of the false charges that Singham and others had made against me and then to publish it as a journalistic "report." The headline of Jaschik's article paralleled the headline in Singham's column in the *Plain Dealer* and mimicked its bias: "The Poster Child Who Can't Be Found."[21] In other words, without investigating the case, Jaschik gave a platform to Mano Singham's inventions, adding another false claim—that the Colorado case was of

---

[21]Scott Jaschik, "The Poster Child Who Can't Be Found," *InsideHigherEd*, March 14, 2005, http://www.insidehighered.com/news/2005/03/14/horowitz3_14

special importance to my campaign, when in fact it was one of five examples I had offered in an article in *The Chronicle of Higher Education* as an indication that there was a problem which the Academic Bill of Rights was designed to address.

Jaschik did call to interview me for his piece, and correctly reported that I was trying to get both the university and the student to provide a definitive response to the charges that Singham had irresponsibly made. But summarizing groundless charges about an alleged "poster child" who couldn't be found, as Jaschik did, merely added authority to a malicious and groundless attack.

When I voiced my objections to Jaschik, he did make an effort to investigate for himself. But he limited his inquiries to two interested and hostile parties—the university administration and the professor—whom (contrary to Singham) he discovered did actually exist and whom he named. This was Robert Dunkley, an assistant professor of Criminology. Both the Administration and Dunkley, of course, had an interest in suppressing the facts of an embarrassing student complaint and were busy covering their tracks.

When my office called the university, for example, its spokeswoman, Gloria Reynolds, would not disclose the grade the student had complained about on the original exam, and which caused her to make her successful appeal. On the advice of the university lawyers, as Reynolds explained to my office, she would only release the student's final grade for the class; that is, the grade she received *after* she had successfully appealed the exam and secured an upward adjustment. Neither the university nor *InsideHigherEd.com* made any effort to clarify this confusion about the grades or clarify it to the public. My critics took advantage of this confusion to assert that my claim (actually the student's claim) that she had originally gotten an "F" was wrong. "Reynolds added the student did not receive an F," Jaschik reported. Actually, since Reynolds withheld the relevant information and referred only to the final grade in the class, there is absolutely no factual basis for doubting the student's word that she originally got an "F" *on the exam.*

Reynolds also provided a copy of Professor Dunkley's new version of the exam, without explaining that it was only a reconstructed version, not the original, which Dunkley had illegally destroyed. The reconstructed version differed in details from the exam the student remembered. This difference in details between the exam Dunkley reconstructed and the original as the student remembered it was also unscrupulously exploited by Jaschik and my critics, who used the discrepancy to claim that I had made up the question itself.

In fact, the new exam question was so close to what the student had originally claimed as to justify my contention and hers that the question was abusive—although neither Jaschik nor my critics would acknowledge this point. The question, as remembered by the student, was: "Explain why George Bush is a war criminal." The question as reconstructed by Dunkley was: "Make the argument that the military action of the US attacking Iraq was criminal." This was only marginally different in wording and in concept from the student's original claim—since Bush, as President, would be legally responsible for the decision to go to war. If Jaschik and my detractors had been interested in students' academic freedom they would have acknowledged this. But they weren't. Instead, on the basis of this minor difference on a reconstructed exam, they represented me as a liar.

In his article, Jaschik ignored the fact that the exam the university produced was not the original exam, and failed to mention the close similarity between the question as the student and I had reported it and the reconstructed question supplied by Professor Dunkley. Jaschik also concealed the fact that the student's formal and successful appeal of her original grade on the exam had resulted in an adjustment of that grade significantly upwards by the university. This sowed the confusion as to what grade my critics and I were talking about. Instead of untangling the facts, Jaschik reported the deceptive and unsupported claims of Dunkley and the truncated account of the final grade from the administration as though they were the only facts available. Consequently, his second "corrective" story merely refurbished and strengthened the original false accusations by Mano Singham. This was captured in his title: "Tattered Poster Child:"[22]

Here is Jaschik's summary: "While a Northern Colorado spokeswoman acknowledged Monday that a complaint had been filed, she also said that the test question was not the one described by Horowitz, the grade was not an F, and there were clearly non-political reasons for whatever grade was given. And the professor who has been held up as an example of out-of-control liberal academics? In an interview last night, he said that he's a registered Republican."

This is a summary of false positives. I had never claimed that Professor Dunkley was an example of an "out-of-control liberal" or characterized his politics at all. So his claim to be a Republican was irrelevant and had no bearing on anything I said. Its only utility was to make me look ridiculous to readers not acquainted with the facts. The spokeswoman's claim that the grade was not an F was also meaningless, since she was referring to the final grade, not the exam grade—which was the only grade the student had complained about. The spokeswoman's claim that the test question was not the one described by me was equally deceptive, since the only exam she had in her possession was one that Dunkley had made up after the fact, not the original exam the student had complained about. Moreover, the questions on the made-up exam and the one the student remembered were virtually the same. Finally, the spokeswoman's claim that the student's exam grade was not given for political reasons was merely her opinion ungrounded in any facts.

I wrote a lengthy refutation of all the false claims made by Singham and his followers in an article called "The Case of the Colorado Exam."[23] I submitted the article to Jaschik, who refused to print it—no explanation offered—and also refused to post a

---

[22]Scott Jaschik, "Tattered Poster Child," *InsideHigherEd*, March 15, 2005, http://www.insidehighered.com/news/2005/03/15/horowitz3_15

[23]David Horowitz, "The Case of the Colorado Exam," *FrontPageMag.com*, April 21, 2005, http://archive.frontpagemag.com/readArticle.aspx?ARTID=9017

correction of the false information he had published. All he agreed to was to provide an easily ignored link to my article from his site.

The result of Jaschik's misreporting was that the false charges have become an urban legend in the campaign against my efforts in behalf of students' academic freedom. If one enters the words "David Horowitz+Colorado Exam" into the Google search engine, one will retrieve 60,000-plus references, virtually all of them repeating the false charges spawned by Mano Singham's column as though they were true. A long passage from Jaschik's misleading article "Tattered Poster Child" is also excerpted verbatim in Michael Bérubé's book as an "answer" to "Conservative Complaints" about faculty abuses of students' academic freedom.[24] This doesn't say much for the research methods of some university professors.[25]

The parallel elements in the Colorado and Bloomsburg cases are too obvious to ignore. A student complains about an exam question and I report her complaint. Instead of looking into the complaint, my opponents and detractors claim that I invented the student, the professor and the exam question itself. When these tactics fail, the critics accuse me of putting words into students' mouths and conducting a witch-hunt of academic liberals. The malicious spin is then spread across the Internet by professor unions and their allies as though they were facts. The goal of these efforts is to deny that such abuses exist, or to claim that they are

---

[24]*What's Liberal About the Liberal Arts?: Classroom Politics and "Bias" in Higher Education*, Michael Bérubé, W.W. Norton, 2006, p. 29; cf. for my review of Bérubé's book, "What's Not Liberal about the Liberal Arts," *FrontPageMag.com*, October 20, 2006, http://archive.front-pagemag.com/ readArticle.aspx?ARTID=1989; Bérubé also wrote on his blog, "Horowitz lied about the student in Colorado"; see Michael Bérubé, "Horowitz Agonistes," February 11, 2006, http://www.michael-berube.com/index.php/ weblog/comments/853/. This blog comment appeared in February 2006, a year after I had corrected Jaschik's erroneous reports.

[25]Bérubé was aware of the facts—they were presented to him in a long and detailed email exchange with a professor on his own blog. He just chose to ignore them: "Horowitz Agonistes," op. cit.

so rare as to require no remedies other than those already in place; moreover, that to stigmatize the students' advocate and sponsor of reform as a liar who wants to discredit professors and restrict their speech.

In October the Republican majority on the Pennsylvania Committee on Academic Freedom was presented with a draft report of its proceedings. The report was submitted by Representative Gib Armstrong, the author of the legislation creating the committee. The "Summary of Testimony" contained in the report revealed that when the hearings began, not a single public university in the state of Pennsylvania had a provision to protect students' academic freedom. The report noted that in response to the hearings, two major universities—Temple and Penn State—had already adopted new academic freedom policies that were in fact specific to students. Texts of the new policies appeared in the appendix, and among its recommendations was a suggestion that other universities should consider making their academic freedom policies "student-specific" as both Penn State and Temple had done.[26]

Since it was my efforts that had led directly to the creation of the committee and to the adoption by Temple and Penn State of these new policies protecting students, the hearings by any measure were a significant achievement of the academic freedom campaign. Yet Scott Jaschik reported the result of the hearings in *InsideHigherEd* with this headline: "From Bad to Worse for David Horowitz."[27] It was exactly the line put forth in the press releases issued by the teacher unions, which had opposed my campaign from the beginning.

Jaschik's article began by misrepresenting the very nature of the hearings, describing the committee as a "legislative panel that was

---

[26]David Horowitz, "Pennsylvania's Academic Freedom Reforms," *Students For Academic Freedom*, December 1, 2006, http://www.studentsforacademicfreedom.org/index.php?option=com_content&task=view&id=2324&Itemid=40s

[27]Scott Jaschik, "From Bad to Worse for David Horowitz," *InsideHigherEd*, November 22, 2006, http://www.insidehighered.com/news/2006/11/22/tabor

looking for examples of violations of students' rights because of their political views." In fact the committee made no systematic effort to gather student claims about political abuses, nor did it ask university administrators to do so. On the first day of the hearings, the committee chairman, Rep. Tom Stevenson, declared in so many words that the committee would *not* look at specific abuses involving students and professors: "This committee's focus will be on the institutions and their policies, not on professors, not on students."[28]

One of the prime reasons the committee did not focus on student complaints was explained in the finding of the draft report that there was no university-provided basis or procedure for such complaints. Students had no formal academic freedom rights; there was no grievance machinery to deal with student academic-freedom complaints, and students were not informed by the university that professors were obligated to respect intellectual diversity, to refrain from harassing students for their political views, or to assign texts reflecting more than one perspective on controversial matters—all of which were concerns of the academic freedom campaign.[29]

Having misleadingly claimed that the committee set out to find "violations of students' rights because of their political views," Jaschik then reported—not surprisingly—that it had failed to find such violations. Thus, according to Jaschik, it had delivered a devastating rebuttal to my claims. This was exactly the message of the professor unions—that there were no abuses or, as the head of one of the unions put it, the hearings were "a solution in search of a problem."[30]

---

[28]Public Hearing of Select Committee on Academic Freedom in Higher Education, held at William Pitt Union Ballroom, 5th Avenue & Bigelow Boulevard, Pittsburgh, Pennsylvania, November 9, 2005, p. 4

[29]David Horowitz, "The Campaign for Academic Freedom," *Students For Academic Freedom*, http://www.studentsforacademicfreedom.org/documents/2064/the-campaign-for-academic-freedom

[30]William Scheuerman, president of an American Federation of Teachers union; Cara Matthews, "Conservative Group Seeks College 'Bill of Rights'," *Students For Academic Freedom*, October 12, 2005, http://www.studentsforacademicfreedom.org/news/1184/GannetetNewsConservGroupSeeks101305.htm

Jaschik's article summarized the committee's "final report" in these words: "A week ago, it looked like David Horowitz had a few things to be thankful for in the emerging report of the Pennsylvania legislative panel that was looking for examples of violations of students' rights because of their political views.... Horowitz pointed to the committee's recommendation that colleges adopt policies to protect student rights. And he liked the many pages included in the draft report that summarized testimony by Horowitz and some of his allies. Those are all gone in the final version of the report the committee approved Tuesday, which is being hailed by academic groups as completely vindicating their views."

It's true that most of the parts of the report that I endorsed were cut from the "final version of the report" referred to by Jaschik. But, as Jaschik knew, this was the result of an eleventh-hour *coup* by the Democratic members of the committee, all of whom had voted against the creation of the committee in the first place. The Democrats were provided with a majority by two Republicans who defected to their cause; one of them had also voted against the enabling resolution. Jaschik does report my claim that the final result was a "theft" by the opposition, but he also says that the committee was "Republican controlled," which in the matter of the final report it was not. Because the Republicans—faced with an insuperable majority and the end of the legislative term—then signed on to the final report, Jaschik was able to claim that the rejection of the original report reflected the sense of the whole committee, when it did not.

The night before the actual vote, one of the Republican defectors, Representative Lynn Herman, rewrote the draft report. In doing so, he removed all references in the recommendations to the need to create "student-specific rights," and inserted a ludicrous conclusion: that abuses of student rights were "rare." Of course they were rare—students had no rights and no grievance procedures through which to air their complaints, and therefore no protection from faculty reprisals.

Herman also deleted the entire "Summary of Testimony" in the report, which documented the absence of student protections in existing university regulations. The cynical nature of this scam was so transparent that Herman did not even bother to replace the deleted section with a different version. The final report therefore contains no summary of what actually transpired at the hearings. All this might have interested a reporter less eager than Jaschik to make a partisan case. That case was summed up by an opponent of the academic freedom campaign quoted by *InsideHigherEd:* "This committee spent a lot of time and a lot of money trying to find some shred of evidence of a real problem and they couldn't find one because there is not one."[31]

Interviewing me for his article, Jaschik pressed the issue of student abuses, the cornerstone of the professor-union campaign against an Academic Bill of Rights. Did I really think there were abuses of students? If I did, where were they? Jaschik asked the question as though he had an interest in my answer. If he actually had such an interest, he might long ago have assigned his reporters to find out for themselves. They could have begun with the case of Jennie Mae Brown, whose complaint led to the hearings. Jennie Mae Brown was an Air Force veteran of the war in Iraq who had taken a physics course at one of the Penn State campuses and was subjected to harangues by her professor against the military and the war. When she voiced her complaint to Representative Gib Armstrong, it inspired him to sponsor legislation creating the Committee on Academic Freedom. Alternatively, Jaschik could have assigned a reporter to interview the dozens of students who filed complaints with Armstrong during the hearings, but on condition that their names not be divulged.

Jaschik's agenda, like that of the committee Democrats, was not to find out the truth but to carry out a partisan political

---

[31]Scott Jaschik, "Who Won the Battle of Pennsylvania?," *InsideHigherEd,* November 16, 2006, http://www.insidehighered.com/news/2006/11/16/tabor

agenda. Instead of looking into the problem, Jaschik pressured me to come up with yet another example of what I considered to be an academic abuse—so that he could refute it. Aware of his agendas, I attempted to frustrate them by offering a case he could investigate himself. I mentioned my experience at Bloomsburg—the complaints I had heard from John Boyer and Jason Walter.

Since I had been manhandled by Jaschik before, I was careful not to make the claim that the stories I had been told were true. I told Jaschik I hadn't seen the exam, and hadn't attended the inquisitorial proceeding orchestrated by Professor Zoelle and Professor Smith after the students had met with me. I gave him the names of students he could contact, and mentioned several professors, including Dean Agbango. I also suggested he speak to the president of the university herself. Jaschik performed none of these journalistic tasks. Instead he followed the course he had taken in previous cases, including the one involving the Colorado exam. He interviewed only Professor Zoelle and reported her comments as thought they were fact: "Reached while en route to her Thanksgiving vacation, Zoelle said that Horowitz was 'absolutely incorrect.'"

What these episodes demonstrate is the lengths to which my academic opponents are willing to go to protect their ability to use the classroom to advance their political agendas, even at the expense of their students' educations. The very modest proposal of the academic freedom campaign which has aroused such opposition is that university administrations should take steps to provide students with reasonable protections, and that they should restore professional academic standards. These include faculty respect for political differences, for the pluralism of ideas, and for fairness when dealing with matters that are controversial. The problem of such academic abuses is not an invention. It is real, and it is not going to disappear of its own accord.

PART V

Indoctrination U.

The Professors

W hen *The Professors* was first published in February 2006, it was greeted by cries of outrage from the academic left. The author was denounced as a reincarnation of Joseph McCarthy and his book as a "blacklist," although no evidence existed to support either claim and both were the opposite of the truth. Far from being a "blacklist," the text explicitly—and in so many words—defended the right of professors, without fear of political reprisal, to teach views that were unpopular. The author also publicly defended the First Amendment rights of Ward Churchill, the most notable case of a professor under attack for his political views.

The very nature of the attacks, on the other hand, served to confirm its analysis. *The Professors* describes a segment of the university that has supplanted scholarly interests with political agendas, and has corrupted intellectual discourse in the process. Its hundred-plus profiles are of professors who regard educational institutions as instruments of social change, and who understand their task as inculcating sectarian doctrines to promote such change.

An ironic aspect of this ambition is that those who regard themselves as academic progressives are more accurately understood as academic reactionaries, determined to turn back the clock to a time when universities were largely denominational

---

Originally published September 12, 2007, as "The Professors: New Preface," http://archive.frontpagemag.com/readArticle.aspx?ARTID=28040

and their mission was to instill religious creeds. This process has been under way for more than three decades, with disquieting results. Under the influence of tenured radicals, American liberal arts faculties have become more narrow-minded and intellectually repressive than at any time in the last hundred years.

Today we would call such practices "indoctrination," a project antithetic to the very idea of a democratic education. In a democracy, educators are expected to teach students *how* to think—not *what* to think. In teaching controversial issues, they are expected to refrain from telling students which side of the controversy is "politically correct." Instead, they are tasked with developing students' abilities to think for themselves.

Professional restraint is thus a condition of academic freedom as applied to the instruction of students. Fortunately, outside liberal arts faculties it is still observed by most members of the academic community, regardless of their political disposition. Stanley Fish, himself a distinguished liberal academic, has summarized this discipline with admirable clarity: "Academic freedom is the freedom of academics to *study* anything they like; the freedom, that is, to subject any body of material, however unpromising it might seem, to academic interrogation and analysis.... Any idea can be brought into the classroom if the point is to inquire into its structure, history, influence and so forth. But no idea belongs in the classroom if the point of introducing it is to recruit your students for the political agenda it may be thought to imply."[1]

In keeping with a consensus on academic freedom that has lasted for nearly a century, most universities stipulate that the pursuit of knowledge should be "disinterested"—that faculty should observe the principle of neutrality on controversial matters, and that they should refrain from indoctrinating their students. These precepts are eloquently set forth in the classic

---

[1]Stanley Fish, "Conspiracy Theories 101," *New York Times*, July 23, 2006, http://www.nytimes.com/ref/opinion/23fish.html?_r=0

statements on academic freedom of the American Association of University Professors.

By contrast, the faculty radicals described in *The Professors* have taken the position that political activism should be an integral part of university curricula. As *The Professors* demonstrates, such radicals have exerted a disturbingly large influence over liberal arts studies. Entire academic programs—Women's Studies and Peace Studies are prime examples—require students to subscribe to a left-wing ideology in order to qualify as good students and receive good grades.[2] Faculty radicals also dominate many professional academic organizations, including the American Association of University Professors, and seek to use their offices for political ends. Professional groups such as the American Historical Association regularly pass formal resolutions on such public controversies as the war in Iraq. In doing so, they promote the illusion that a controversial political judgment can be resolved as a matter of scholarly expertise. This is itself a corruption of the academic idea and only serves to discredit the profession. In 2007, an AHA resolution condemning the Iraq War was passed by a determined minority who exploited the scholarly prestige gained in historical fields far removed from the Middle East to promulgate a fashionable left-wing political judgment on current events.

Such developments in the academy threaten the very idea of an academic standard, and constitute a dangerous trend in higher education. *The Professors* was written to identify the academic sources of this problem and to describe the attitudes behind it. Its text consists of a series of profiles accompanied by a 17,000-word explanatory essay. The essay outlines the problem and explains the methodology. The profiles depict more than a hundred academics who, in their classroom curricula, campus behavior or

---

[2]Analyses of more than a hundred examples of such indoctrination curricula can be found under the category "Indoctrination Studies" at http://www.discoverthenetworks.org/viewSubCategory.asp?id=522

published statements, support the view that political activism is integral to the academic mission.

This activist intrusion into scholarly disciplines is illustrated by a statement made by Princeton professor Joan Wallach Scott, an influential left-wing academic and ideological feminist, who was not included in the original text: "As feminist and historian," Scott wrote in the preface to her principal academic work, "my interest is in the operations of power—how it is constructed, what its effects are, how it changes. It follows that activism in the academy is both informed by that work and informs it."[3]

Scott is a member of "Historians Against the War." She is also a leading figure in the American Association of University Professors, an organization historically associated with the academic freedom tradition, which has recently strayed from that mission. From 1999 to 2005, Professor Scott was head of the AAUP's Academic Freedom Committee; but the only freedom Professor Scott appears to have been concerned with was the freedom to express radical views. By her own account, her principal concerns were the fates of Professor Sami al-Arian, an indicted Palestinian terrorist (eventually deported) and Tariq Ramadan, an academic barred by the State Department because of his connection to terrorist organizations.[4] Scott is on record as stating that all but one of the academic freedom problems the AAUP tracked from 9/11 to 2005 were instigated by the "pro-Israel bloc."[5]

---

[3]Joan Wallach Scott, *Gender and the Politics of History*, Columbia University, 1988, introduction

[4]For details on Tariq Ramadan, see Paul Berman, "Who's Afraid of Tariq Ramadan?" June 4, 2007, http://www.newrepublic.com/article/who%E2%80%99s-afraid-tariq-ramadan

[5]Jane Adas, "Princeton Panelists Share Cautionary Tales of Dangers to Academic Freedom," *Washington Report on Middle East Affairs*, December 2005,http://wrmea.com/archives/December_2005/0512046.html. See also the author's discussion of Joan Wallach Scott in *Indoctrination U.*, pp. 39–45.

The current president of the AAUP, Cary Nelson, is also a well-known political activist, author of *Manifesto of a Tenured Radical*. During a debate at a conference in 2007, Professor Nelson said: "You cannot take politics out of my classroom anymore than you can take it out of life. It's built into my subject matter and it's been built into my subject matter for the whole 37 years in which I've taught."[6] Professor Nelson went on to criticize what he regarded as the timidity of colleagues who refrained from expressing their political views in the classroom.

Attitudes like these go far in explaining the unscholarly responses that *The Professors* elicited. Professor Nelson's review in the AAUP's journal, *Academe,* began with this injunction: "Please ignore this book. Don't buy it. Don't read it. Try not to mention it in idle conversation."[7] These were strange instructions for an educator, but not so strange for a political activist outraged by the fact that his agendas were being scrutinized.

To combat the author of *The Professors* (no other verb will do), the American Federation of Teachers organized a coalition of left-wing organizations it called "Free Exchange on Campus."[8] The union issued a press release touting its newly created organization: "Free Exchange on Campus ... has condemned a new book that attacks individual professors for their personal political beliefs. The book is *The Professors: The 101 Most Dangerous Academics in America*, by David Horowitz, who is also the author of the so-called Academic Bill of Rights legislation making its way through-

---

[6]A transcript of the debate can be found at "Political Indoctrination and Harassment on Campus: Is there a Problem?," *FrontPageMag.com,* March 23, 2007, http://www.frontpagemag.com/Articles/ReadArticle. asp?ID=27446

[7]Cary Nelson, "Ignore This Book," *Academe,* November-December 2006, Vol. 92, No. 6, pp. 81–82, 84, http://www.jstor.org/stable/40253534

[8]The organizations included the ACLU, People for the American Way and Campus Progress—a student organization created by George Soros and former Clinton chief of staff John Podesta; Jacob Laksin, "Truth-Free Exchange on Campus," *FrontPageMag.com,* April 14, 2006, http://www.frontpagemag.com/Articles/ReadArticle.asp?ID=22018

out the states. The book is essentially a blacklist of academics, says Free Exchange on Campus, and is based on inaccurate and misleading information."[9]

Any fair-minded reader of *The Professors* will readily see that these political sound-bites bear no relation to the text. *The Professors* does not "attack individual academics for their personal political beliefs," nor does it suggest that professors should be fired for their political beliefs. It cannot be described by any reasonable standard as a "blacklist." The author makes quite explicit in the introduction that he did not design the text to attack professors' political beliefs: "This book is not intended as a text about left-wing bias in the university, and does not propose that a left-wing perspective on academic faculties is a problem in itself. Every individual, whether conservative or liberal, has a perspective and therefore a bias. Professors have every right to interpret the subjects they teach according to their individual points of view. That is the essence of academic freedom."[10] A defense of unpopular professorial views could hardly be more clearly expressed.

Yet, the cynical misrepresentation of *The Professors* as a McCarthy "witch-hunt" is the substance of virtually all the hostile responses to this book. Not a single academic who condemned *The Professors* bothered to address its argument, or demonstrated a familiarity with the 17,000 words of explanatory material. Instead critics read their own agendas into the profiles and responded to whatever it was they had made up. It is true that the profiles describe professors' political beliefs, and that the author occasionally expresses an opinion about professorial statements that are overtly racist or anti-Semitic or simply incoherent. But

[9] "Academic Freedom in the 21st-Century College and University: Academic Freedom for All Faculty and Instructional Staff," *American Federation of Teachers*, October 2007, pp. 15, 21, http://www.aft.org/sites/default/files/academicfreedomstatement0907.pdf

[10] David Horowitz, *The Professors: The 101 Most Dangerous Academics in America*, Regnery, 2006, p. xxvi

the clear (and limited) purpose of the book is to demonstrate that the individuals are political activists before they are scholars.[11]

The book's introductory essay also explains that there are four specific "disturbing patterns of university life" to which the author objects. None of these patterns involves the expression of unpopular views inside or outside the classroom. All are viewpoint-neutral. The four problem areas are: "(1) promotion far beyond academic achievement; (2) teaching subjects outside one's professional qualifications and expertise for the purpose of political propaganda; (3) making racist and ethnically disparaging remarks in public without eliciting reaction by university administrations, as long as those remarks are directed at unprotected groups, e.g., Armenians, whites, Christians and Jews; and (4) the overt introduction of political agendas into the classroom and the abandonment of any pretense of academic discipline or scholarly inquiry."

The Professors does identify several academics as "Communists" (Bettina Aptheker, Angela Davis, Manning Marable and Harry Targ). But these are references to their actual membership in a faction of the Communist Party, certainly a relevant aspect of the resumes of professionals whose expertise is ideas. Two professors, Bill Ayers and Bernardine Dohrn,[12] are described as terrorists, but this is also an accurate and literal description. Both were leaders of the Weather Underground, a terrorist organization whose relevance to their academic activities the body of the text makes clear. *The Professors* also describes tenured professors who are

---

[11]The fact that their activism is oriented towards the left is explained by the well-documented absence of conservatives on liberal arts faculties. For documentation of the vanishing presence of conservatives on university faculties, see: "Studies on Faculty and Campus Diversity," *Students For Academic Freedom*, July 4, 2006, http://www.studentsforacademicfreedom.org//index.php?option=com_content&task=view&id=1893&Itemid=40

[12]Dohrn and Ayers raised Kathy Boudin's child during the 20 years she was in prison. For an account of the Weather Underground, see Peter Collier and David Horowitz, *Destructive Generation*, Summit, 1989.

crude racists and anti-Semites (Amiri Baraka, Hamid Dabashi, and Leonard Jeffries, among others); convicted torturers (Maulana Karenga); supporters of Islamic terrorism (Shahid Alam and Hamid Algar, among others); and bearers of academic credentials that are fraudulent (Ward Churchill, Michael Vocino). Since professors are hired through an elaborate system of professional standards and review, these cases demonstrate that the system is broken, which is the purpose of the collective portrait the book set out to construct.

Penn State professor and AAUP board member Michael Bérubé was also one of many politically inspired assailants to misrepresent the book's purpose. In at least three separate commentaries, Professor Bérubé has ridiculed *The Professors* and its author without addressing the book's argument.[13] When he and the author met at a lunch arranged by *The Chronicle of Higher Education*, Bérubé conceded he had not actually read the explanatory text, which defines what the book is about.[14] Like other critics, Bérubé merely sampled the profiles and guessed what purpose they might serve, imputing to the author agendas he did not have, while refuting claims he did not make.[15]

---

[13]These can be found on his blog at http://www.michaelberube. com/index.php/search/results/d5e834cf773b078284c542fe944de924/, and in Jennifer Jacobson, "Dangerous Minds," *Chronicle of Higher Education*, February 17, 2006, http://chronicle.com/article/Dangerous-Minds/14710/. Jacobson interviewed Bérubé about the book.

[14]Bérubé subsequently wrote a book defending the academic left called *What's Liberal About the Liberal Arts?: Classroom Politics and "Bias" in Higher Education*, W.W. Norton, 2006, in which he continued his attacks on the author. A review of Bérubé's book by the author can be found here: David Horowitz, "What's Not Liberal about the Liberal Arts," *FrontPageMag.com*, October 20, 2006, http://www.frontpagemag.com/Articles/ReadArticle.asp?ID=25020

[15]Bérubé also conceded that the profile of himself—which claimed that he viewed the classroom as a vehicle of social transformation, and which he ridiculed as an ignorant misrepresentation of his views—resembled criticisms of his work also made by Stanley Fish in *Professional Correctness*, Oxford University Press, 1995; a book which drew a very different response from Bérubé.

In urging others not to read *The Professors*, AAUP president Cary Nelson similarly ignored what it actually said. After calling the book "a faculty blacklist," Nelson complained that "the entries ... purport to be accounts of a hundred faculty careers. Yet most of them ignore the chief publications at the core of those careers." If Nelson had bothered to read the methodological essay provided, he would know the book's profiles did not purport to be anything of the kind. They were not written as accounts of academic careers, but were compiled to illustrate patterns among individuals who confused their activist agendas with an academic calling. The profiles assemble statements and activities of academics which reflect a belief that scholarship and political activism are integral to each other. They also document violations of academic protocol in the four categories listed above. The one thing they do *not* do is what Professor Nelson claims—attempt to provide accounts of intellectual careers (something that could hardly be accomplished in a format limited to four pages for each entry).

The abusive term "blacklist" is one of two main charges deployed by critics to discredit the author and prevent readers from evaluating his argument. The other is to claim that the book is factually challenged and "contains numerous errors, misrepresentations and distortions ..."[16] These baseless allegations make up the bulk of the union-sponsored 50-page response, called "Facts Count," which critics such as Nelson merely repeat: "Horowitz's entries are fundamentally acts of misrepresentation and erasure...."[17]

"Facts Count"—the union report—is based on the complaints of twenty of the professors profiled. To make sure that even the dimmest reader would not miss the point, Free Exchange included a permanent feature on its website called "Horowitz Fact-

---

[16]Jennifer Jacobson, "Group Assails Book by Conservative Writer," *Chronicle of Higher Education*, May 19, 2006, http://chronicle.com/article/Group-Assails-Book-by/19492
[17]Cf., Cary Nelson, "Ignore This Book," op. cit.

Checker." The subsequent repetition of this canard by a small army of politically motivated critics has helped create the impression that the author has a bigger problem with facts than do his critics, who describe as a "blacklist" a book that defends the right of professors to hold unpopular views.

The Free Exchange report is itself rich in easily demonstrated factual errors: e.g., "Mr. Horowitz chiefly condemns professors for expressing their personal political views outside of the classroom."[18] In fact, not one individual profiled in *The Professors* is condemned for expressing his or her personal views outside the classroom. To be sure, the political views of professors are described. But that is because the book is about political activists who regard the university as a platform for their activism. It is not, on the other hand, a book whose purpose is to condemn professors for expressing their political views. Insofar as individual professors are "condemned" in the text, they are faulted under the categories of abuse specified in the book's introduction and listed above. The infractions the book alleges are infractions of academic standards, not deviations from political correctness. None of the book's categories includes the expression of personal political views as a culpable academic offense.

A typical complaint about the author's accuracy can be found in comments provided to Free Exchange by Bettina Aptheker, a professor of Feminist Studies at the University of California Santa Cruz. Aptheker criticized the author for "misrepresenting" an anti-war speech she made to UCSC students in which she compared the Bush administration's policies to those of Nazi Germany. In the words of the Free Exchange Report: "Mr. Horowitz claims that Professor Aptheker 'informed students' that 'our agenda should be to overthrow Bush.' Both Aptheker and Free Exchange contend that this is a factual error and misrepresents what Aptheker said."[19]

---

[18]"An Analysis of David Horowitz's The Professors: The 101 Most Dangerous Academics in America," *Center for Campus Free Speech*, Spring 2006, http://www.campusspeech.org/page/cfs/facts-count
[19]Ibid.

The Free Exchange report then refutes the alleged error with this sentence: "Professor Aptheker responds, 'I am inaccurately quoted: I called for the overthrow of George W. Bush by all constitutional and democratic means up to and including impeachment.'" Readers are invited to parse the difference between the two quotes; to guess, first, how the Constitution provides for the "overthrow" of an elected President, and second, how the citizens of a country which is to be equated with Nazi Germany could have access to "constitutional and democratic means up to and including impeachment." Even if Professor Aptheker could be taken at her word, and even if she did make this qualification in her speech, the journalist who reported her remarks in the Santa Cruz student paper (which is the book's source for her remarks) failed to note them. In other words, if the quote misrepresents what she said, the fault can hardly be attributed to the author of *The Professors*.

Professor Aptheker also claims the author misidentified the date of her departure from the Communist Party as taking place after the fall of the Berlin Wall. The author is willing to accept her word on this matter and stands corrected. The Aptheker profile in the original text presumed she had been expelled with her long-time friend and political ally Angela Davis in a noted group ejection that occurred after the fall. Aptheker objects that she actually left the Party ten years earlier over the rejection of a manuscript she had written for the Party's official publishing house. What Aptheker does not mention is that she contributed to the author's error *by concealing the fact that she had left the Party when she did.* She only revealed this deception twenty-five years later in her autobiography, which appeared after the publication of *The Professors*.[20] According to the autobiography, Aptheker concealed her Party resignation so that her departure would not be taken as a

---

[20]Bettina Aptheker, *Intimate Politics: How I Grew Up Red, Fought for Free Speech, and Became a Feminist Rebel*, Seal Press, 2006, and David Horowitz, "The Political Is Personal," *FrontPageMag.com*, November 10, 2006, http://www.frontpagemag.com/Articles/ReadArticle.asp?ID=25418

sign of protest against the Soviet Union.[21] In other words, while she left the Party she did not abandon her commitment to communism, which is exactly what the passage in *The Professors* was written to reflect—that she remained committed to the communist cause even after the fall of the Berlin Wall.

This minor error in the text of *The Professors*, abetted by Aptheker's own admitted deception, is one of only six identified in the Free Exchange report that can actually be regarded as factual errors, and not merely another name for differing interpretations. Like the others, it has been corrected in the paperback edition.

Aptheker's autobiography provides powerful evidence, on the other hand, to support the substantive claims *The Professors* makes about her ideological agendas in the classroom. In her memoir, Aptheker reveals that she was responsible for designing key elements of the Women's Studies curriculum at UC Santa Cruz. By her own account, she designed them as elements of a program whose purpose was not academic but was to train students to be political radicals: "I redesigned the curriculum [for the introductory course] and retitled it 'Introduction to Feminism,' making it more overtly political, and taught the class in the context of the women's movement.... Teaching became a form of political activism for me, replacing the years of dogged meetings and intrepid organizing with the immediacy of a liberatory practice...."[22] This is eloquent confirmation by a harsh critic of *The Professors* that the academic abuses it set out to document are real.

Professor Aptheker is not unique among the author's critics in defaming him without evidence, as a seventy-page point-by-point response to the Free Exchange report written by Jacob Laksin makes clear.[23] Reviewing each of the Free Exchange charges,

---

[21]Aptheker, op. cit, pp. 405–6
[22]Ibid.
[23]Jacob Laksin, "Discounting the Facts," *FrontPageMag.com*, June 15, 2006, http://archive.frontpagemag.com/readArticle.aspx?ARTID=4039. Laksin was a colleague of the author and employee of the David Horowitz Freedom Center.

Laksin concludes: "'Facts Count' is a tendentious document that misrepresents and distorts the arguments of *The Professors* in order to attack the book and its author, and is not above fabricating evidence to make its case. Time and again the report insists that *The Professors* cites no evidence for a given claim when even a cursory reading of the text and its sources would confirm the opposite. Time and again, the report rebuts arguments that appear nowhere in *The Professors,* but are the inventions of the Free Exchange authors themselves. The overall impression created by these methods is that either these authors have not read the book or else they are unwilling honestly to engage with its arguments."[24] Free Exchange failed to respond to Laksin's refutation.

The unsubstantiated claims that the author misrepresented his subjects, and that his text is factually inaccurate, were also categorically dismissed by one of the academics profiled. Dana Cloud, a professor of Communication Studies at the University of Texas, had led a protest against the book's author when he spoke at her campus, and has been candid about her own use of the classroom for political agendas. But she was firm in her conclusion that *The Professors* was an accurate account of what its subjects proposed: "There are organizations and professors who have devoted themselves to refuting Horowitz's 'facts' about their publications and activism," wrote Professor Cloud; "I believe this also is a wrong approach, because his 'facts' about faculty syllabi and political affiliations are not in question."[25]

The new paperback edition of *The Professors* corrects the six trivial errors in the original 110,000-word text that have been unearthed by its critics. Since it can be assumed that the book was reviewed by a hundred and one subjects, each with an axe to grind, and virtually all of them with Ph.D.s, it can be said that few books

---

[24]Ibid.
[25]Dana Cloud, "David Horowitz and the Thought Police," *CounterPunch*, March 8, 2007, http://www.counterpunch.org/2007/03/08/david-horowitz-and-the-thought-police/

have come under more copious scrutiny. This is what its detractors discovered: in addition to mistaking the date of Professor Aptheker's secret resignation from the Communist Party, the text referred to Professor Emma Perez as *Elizabeth* Perez in one of three mentions of her name; it identified Dean Saitta as the director of the Museum of Anthropology at the University of Denver in 2005 when he left the post in 2003; it described Beverly Aminah McCloud as a member of the Nation of Islam when she is only an admirer of the Nation of Islam and its racist leader Lewis Farrakhan; and it misattributed a quote from a symposium on 9/11 to Eric Foner, whose sentiments, expressed in the same symposium (and on the same page of the *London Review of Books*) were identical (and are now included in the present text). This, insofar as the author is able to tell, is an accounting of all the errors unearthed, which his academic detractors have described as "numerous" and evidence of the untrustworthiness of his research. What does that say about *their* scholarly methods?

In an early review of *The Professors*, Harvard scholars Abigail and Stephan Thernstrom offered this observation: "Academics on the left like to pat themselves on the back for daring to 'speak truth to power.' David Horowitz's *The Professors* speaks some uncomfortable truths to them—to those who run American higher education today. They will hate this scathing critique, but will be hard-pressed to answer his charges."[26]

The exceptionally low standards displayed by academic critics of *The Professors* underscore the problems it set out to address. In their attacks on the book and its author, those critics have subordinated intellectual principles to political ends. A crafty (and ruthless) politician once remarked: "In political conflicts the goal is not to refute your opponent's argument, but to wipe him from the face of the earth."[27] Michael Bérubé, among others, appears to have adopted a similar scorched-earth policy towards the author of

---

[26]This was a blurb that appeared on the jacket of the hardcover text.
[27]The politician was Lenin.

The Professors. In a moment of candor on the academic blog "Crooked Timbers," he complained about his lunch meeting with the author, which had been arranged by *The Chronicle of Higher Education:* "[It] grants Horowitz, and his complaints about academe, a certain legitimacy."[28] This legitimacy was something Bérubé was determined to torpedo: "My job is to contest that legitimacy, and to model a way of dealing with Horowitz that does not give him what he wants, namely 1) important concessions; or 2) outrage." To implement such a strategy, Bérubé recommended that opponents of the book resort to "mockery and dismissal."[29]

It proved to be the model not only for Bérubé's responses but for his colleagues' as well. In a comment on the book to the Columbia University *Spectator,* Professor Todd Gitlin dismissed the author as "bonkers;" at a public rally to protest the "Academic Bill of Rights," Professor Joan Wallach Scott referred to the author's academic freedom campaign as "the pro-Sharon lobby," i.e., a Zionist plot; and in the official journal of the American Association of University Professors its president, Cary Nelson, advised academics to ignore the book.

These are expressions of a mentality that seeks to suppress rather than engage an opposing point of view. This is the way political operatives think, not the way academics and scholars should conduct themselves. It is antithetic to the scientific method, which academic professionals are obligated to follow. The scientific method pursues the truth disinterestedly, submits hypotheses to opposing perspectives, and tests claims against the evidence. This is the very basis of academic freedom, which is freedom within a professional discipline governed by scientific method.

---

[28]Michael Bérubé, "Discipline and Puzzle," *Crooked Timber,* March 29, 2007, http://crookedtimber.org/2007/03/29/discipline-and-puzzle/
[29]Ibid.

2

The Two Universities of Texas

There are two universities operating under the name "University of Texas." The first is a world-class school of scientific inquiry and professional training. It examines phenomena and draws conclusions when all the evidence is presented and inquiries are complete. But there is a second University of Texas which is quite different in its methods and goals. This university's faculty regard themselves as activists, not scholars, and their method is that of authority, not science. Their conclusions are ready-made and their inquiries are designed to search out facts that will confirm what they already know. Their curriculum is designed not to teach students how to conduct a disinterested inquiry, but to convert them to a sectarian ideology and recruit them to its causes.

Students in this second university are taught to respect dogma rather than evidence. They are offered a curriculum that is relentlessly one-sided and denies legitimacy to dissenting points of view. Students are in this school are being given an indoctrination, not an education. Among the departments and programs at the second University of Texas that are parties to this scam are the Communications Studies Department, the Center for Women's and Gender Studies and the Division of Rhetoric and Writing.

The stated mission of the Center for Women's and Gender Studies does not propose a disinterested inquiry into the history

Originally published February 20, 2007, as "The Two Universities of Texas," http://archive.frontpagemag.com/Printable.aspx?ArtId=62

and condition of women or the nature of gender and its place in different societies. Instead, its stated mission is "to advance knowledge and understanding about ... the role that gender plays in *structuring* society." (emphasis added) The idea that gender structures society is an ideological claim, not a program for scholarly investigation. This claim is the organizing principle of gender feminism, a radical sect of the broader movement. Not surprisingly, the reading lists for courses in the department are almost exclusively drawn from radical feminist texts.

Graduate students in an Introduction to Women's and Gender Studies course, for example, are provided with a reading list that includes scores of texts written from a radical viewpoint. Only one text blatantly criticizes the radical feminist perspective. This is a book written by two founders of women's studies who subsequently left the field, because they felt it had become devoted to a political ideology to the point that its practitioners regularly denied scientific findings which conflicted with their political agendas. But this is the way the course syllabus for the introductory class refers to the book: "Daphne Patai and Noretta Koertge, professing feminism, *passim* (note that this represents anti-women's studies—prepare to refute it)." This is the instruction of a political ideologue, not an academic scholar.

This is one example; a glance at other curricular offerings in this and related programs reveals similarly unprofessional agendas. Many of the professors who teach these courses are neither trained historians nor sociologists nor economists; yet the subject matter they teach will often be the history of radical movements, globalization, race, or all three. "Communications and Social Change," taught by a professor of communications studies, is such a course. It has no academic rationale except to recruit students to the causes favored by its Marxist instructor: "After the historical survey of social movements, the second part of the course asks you to become involved as an observer and/or as a participant in a local social movement." The course requires only two texts—both by Marxists (Howard Zinn and UT's own Robert Jensen), both situated on the extreme left of the political spectrum. There's no harm in reading Zinn or Jensen, but a properly academic course would include their critics on the right and left.

There are enough such courses at the University of Texas that students can enroll in a degree-granting curriculum which has no academic component but is a comprehensive training program in the theory and practice of radical politics.

What is the rationale for lending the prestige of this university, which is the prestige of science, to ideological causes? What is the justification for deceiving students into thinking that they are getting an education, when in reality they are getting a political indoctrination? And how can any self-respecting liberal countenance academic programs in which there is only one side presented about the most controversial issues of the day?

3

Secular Creationism

A year ago the biggest issue in education after budgets was whether "Intelligent Design" should be taught in the nation's schools. Opponents called it a form of "creationism" and the press treated the ensuing legal battle as the biggest clash between faith and science since the Scopes monkey trial.[1] In a stinging rebuke to the religious right, a Pennsylvania judge ruled that "Intelligent Design" had no place in classrooms because it was "a religious view, a mere re-labeling of creationism, and not a scientific theory," thus violating the separation of church and state.[2]

Yet at that very moment professors in American universities were teaching a form of secular creationism as contrary to the findings of modern science as the Biblical claim that God had made the world in seven days. The name of this theory is "social constructionism," and its churches are Women's Studies departments in universities across the United States. The feminist theory of social construction maintains that the differences between men and women—apart from obvious anatomical ones—are not biologically determined but are created by a patriarchal social structure that is designed by men to oppress women. It is "patriarchal society" that turns naturally bisexual infants into male and

Originally published March 19, 2007, as "Secular Creationism," http://archive.frontpagemag.com/Printable.aspx?ArtId=25533
[1] "Judge Rules against Intelligent Design," *Associated Press*, December 20, 2005, http://www.nbcnews.com/id/10545387/#.VK2M-WAtFJQ
[2] Ibid.

female personalities by conditioning them from birth to adopt gender roles—the one aggressive, masculine and destined to command, the other passive, feminine and slated to obey.

Critics of feminism such as Christina Hoff Sommers and neuroscientists such as Harvard's Stephen Pinker have pointed out that this view contradicts the findings of modern science—evolutionary psychology, neuroscience and biology.[3] For example, men are known to cluster in significantly greater numbers at the high end of testing for mathematical aptitude, though they cluster in greater numbers at the low end of that bell curve as well. The scientific evidence is summarized in a recent book, *Sex Differences in Cognitive Ability,* whose author, Diane Halperin, is president of the American Psychological Association and was a social constructionist herself before reviewing the scientific literature. She concludes: "Socialization practices are undoubtedly important, but there is also good evidence that biological differences play a role in establishing and maintaining cognitive sex differences, a conclusion I wasn't prepared to make when I began reviewing the relevant literature."[4] Similarly, male aggression and competitiveness are not created out of whole cloth by a patriarchal system of dominance, as Women's Studies feminists argue, but are to a significant degree hormone-instigated. In other words, according to modern science, the cause lies not in patriarchal hierarchies but in the genes.

Yet here is a typical statement from the official course description for "Feminist Political Theory 433" as taught at the University of Arizona by a full professor of Political Science and recipient of a coveted MacArthur Foundation fellowship: "Because gender is socially constructed, it is instructive to study how gender ideologies—which profoundly shape today's intellectual inquiries and political realities—have been articulated in the form of political

---

[3] http://archive.frontpagemag.com/bioAuthor.aspx?AUTHID=2171; http://archive.frontpagemag.com/bioAuthor.aspx?AUTHID=3364

[4] Diane F. Halpern, "What Have You Changed Your Mind about? Why?" *Edge,* 2008, https://edge.org/response-detail/10981

theory."[5] Obviously the premise of this course must be accepted by students, or there is no course. Yet this statement asserts a claim that is not scientifically founded, and in fact is scientifically contradicted. In other words, students are *required* to believe a religious myth in order to get their academic grade.

Here is a parallel statement from the Kansas State University catalogue: "To qualify for a Bachelor of Arts or a Bachelor of Science in Women's Studies at Kansas State University, students will have demonstrated their familiarity with key Women's Studies concepts such as the social construction of gender, oppression of and violence against women, heterosexism, racism, classism, and global inequality." In other words, students cannot graduate from the Kansas State Women's Studies program unless they believe in the ideology that makes up its core, and demonstrate that they do believe in it. Yet the ideological premise is scientifically challenged—a fact that the program does not acknowledge. In the catalogue descriptions of more than a hundred Women's Studies courses which I have personally examined, these are common themes.

Indoctrination in dogmatic creeds such as gender feminism was once alien to the very idea of a modern research university. Now it has become an orthodoxy. Problematic dogmas have become the basis of entire programs funded by taxpayers. This is made possible by university authorities who have abdicated their responsibility to enforce university standards, while professional scholars who observe those standards are intimidated by academic radicals who will denounce as sexist, racist and homophobic anyone who gets in their way.

---

[5]David Horowitz and Tom Ryan, "Abusive Academics," *FrontPageMag.com*, January 19, 2007, http://archive.frontpagemag.com/readArticle.aspx?ARTID=540

4

The End of the University As We Have Known It

Alarms about the political subversion of the academic curriculum were first sounded more than a quarter of a century ago with such books as *The Closing of the American Mind*, *Illiberal Education* and *Tenured Radicals*. Lesser known but more specifically documented texts followed, including *Zealotry and Academic Freedom* by Neil Hamilton (1995) and *Professing Feminism: Education and Indoctrination in Women's Studies*, by Daphne Patai and Noretta Koertge (1994). In addition, several websites including *noindoctrination.org* and *studentsfor-academicfreedom.org* have collected many student testimonies of academic abuses, stemming from the introduction of political agendas into the academic curriculum. Several organizations including the National Association of Scholars and the American Council of Trustees and Alumni have contributed to these efforts.

In 2003 I began a campaign for an "Academic Bill of Rights" to protect students from being proselytized in university classrooms. Partly under the pressure of that campaign, hearings have been held in the Pennsylvania and Missouri legislatures and the accumulation of evidence that such practices are widespread has reached a critical mass.

These activities have been strongly resisted by the teacher unions who have conducted a campaign of reckless *ad hominem* attacks against their critics, stubbornly denying the facts while

Originally published November 16, 2007 as "The End of the University As We Know It," http://archive.frontpagemag.com/Printable.aspx?ArtId= 28814 avoiding the issues they raise.[1] Now the American Association of University Professors has issued a report, called "Freedom in the Classroom," to answer the critics in a less inflammatory style.[2] Not surprisingly, given its dismal record during these efforts, the AAUP report is not a defense of academic freedom, as its title implies, but an attack on the academic rights of students and a defense of indoctrination in the classroom. It marks a return to principles that guided universities when they were instruments of religious sects, and their curricula were governed by the authority of the church rather than the method of scientific inquiry.

My own views on indoctrination are set forth in both the recently published *Indoctrination U.* and a previous book called *The Professors*, with which members of the AAUP committee responsible for this new report are quite familiar. With my colleagues Jacob Laksin and Tom Ryan, I have also posted Internet analyses of the syllabuses of 200 courses that are designed to indoctrinate students, and that violate existing university regulations.[3] These analyses make up more than 100,000 words of text. Stephen Balch, president of the National Association of Scholars, has also written extensively on indoctrination in Schools of Education and Social Work programs, and published a report on the latter.

The AAUP report examines none of these studies or the issues they raise. Instead, its entire discussion of indoctrination is focused on a four-year-old complaint by a group called the "Committee for a Better Carolina," about the assignment of a single text by the University of North Carolina as part of its freshman summer reading program. The University had required all incoming

---

[1]For documentation, see my recent book, *Indoctrination U.: The Left's War Against Academic Freedom*, Encounter, 2007

[2]"Academic Freedom for Students and Faculty," *American Association of University Professors*, February 2005, http://www.aaup.org/our-work/government-relations/past-campaigns-academic-bill-rights/aaup-policies-classroom

[3]Analyses of more than a hundred examples of such indoctrination curricula can be found under the category "Indoctrination Studies" at http://www.discoverthenetworks.org/viewSubCategory.asp?id=522

freshman to read the socialist writer Barbara Ehrenreich's *Nickled and Dimed*, a journalistic tract on poverty and the evils of the capitalist system. The Committee for a Better Carolina did not argue that the Ehrenreich text should not have been assigned. It argued that if college freshmen were going to be required to read a partisan text on a contested issue, they ought to be provided with another point of view for comparison. According to the AAUP's own statements on academic freedom, the assignment of two or three texts in this context would have been the appropriate educational practice, although the AAUP refused to concede even this point. The complaint lodged by the Committee for a Better Carolina not only objected to the assignment of one extremely partisan text but argued that it was a case of "indoctrination."

Obviously the assignment of any one book is not a *prima facie* case for indoctrination. The AAUP jumped on this confusion, and was right to make the point in its report. But it was not right to make this its sole reason to reject the North Carolina complaint as a prelude to setting its new guidelines on indoctrination. Why belabor a point that its principal critics would so readily agree with, unless its real purpose was to distract attention from the more serious issues its critics have raised?

The Committee for a Better Carolina was not constructing a formal argument about the nature of indoctrination in university courses. It was addressing a specific case, which it found problematic and was reasonable in doing so. Was there a basis for the committee's concern? As professors Neil Gross and Solon Simmons have shown in a recent Harvard study, 95 percent of the professors on liberal arts faculties are likely to share liberal or left-wing approaches to social issues—such as the causes of poverty and its remedies.[4] In these circumstances, concern that the assignment of a single polemic by a socialist author might be an attempt to

---

[4]Neil Gross and Solon Simmons, "The Social and Political Views of American Professors," *Intellectual Takeout*, September 24, 2007, http://citeseerx.ist.psu.edu/viewdoc/download?doi=10.1.1.147.6141&rep=rep1&type=pdf

enforce an existing faculty prejudice is not unreasonable. But the AAUP report never gets to the level of such specific substantive objections. Instead it uses the Committee for a Better Carolina's complaint as an opportunity to disparage its critics as philistines with no appreciation for the fine points of an academic discourse or the freedoms that make it possible.

In fact, despite this snobbery, the AAUP's own academic-freedom principles strongly support the Committee for a Better Carolina's concerns. The AAUP's well-known statements on academic freedom instruct professors—and in so many words—to provide students with "divergent opinions" on "controversial matters," and to be fair-minded in doing so. Here is the AAUP's classic guideline, as set forth in its famous 1915 *Declaration of Principles on Academic Freedom and Tenure:* "The university teacher, in giving instructions upon controversial matters, while he is under no obligation to hide his own opinion under a mountain of equivocal verbiage, should, if he is fit in dealing with such subjects, set forth justly, without suppression or innuendo, the divergent opinions of other investigators ... and he should, above all, remember that his business is not to provide his students with ready-made conclusions, but to train them to think for themselves, and to provide them access to those materials which they need if they are to think intelligently."

The AAUP's long-standing (but now abandoned) position is quite clear. If a professor is "fit to deal with such matters" (e.g., the nature and causes of poverty), that professor should present students with the divergent positions of others and "provide them access to those materials which they need if they are to think intelligently." It is not outlandish to suppose this would mean providing an alternative text. In fact, this has been the core principle for distinguishing education from indoctrination in the modern research university—until now, for the 2007 AAUP report simply ignores the principle.

Not surprisingly, the report also fails to look at the ideologically one-sided nature of the North Carolina faculty, along with the fact that the text assigned was written by an ideological radical. Instead it lectures the plaintiffs: "The Committee for a Better Carolina could not possibly have known whether the assignment of Ehrenreich's *Nickel and Dimed,* which explores the economic difficulties facing low-wage workers in America, was an example of indoctrination or education. It is a fundamental error to assume that the assignment of teaching materials constitutes their endorsement. An instructor who assigns a book no more endorses what it has to say than does the university library that acquires it."

But is this really the case? The text was assigned not by an individual teacher but by the university administration—and to incoming freshmen. This is quite different from the decision of a faceless librarian to stock a book on a library shelf. In addition, the Ehrenreich text was only one of a series assigned summer readings. The previous year's required selection—a book on the Koran—had also provoked a public reaction because of what was perceived as its overly sympathetic attitude towards Islam, coming on the heels of the 9/11 attacks. The fact that the university faculty ignored the complaints and assigned a radical text—again without providing critical materials—can hardly be regarded as unimportant. The report committee was aware of these facts, but ignored them.

The AAUP's suggestion that a teacher might assign a text in order to disagree with its conclusions may seem reasonable in the abstract but, in the specific case presented, it was an evasion. While the Committee for a Better Carolina could not prove its claim that there was indoctrination on the basis of this assignment, the AAUP could not prove there was none. To do so it would have had to produce the class lessons of the North Carolina faculty demonstrating that they did not endorse the contentious theses of Ehrenreich's neo-Marxist tract.

In focusing on this complaint without really dealing with it, the AAUP report is able to ignore the hundreds of syllabi, posted on the Internet, which are clearly designed to indoctrinate students. Instead of addressing this serious issue, the AAUP report avoids it by reiterating principles over which there is no disagreement. For example: "Indoctrination occurs whenever an instructor insists that students accept as truth propositions that are in fact professionally contestable." Agreed. And: "Instructors indoctrinate when they teach particular propositions as dogmatically true." Agreed. Another sound principle in the report is this: "It is not indoctrination when, as a result of their research and study, instructors assert to their students that in their view particular propositions are true, even if these propositions are controversial within a discipline." Agreed.

Just to be clear, here is the way I would formulate the principle: *When professors teach a point of view that is contested within the spectrum of scholarly or intellectually responsible opinion, they should make their students aware that it is contested, and must not teach their point of view as though it were scientifically established fact.*

This definition is not without problems. Outside the hard sciences, where contested issues can be resolved by experiment and authorities certified by objective measures, the question of what constitutes "scholarly or intellectually responsible opinion" is obviously itself controversial, and cannot be resolved at the margins. In the circumstances, it is probably better to err on the side of acknowledging challenges to an orthodoxy in the humanities and social sciences, even if those challenges are marginal, than to make absolute claims to truth that these disciplines cannot sustain. The process of making such acknowledgements is a way of teaching students about democratic ways of thinking, and teaching them to respect the pluralism of ideas.

Because respect for the contested nature of non-scientific opinions is the foundation of an educational discourse (and a democratic culture), it is disturbing when the AAUP report states that it is not necessary for liberal arts professors to observe this principle, if they can enforce a consensus among their faculty peers: "It is not indoctrination for professors to expect students to comprehend ideas and apply knowledge that is accepted as true within a relevant discipline." Note that the AAUP statement does not say "within the spectrum of scholarly and intellectually responsible opinion," or "within the spectrum of scientific opinion." Instead the AAUP report says a dogma can be taught as truth if it is accepted as true "within a relevant discipline."

This is a striking departure from the past and a very troubling doctrine. In the humanities and the liberal arts, no doctrine or ideology should be taught as "truth." Teaching an orthodoxy as truth is the mission of authoritarian institutions, and the antithesis of a liberal education. More worrying still is the fact that this is an attempt to ratify a transformation of the university that is already well advanced.

Since the 1960s, many newly minted academic disciplines have appeared that are not the result of new scholarship or scientific developments but of political pressures brought to bear by ideological sects. The discipline of Women's Studies, which is academically the most important of these new fields, freely acknowledges its origins in a political movement and defines its educational mission in political terms. Thus, the preamble to the Constitution of the National Women's Studies Association proclaims:

> *Women's Studies owes its existence to the movement for the liberation of women; the feminist movement exists because women are oppressed. Women's studies, diverse as its components are, has at its best shared a vision of a world free not only from sexism but also from racism, class-bias, ageism, heterosexual bias—from all the ideologies and institutions that have consciously or unconsciously oppressed and exploited some for the advantage of others.... Women's Studies, then, is equipping women not only to enter the society as whole, as productive human beings, but to transform the world to one that will be free of all oppression.*[5]

---

[5]National Women's Studies Association Journal, Vol. 14, No. 1, pp. xix–xx, Spring 2002, *Project Muse,* from the Founding Preamble: Adopted January 13–16, 1977, https://muse.jhu.edu/login?auth=0&type=summary&url=/journals/nwsa_journal/v014/14.1preamble.html

This is the statement of a political cause, not a program of scholarly inquiry.

In the face of such attitudes, now firmly entrenched in the university culture, when the professors' guild says that it is not indoctrination "to expect students to comprehend ideas and apply knowledge that is accepted as true within a relevant discipline," what it is really saying is that the training of students in sectarian ideologies, such as feminism, is an acceptable function of a university education. This is an abrogation of academic freedom, a severing of the link between scientific method and academic professionalism. It undermines the very concept of a university education as it has been understood for the last hundred years, ever since American institutions of higher learning declared their independence from religious denominations.

In issuing its defense of indoctrination, the American Association of University Professors is fully cognizant of the fact that numerous academic disciplines have incorporated sectarian ideologies as "scholarly truths" and view their academic mission as instilling these doctrines in their classrooms. These ideological programs include Women's Studies, African American Studies, Peace Studies, Cultural Studies, Chicano Studies, Gay Lesbian Studies, Post-Colonial Studies, Whiteness Studies, Communications Studies, Community Studies, and recently politicized disciplines such as Cultural Anthropology and Sociology. At the University of California Santa Cruz, the Women's Studies Department has dropped all pretense of being a scholarly discipline and has renamed itself the "Department of Feminist Studies" to signify that it is a political training facility, and has been able to do so without a word of complaint or caution from university administrators or the AAUP.

The AAUP's new doctrine is a transparent attempt to justify the transformation of the university into a home for these sectarian creeds by shielding them from the scrutiny of scientific method. In the new dispensation, political control of a discipline is the sole basis for establishing "truth" and closing off critical debate. The idea that political power can establish "truth" is a conception so incompatible with the intellectual foundations of a liberal education that the AAUP committee could not state it so baldly. Hence the disingenuous compromise of "truth within a relevant discipline."

The architect of this compromise is unknown but one can suppose Professor Robert Post, as one of the nation's leading experts on academic freedom and a member of the AAUP committee, played a key role in its final formulation. Some years ago, Post wrote a first-rate summary of the principles that have informed university governance since 1915. The essay was called "The Structure of Academic Freedom" and appeared in *Academic Freedom After September 11*, a collection of articles by liberal and left-wing scholars.[6] "[A] key premise of the '1915 Declaration,'" Post wrote, "is that faculty should be regarded as professional experts in the production of knowledge." Post explains: "The mission of the university defended by the 'Declaration' depends on a particular theory of knowledge. The 'Declaration' presupposes not only that knowledge exists and can be articulated by scholars, but also that it is advanced through the free application of highly disciplined forms of inquiry, which correspond roughly to what [philosopher] Charles Pierce once called 'the method of science' as opposed to the 'method of authority.'"[7]

The method of authority, of course, is precisely the method now recommended by the AAUP committee—the authority of the discipline. This is precisely the method employed in Women's Studies departments throughout the university system. Thus, virtually every Women's Studies curriculum is premised on the controversial thesis that gender is "socially constructed." Women's Studies' curricula are designed to present and explore this doctrinal claim as

---

[6]Beshara Doumani, ed. *Academic Freedom After September 11*, New York, Zone Books, 2006, p. 69

[7]Post is referring to the AAUP's 1915 "Declaration of Principles on Academic Freedom and Academic Tenure," http://www.aaup.org/NR/rdon lyres/A6520A9D-0A9A-47B3-B550-C006B5B224E7/0/1915Declaration.pdf

though it were an established truth; students in Women's Studies are expected to apply it as knowledge and accept it as truth.

The social construction of gender, which is academic nomenclature for asserting the primacy of nurture over nature, is an idea that is important to an ideological movement—radical feminism—which proposes the use of political means to reshape social relations. But the claim itself is refuted by the findings of modern neuroscience, evolutionary psychology, and also biology (as any reader of Stephen Pinker's *The Blank Slate* would know). To force students to accept as true a doctrine which is contested by biological scientists is precisely what is meant by indoctrination. Yet the AAUP has found a way to redefine indoctrination so that it no longer is. Under the principle of "truth within a relevant discipline," it is not indoctrination for Women's Studies professors to assert a dogma as truth, because it is a feminist "truth" and all Women's Studies professors are required through the hiring process to be radical gender feminists, since the discipline so defines itself; and they are obliged to believe it.

At the time its report was finalized, the AAUP issued a new edition of its official journal, *Academe*, featuring two articles defending feminist indoctrination of university students. The first article, titled "Impassioned Teaching," was written by one of its regional presidents, Pamela Caughie, head of the Women's Studies Department at Loyola University in Chicago. Caughie wrote: "I feel I am doing my job well when students become practitioners of feminist analysis and committed to feminist politics."[8] This is the attitude of a professor seeking to indoctrinate her students in feminist dogmas—not to educate them about women. In the same issue of *Academe*, Professor Julie Kilmer describes how it is necessary to publicly expose and intimidate students who "resist" such indoctrination, while providing suggestions as to how to do it. The publication of two such articles can hardly be regarded as

---

[8] Pamela Caughie, "Impassioned Teaching," *Academe*, July-August, 2007, Vol. 93, No. 4, pp. 54–56, http://www.jstor.org/stable/40253083

coincidental. They identify the downward slope on which the AAUP now finds itself.[9]

It is a slope that is slippery in more ways than one. The doctrine of "truth within a relevant discipline" may work in one direction when the discipline is controlled by ideological leftists, but in quite another if a discipline should come under the aegis of different political factions. Suppose, for example, antagonists of Darwin's theory of evolution were to establish a new academic field of Intelligent Design Studies. What academic principle would then prevent them from teaching their contested theories as truth? The same would apply to conservatives or Republicans, or 9/11 conspiracy theorists, or animal rights activists, or racists—in fact, to any political movement that was able to take control of a university department and structure its curriculum as a new academic "discipline."

Far from setting off alarm bells for the current AAUP leadership, this prospect is apparently acceptable—although one suspects that behind this acceptance is a smug confidence that the prospect is hopelessly remote. Thus, Michael Bérubé, a member of the AAUP's National Council, has already endorsed such an idea and in so many words: "I don't see that there's anything wrong with a situation in which students learn to practice feminist analysis and become committed to feminism.... I don't see that there's anything wrong with a situation in which students learn to practice conservative analysis and become committed to conservatism."[10]

Like many of his colleagues, Bérubé argues that indoctrination is not really indoctrination if students are "free not to do those things without penalty"—that is, if they can object to a professor's

---

[9]Julie Kilmer, "Retain Your Rights As A Liberal Educator," *Academe*, July-August, 2007, Vol. 93, No. 4, pp. 56–57, http://www.jstor.org/stable/40253084

[10]Michael Bérubé, "Freedom to Teach." *InsideHigherEd.com*, September 11, 2007, http://www.insidehighered.com/views/2007/09/11/berube. See response by Bérubé to Professor Ethan's comment, September 12, 2007, in the Comments Section, which starts, "I don't care for Professor Kilmer's take on student "resistance" any more than Tim Burke does, Prof. Ethan."

classroom advocacy without fear of reprisal.[11] But how would students know in advance that there was no penalty for refusing to embrace a professor's political assumptions? How would they deal with Professor Kilmer's threats to "expose" them and break down their "resistance?" How would a Women's Studies major be able to resist the feminist assumptions of the Women's Studies curriculum and still be judged a good student by its ideologically committed and monolithic faculty? Especially if its professors are advocating one and only one point of view in their classrooms, and are doing so by utilizing a mode of discourse which Pamela Caughie has described, and promoted, as "impassioned teaching"?

Caughie's article with that title is subtitled: "Don't be afraid of classroom advocacy; it's not the same as indoctrination." In it she explains: "I can hardly teach feminism as if it were simply an object of analysis and not a vital force in my life."[12] But what student realizing that feminist dogmas are a vital force in the life of their professor would take the risk of challenging them in class, considering that their grade is dependent on the professor's approval? If Caughie cannot teach without proselytizing, she should seek employment with a feminist advocacy organization, not a modern research university, which claims to operate under guidelines instituted to separate it from the religious institutions of the past.

Even the term "impassioned teaching" is a significant departure from previous AAUP statements on academic freedom, which drew a clear line between political advocacy and scholarly discourse. For example, the AAUP's 1940 statement on academic freedom, which is part of the template of most modern research universities, states that scholars and educators should be "restrained" rather than impassioned, and should show appropriate respect for divergent views: "As scholars and educational officers ... [professors] should at all times be accurate, should exercise

---

[11]Ibid.
[12]Caughie, op., cit.

appropriate restraint [and] should show respect for the opinions of others...."

Under these guidelines, professors are obligated to hold back their ardor, to teach students to be skeptical, to assess the evidence, to respect the divergent opinions of others, and to support the pluralism of ideas on which democratic culture is based. It is their obligation to provide students with materials that would allow them to weigh more than one side of controversial issues, to learn to think intelligently and to think for themselves. That is why the AAUP's new position is so shocking a departure, and so disturbing a betrayal of academic freedom. The current AAUP leadership has laid down a challenge that everyone concerned about the future of the academy must answer; for if the attitudes enshrined in the new report become an academic standard, it will spell the end of the modern research university as we know it.

5

The Hazards of Speaking on a College Campus

For a conservative, the hazards of speaking on a college campus are more extensive than you might think. Once the security guards are in place—as they inevitably must be—the risk of getting pied or physically attacked or having one's speech shut down by raucous protesters is actually a lesser problem than others one regularly encounters at these events.

Far more prevalent is the problem presented by the generally hostile environment a conservative normally encounters on any campus. This includes destruction of flyers advertising one's event, failure of the campus newspaper to publicize it, and failure of professors to recommend or even require student attendance as they regularly do for radical speakers. Equally troublesome for a visiting conservative is the pervasive mindset of a community that is constantly brow-beaten by leftist propaganda and is the subject of relentless intimidation by leftist bigots who will readily call anyone who disagrees with them a racist, a sexist or an Islamophobe. This creates a conventional wisdom that institutionalizes falsehoods such as "Israel is occupying stolen Arab lands," "Israel is an apartheid state," or "Jews control American policy." The same oppressive atmosphere makes lunatic positions—such as the claim that the American government or the Israeli Mossad blew

Originally published October 24, 2008, as "The Hazards of Speaking on a College Campus," http://archive.frontpagemag.com/ReadArticle.aspx? ArtId=32780 up the World Trade Center—seem plausible. When I spoke at Central Michigan University last week, for example, my speech was competing with another event, organized by Michigan faculty, which featured a once-deported Muslim professor, now re-admitted on visa, who argued that 9/11 was an Israeli plot.

At the same time, reasonable statements a visiting conservative is likely to make—e.g., that the Arabs are guilty of a sixty-year war of aggression whose goal is to destroy the Jewish state—seem one-sided, hard-to-believe and therefore "extreme." So any statement made by such a visitor can seem ludicrous and absurd to a campus audience which is likely never to have been confronted by conservative arguments—perhaps never to have heard them presented by an adult member of the academic community.

In this fertile ground, the campus press becomes the most hazardous land mine for a visiting conservative. As a result of changes made twenty and thirty years ago, campus newspapers are independently owned while still drawing on institutional support from universities who give them exclusive distribution rights, and allow them to bear the names of traditional campus newspapers, thus associating them with the university community. This arrangement allows university administrators to wash their hands of responsibility for the journalistic contents of the papers while providing them with a captive campus audience.

On my campus visits, I have occasionally had really fine student reporters cover my events, and I have had honest but incompetent student reporters garble my remarks. But I have also had ideologically hostile campus reporters who garbled my remarks with political intent. The resulting caricatures have provided useful fodder for the many leftist websites gunning for me on the Web. The fact that this ammunition comes with the apparent imprimatur of venerable institutions increases its power to produce significant damage. It is this hazard to one's reputation as a public intellectual that presents the most troublesome risk to a conservative who is imprudent enough to accept an invitation to come to a university to speak.

A case in point is the recent visit I made to Brown University during the Islamo-Fascism Awareness Week I had organized. I have a long history with *The Brown Daily Herald* which covered my visit. In 2001, its liberal editors published an ad I wrote called "10 Reasons Why Reparations for Slavery Is a Bad Idea and Racist Too." The editors stood up courageously when they were attacked by the campus left, which stole an entire edition of the paper in retaliation and destroyed the copies. The leftists then threatened to repeat the vandalism every day until the editors paid them money, gave them a free full-page ad and agreed to have their representatives form a committee that would oversee the editorial content of the paper from then on. When Brown's president gently reminded these youthful totalitarians that a free press was a pillar of American democracy, 60 Brown professors signed an open letter condemning the president for her remarks and defending the vandals.

This history is a necessary background to the paper's report on my speech at Brown last week. The assault began with the story's headline: "Horowitz Lambastes Islam in Near Empty MacMillan (Hall)."[1] These seven words consist of one damaging lie and one misleading half-truth. The half-truth is the statement regarding the poor attendance at my speech. As I have already pointed out, there is not a level playing field for conservatives at Brown or any university. Brown has one notable conservative faculty member in its entire liberal arts program, and thus only one professor who might encourage his students to come to this event or spring to my defense if the event were attacked. But this professor did not attend. Nor did I expect him to attend. It would be, to put it bluntly, dangerous from a career point of view for him to be associated with me in any way, a fact we both understand. Consequently we have never met, although I have spoken at Brown twice. Since

---

[1]Ben Schreckinger, "Horowitz Lambastes Islam," *The Brown Daily Herald*, October 23, 2008, http://www.browndailyherald.com/2008/10/23/horowitz-lambastes-islam/

this is a normal situation on university campuses, my usual speaking audience is a couple of hundred students. If I were a leftist with my level of notability, there would be double that number or more.

Although I normally speak to hundreds of students despite these handicaps, there were only about 50 in MacMillan Hall that night. This was the half-truth. The reason for the poor attendance was that the event had been scheduled on the night of the 6th game of the playoffs between the Boston Red Sox (the "home team" for New England) and the Tampa Bay Rays. The schedule for my speech had been in place before Boston unexpectedly beat Anaheim in the semifinals. The omission of this not insignificant fact from both the article and the headline was hardly accidental—particularly since the reporter had a "Go Red Sox" sticker on his laptop cover.

So much for the half-truth. The lie in the article headline is that I attacked Islam as a religion. I did say that Islam had problematic elements, in particular the genocidal saying or *hadith* attributed to its Prophet which says: "The Day of Judgment will only come when Muslims fight Jews and kill them, when the Jews hide behind the rocks and the trees and the rocks and the trees cry out 'Oh Muslim, there is a Jew hiding behind me, come and kill him!'" This *hadith* was a focus of our Islamo-Fascism Awareness Week this fall and therefore an inevitable subject of my talk.

However, throughout my talk and in my discussion of this *hadith* in particular, I went out of my way to say I was not condemning or attacking or "lambasting" Islam as such. "There are both good Muslims and bad Muslims," I said repeatedly, "just as there are good Christians and bad Christians and good Jews and bad Jews." I went further. I pointed out that at a speech I gave at the University of Virginia the night before, there were 30 or so Muslim students in the audience, who so identified themselves when I asked for a show of hands. I asked for the show of hands after a Muslim student questioned whether the Prophet had ever said such a thing. The student said she had never heard of this famous *hadith*. I then asked for the Muslims to indicate whether any of them had heard of this *hadith*. None of them had.

This genocidal *hadith* is not incidental to the Islamo-fascist *jihad*, which was the subject of my talk. It is written into the Hamas charter. It is obviously a motivating force behind the genocidal agendas of Hezbollah, Hamas, the Muslim Brotherhood and the Iranian regime. I used the University of Virginia episode to illustrate the fact that there were Muslims who were innocent of these agendas. I repeated for the Brown students my belief that probably the majority of Muslims were innocent of those agendas, and not part of the Islamic *jihad*.

Yet the *Daily Herald* article ignored these facts to accuse me of attacking Islam and provided "evidence" which will be used on numerous Islamist and leftist websites where I am being maligned as one of the nation's top "Islamophobes."[2] The article began with an introductory joke I told when I said that I hoped the students had checked their pies at the door.[3] This was a reference to a recent incident in which *New York Times* columnist Thomas Friedman had been so assaulted at Brown. The *Herald* article then pointedly described me as "a Jewish writer and activist who holds adamantly pro-Israel views," and opened its account of my remarks with the following sentence: "'You have one of the worst faculties in the United States,' [Horowitz] said, 'These people are communists—they are totalitarians.'" This was the last point in the article where any Brown reader would still be interested in anything I said, or would regard me as anything but a foaming-at-the-mouth ideologue.

The alleged quotation was a travesty, a gross distortion of the statement I actually made. I did not and would never say that the entire faculty of any school north of Havana was made up of communists and totalitarians. (I wouldn't even make such a blanket

---

[2]Ibid., "Smearcasting: How Islamophobes Spread Fear, Bigotry and Misinformation," *Fairness & Accuracy in Reporting*, October 2008, http://www.smearcasting.us/FAIR_Smearcasting_Final.pdf

[3]Ben Schreckinger, "David Horowitz Speaks with *The Herald*," *The Brown Daily Herald*, October 17, 2008, http://www.browndailyherald.com/2008/10/17/david-horowitz-speaks-with-the-herald/

statement about Castro's school, which might have many silent dissenters in its ranks.) But mangling my statement was only part of the problem. The reporter also deliberately left out the context of my remark. As is my custom, if I have been to a school before, I reference a previous visit. In this case, since my relationship to Brown has a greater significance than is the case with most schools, I went over the details of the controversy surrounding my reparations ad—including the trashing of the *Herald* by student leftists, and the support for this attack on a free press by the 60 Brown faculty members who signed the letter defending the destruction of the newspaper. I then said that *these* professors had the mentality of communists and totalitarians. Since there were sixty of them supporting the attack on a free press, I did say that I thought Brown had the worst faculty—the most overtly political and anti-democratic—in the country.

There is little point in reviewing the other distortions in the *Herald* story, which included misquoting the genocidal *hadith* to make it look as though I were exaggerating its implications, and claiming that I said, "the Koran left little room for interpretation when compared to the Hebrew and Christian bibles." In fact, I said that Islam was a fundamentalist religion whose *traditions* historically did not allow for an interpretive distance from its texts—a point made by many scholars of Islam.

My speech at Brown is over, but I am now left to deal with the caricature in *The Brown Daily Herald*, which will resurface in attacks on me by equally unscrupulous leftists on the web. I cannot repair the damage to my relationship with Brown, or my reputation with untold Brown alumni and other friends of the Brown community who will read the *Herald* account. When I ask myself why the *Herald*, which despite its liberal bent has been pretty respectful of my views in the past, would send such a dishonest and hostile reporter to cover my event, the answer I come up with is this: he probably was the only one willing to volunteer for the job while the others went to watch the Red Sox.

6

Indoctrination U. *Revisited*

I had three goals in writing *Indoctrination U.*, a book published in 2008. The first was to describe the campaign I launched in the fall of 2003 for an Academic Bill of Rights; the second was to provide case studies of the classroom abuses the Academic Bill of Rights was designed to correct; and the third was to document the bare-knuckle tactics of the bill's opponents, who have conducted themselves in a manner more appropriate to a barroom brawl than to a discussion of academic issues.

From its inception, the proposal for an Academic Bill of Rights inspired fierce controversy. A recently published book, *The Academic Bill of Rights Debate,* summarizes its impact: "Few academic topics have created such a furor in so short a time.... By November of 2006, it had already generated 74 articles in major newspapers, at least 143 articles in all newspapers nationwide, 54 television and radio broadcasts, 47 newswire articles, 20 articles in *The Chronicle of Higher Education,* 73 articles in *InsideHigherEd.com,* dozens of articles in major magazines, and some 154,000 hits in the obligatory Google search."[1]

The Academic Bill of Rights Debate proposes to present the controversy over the bill in an academic manner, but is just another salvo in the partisan attack. Except for the contribution by me, every article in the volume manifests extreme hostility to

---

Originally published April 10, 2009, as "Indoctrination U. Revisited," http://archive.frontpagemag.com/Printable.aspx?ArtId=34790
[1]Stephen H. Aby, ed., *The Academic Bill of Rights Debate,* Praeger, 2007, p. 1

both the bill of rights and its author. The extreme nature of the attacks is well represented in a contribution by Professor Joan Wallach Scott, who describes the Academic Bill of Rights in these words: "It recalls the kind of government intervention in the academy practiced by totalitarian governments (historical examples are Japan, Nazi Germany, China, Fascist Italy and the Soviet Union) who seek to control thought rather than permit a free marketplace of ideas."[2] In point of fact, the Academic Bill of Rights calls for *no* government intervention in the academy and is an effort to *protect* students from thought control. It was specifically designed to thwart faculty attempts to indoctrinate students by presenting professorial opinion as scientific fact and by failing to assign texts critical of faculty orthodoxy.

The Academic Bill of Rights Debate is so one-sided that even its editor, a professor of education at the University of Akron, joins the assault. Instead of providing a dispassionate summary, Stephen Aby's introduction indulges in tendentious attacks on the bill and its author. Although the Academic Bill of Rights is explicitly designed to articulate long-established principles of academic freedom, the debate is introduced with a statement—"The Academic Bill of Rights is a recent and controversial attack on traditional notions of academic freedom"—which is the very opposite of the truth.[3]

Another recent text with a focus on the academic freedom campaign is John K. Wilson's *Patriotic Correctness*. Wilson is the publisher of the webzine *Illinois Academe* and a member of the American Association of University Professors. According to Wilson, "The Academic Bill of Rights is the story of how David Horowitz, pretending to stand up for 'student rights' and moral conduct by professors, led a crusade to have legislators force every college in the country to adopt the most coercive system of

---

[2]Aby, op. cit., p. 197. See pp. 39–45 of the present text for a discussion of Joan Wallach Scott.
[3]Ibid.

grievance procedures and investigations of liberal professors ever proposed in America."[4]

Actually, the "Academic Bill of Rights" contains *no* provision for a grievance machinery and I have never asked legislators to force colleges to do anything. Nor have I ever asked for legislation that would apply to "every college in the country," since even the non-binding resolutions I have sponsored address only public universities. In crafting my proposals for academic reform, I have been careful to respect the independence of academic institutions. I have consequently regarded the problem of enforcement as better left to university faculty and administrators to devise. I have not proposed a single piece of legislation to "force" colleges to adopt *any* reforms, and have never proposed legislation to create academic grievance procedures. Nor have I ever called for "investigations of liberal professors." In fact, I have opposed making the point of view of professors a subject for remedial measures. I have said publicly (and repeatedly) that "bias" is not an issue; that every individual has a "bias" and professors have a right to express theirs in the classroom so long as they do so in a professional manner, and in accordance with the principles of academic freedom. What faculty may *not* do is to impose their bias on students through coercive grading, or by failing to provide them with critical reading materials, or by presenting their personal prejudices as scientific truth.

The unprincipled campaign against the Academic Bill of Rights has been conducted almost exclusively by two left-wing teacher organizations—the American Association of University Professors and the American Federation of Teachers, along with their allies in the education media and the Democratic Party. The two teacher organizations represent less than 10 percent of all professors at institutions of higher learning, but they are able to present themselves as the voice of faculty because the vast majority of

---

[4]John K. Wilson, *Patriotic Correctness: Academic Freedom and its Enemies*, Paradigm, 2007, p. 70

academics have chosen to maintain a discreet silence on these matters—perhaps to avoid becoming targets of similar unprincipled attacks.

The influence of this aggressive political minority should not be underestimated. In a situation where there is widespread misrepresentation of an argument, it is difficult for disinterested parties to get the facts straight. This problem can be seen in the third book to appear about the controversy since the publication of *Indoctrination U.* A publication of the Brookings Institution, *Closed Minds?: Politics and Ideology in American Universities* is the only one of the three texts that attempts to provide a reasonably balanced view of the issues.[5] Written by three academics, including a former university president, *Closed Minds* is promoted by a blurb that praises its "solid empirical research, historical breadth and sober impartiality."

While a far cry from the preceding polemical caricatures, *Closed Minds'* account of the controversy is nonetheless often untrustworthy: "[Horowitz's] proposals included funding for legislative 'watchdog' staffs, investigating student complaints of classroom bias, and imposing annual reporting requirements on public colleges and universities."[6] This statement is wrong on two of three agendas mentioned. I have never supported a legislative watchdog staff or proposed an annual reporting requirement.[7] Both of these have been elements in "diversity" legislation backed by the American Council of Trustees and Alumni, which I have not supported.

A section of *Closed Minds* focuses on a project that I did put my efforts behind, and was central to my campaign. Unfortunately, *Closed Minds* misrepresents this project as well. In 2005,

---

[5]Bruce L.R. Smith, Jeremy D. Mayer, L. D. Fritschler, *Closed Minds?: Politics and Ideology in American Universities*, Brookings, 2008
[6]*Closed Minds?*, op. cit. p. 96
[7]The legislation which I am associated with can be found here: "National and State Legislation Texts," *Students For Academic Freedom*, http://www.studentsforacademicfreedom.org/documents/?c=Legislation-Texts

the Pennsylvania legislature authorized the creation of an Academic Freedom Committee and a series of hearings about the academic-freedom policies of public universities in the Commonwealth. These hearings led directly to the most significant achievement of the academic freedom campaign to date—the creation at Penn State and Temple University of the first academic freedom regulations for students anywhere in the United States. As a direct result of the hearings, Penn State and Temple also created the first (and only) grievance machineries for handling student complaints related to academic freedom.[8]

These events are discussed in *Indoctrination U.* but the authors of *Closed Minds* overlook this text and the achievements it records.[9] Instead, *Closed Minds'* account of the Pennsylvania hearings follows closely the script of the teacher unions and their legislative allies, which—in order to deny the very existence of the problems it addressed—was designed to conceal what the committee actually accomplished. The inaccuracies in *Closed Minds* regarding this episode begin with a false account of the origins of the Pennsylvania Committee on Academic Freedom and the legislation that authorized it. According to *Closed Minds*, "the precipitating event" that led to the creation of the committee was an erroneous claim originating with me, namely that Michael

---

[8]Confusion on this matter has arisen because most universities do provide grievance machinery for students who feel they have been unfairly graded. Administrators who testified at the Pennsylvania hearings played on this confusion to claim that their students' academic freedom was already protected and did not require an Academic Bill of Rights. But the matter of grading is only one area affecting the academic freedom of students. The templates for the existing grievance procedures do not include statements defining academic freedom and consequently do not provide guidelines to students, or a framework for academic freedom complaints. One of the issues brought before the Pennsylvania hearings was that students were unaware of the academic freedom statements of their universities (which in any case did not apply at the time to students). Students would therefore be unaware of any rights they might have. One of the Committee recommendations was to make students aware of their rights.

[9]*Indoctrination U.*, op. cit., pp. 17–18; 71–80

Moore's *Fahrenheit 9/11* was shown in a Penn State biology class prior to the 2004 presidential election. These allegations are used by the authors to discredit the hearings. Following the teacher union script, the authors of *Closed Minds* conclude that the hearings were a "solution" in search of a problem that didn't exist, and that I was the promoter of a false claim that it did.

As the public record reveals, these allegations are false. The event that inspired the authorizing legislation had nothing to do with a showing of *Fahrenheit 9/11* in a biology class. The accurate account of these origins was reported in a *New York Times* article, "Professor's Politics Draw Lawmakers Into the Fray," which appeared on December 25, 2005, shortly after the hearings began. The article, written by reporter Michael Janofsky, identified the "precipitating event" as a Republican Party picnic attended by Republication state legislator Gibson Armstrong. At the picnic, Armstrong was approached by one of his constituents, an Iraq War veteran named Jennie Mae Brown, who complained that she had been subjected to rants against the military by her physics professor at Penn State.[10] This episode inspired Armstrong to begin drafting legislation that eventually led to the creation of the Academic Freedom Committee, and also to consult me for advice on how to proceed. I have re-told this story twice for publication—in an op-ed in the *Los Angeles Times* a month after the Janofsky article appeared, and also in the text of *Indoctrination U.*, so there is little excuse for the three authors of *Closed Minds* to get this wrong.[11]

Not only is *Closed Minds* in fundamental error in stating that a claim about *Fahrenheit 9/11* provided the inspiration for Armstrong's legislation; it is wrong in claiming that the charge origi-

---

[10]Michael Janofsky, "Professors' Politics Draw Lawmakers Into the Fray," *The New York Times*, December 25, 2005, http://www.nytimes.com/2005/12/25/national/25bias.html?_r=0; David Horowitz, "Ideologues at the Lectern," *Los Angeles Times*, January 24, 2006, http://archive.frontpagemag.com/readArticle.aspx?ARTID=5828
[11]*Indoctrination U.*, op. cit., pp. 17–18

nated with me. In fact the claim was made by a member of Representative Armstrong's legislative staff and I heard it from Representative Armstrong himself. I then casually referred to it on a couple of occasions as one of many other classroom examples of professorial abuses that suggested such hearings were needed. At the same time, I provided scores of other cases of similar faculty behavior—all ignored by the Democratic legislators, the teacher unions and the authors of *Closed Minds*. Months before the Pennsylvania hearings began, a biology professor at Penn State protested to Armstrong's staff that the charge was groundless and asked the legislator to provide a source for the charge. When members of Armstrong's staff could not substantiate the claim, I stopped referring to it and never did so again.

Notwithstanding these facts, the authors of *Closed Minds* make the *Fahrenheit 9/11* episode—wholly incidental to the Pennsylvania reform effort—the focus of *five* pages of their book, almost half the space they allot to their entire discussion of the hearings.[12] They do so not because this claim was important either to the testimony before the Pennsylvania committee or to the reform effort itself, but because it was the centerpiece of the attempts by *opponents* of reform—the teacher unions and the Democratic members of the legislative committee—to discredit the hearings and the person they held responsible for them.

The attacks were led by co-chair of the committee itself—Representative Lawrence Curry—described as a "moderate" by the authors of *Closed Minds*. Curry had voted *against* the legislation that created the committee and that authorized the hearings; he then joined the committee as co-chair to sabotage it. Nor did he confine his opposition to the committee chambers and the hearing room. Curry was the keynote speaker at two protest rallies organized by the teacher unions, at which the hearings—then ongoing—were denounced as a "McCarthy witch-hunt," a patent absurdity

---

[12]*Closed Minds?*, op. cit., pp. 129–133

since the committee focused on policies and institutions, not individuals, and no individual names were used.[13] None of these facts is mentioned by the authors of *Closed Minds*.

I was the last witness to testify at the hearing sessions held at Temple University on January 9 and 10, 2005.[14] In my testimony I introduced the signed statement of a pro-life student at Penn State named Kelly Keelan.[15] Keelan described a Women's Studies class she had taken in which her professor instructed students that women should be "proud" of their abortions and then made them all stand and chant, "abortion, abortion." Keelan testified that she was reduced to tears by this demonstration because she felt there was no place for her viewpoint in the class. Nor did such a demonstration have anything to do with the academic study of women. It was clearly about hectoring the students with the aim of persuading them to adopt the professor's pro-abortion views.

This was precisely the kind of abuse the Academic Bill of Rights was designed to prevent. Curry and his Democratic colleagues showed no interest either in Keelan's complaint or in the testimony of Temple student Logan Fisher, who provided similar examples of faculty abuse. Nor did any of the Democratic legislators (or the authors of *Closed Minds*) show any concern about the thirty students who filed complaints with Representative Arm-

---

[13]*Indoctrination U.*, op. cit., p. 80. The hearings were deliberately designed to be as far from a McCarthy witch-hunt as possible. They specifically excluded the mention of any professors' or students' names, precisely to avoid the abuses for which McCarthy was famous. On the first day of the hearings, committee chairman Tom Stevenson laid down the hearings guidelines: "This Committee's focus will be on the [academic] institutions and their policies, not on professors, not on students." The committee strictly adhered to this directive, which didn't dissuade Curry from making his irresponsible attacks.

[14]Most of this testimony is reprinted in Chapter 4 of *Indoctrination U.*, op. cit., pp. 71–80

[15]This part of my testimony is not included in the present volume, but can be found here: David Horowitz, "What I Told Pennsylvania's Academic Freedom Hearings," *FrontPageMag.com*, January 11, 2006, http://archive.frontpagemag.com/readArticle.aspx?ARTID=5964

strong but asked that their names be withheld out of fear of faculty reprisal. Instead, in order to distract attention from these abuses and to create the impression that they did not exist, the Democrats waited until the very end of the hearing session to focus their attention on the erroneous claim about Michael Moore's *Fahrenheit 9/11*, which had been no part of my testimony or that of any other proponent of academic reform during the ten hours of the Temple proceedings.

When it was his turn to question me, Curry wanted to know if I had retracted the statement about the Moore film. I pointed out that the claim did not originate with me and was no part of my testimony and was, in any case, irrelevant to the proceedings. Moreover, I had not repeated the claim once the Penn State professor challenged it. But Curry was uninterested in anything I had done, and persisted in pressing me to say then and there whether I "retracted" the statement. It was a "when-did-you-stop-beating-your-wife?" question. If I admitted to "retracting" the statement, the presumption would be (and was) that it was material to my case for reform, which it was not. If I refused to answer, and thus failed to concede that it was false, I would be guilty of making up stories to establish the need for reform.

Curry's intent in hectoring me over the issue was to stigmatize me for the benefit of hostile education journalists covering the hearings who would be sure to repeat the charge and make it the centerpiece of their accounts of the hearings—which they did. The headline for the lead story appearing the next day in *InsideHigherEd.com* was "Retractions From Horowitz." In the article that followed, editor Scott Jaschik ignored my testimony and that of other witnesses supporting the need for an Academic Bill of Rights, and instead focused relentlessly on the "retraction."

In their version of what transpired, the authors of *Closed Minds* elevate this political sideshow into a defining moment of the proceedings. This fiction is made to seem plausible in their account because it is prefaced by the false claim that the alleged showing of Michael Moore's film was the "precipitating event" that led to the creation of the academic freedom hearings, which it was not. In drawing their own lessons about the hearings, the authors of *Closed Minds* follow the committee's final report, written by the Democrats, which concluded that academic freedom violations on Penn State campuses were "rare."

The authors of *Closed Minds* fail to mention that the committee's final report was the product of an eleventh-hour coup by the Democratic minority who had opposed the hearings and aligned themselves with the teacher unions from the beginning. The result of this coup was an evisceration of the original report and a rewriting of its recommendations. The coup was the work of a coalition of committee members—five Democrats and two Republicans—who had manifested their displeasure with the committee and its work from the outset. One of them, Representative Dan Surra, described the hearings on the opening day as "a colossal waste of time."[16]

The two Republican members of the coup had defected from the committee majority after the Democrats won control of the Pennsylvania House in an election that occurred while the hearings were in session. This created a new committee majority whose members were on record opposing its mandate. After the completion of the original committee report, the anti-reform coalition was able to block a vote of the Republican caucus, which would have ratified the draft. This vote had been scheduled to take place a week before the final report deadline, but the two Republican defectors failed to show up and deprived the caucus of a quorum.[17] Days later, on the eve of the final deadline, the new coalition took control and gutted the report—eliminating its

---

[16]*Indoctrination U.*, op. cit., p. 79
[17]One of Republicans, Lynn Herman, who represented a district containing Penn State University, reported that he had a doctor's appointment as an excuse for missing the caucus. This fiction was designed to prevent the Republican majority from realizing that a coup was in progress.

summary of the evidence. The new majority then rewrote the report's conclusions.[18]

The original draft submitted to the Republican caucus contained a lengthy "Summary of Testimony," which reviewed the ten months of hearings and reported their findings.[19] On the basis of the summarized evidence, the draft concluded that there were *no* academic freedom protections for Pennsylvania students in place at Pennsylvania's public universities. It found that the existing academic-freedom provisions were contained exclusively in employee handbooks and teacher-union contracts and did not apply to students. The original draft therefore recommended that *"student-specific* academic freedom rights" be adopted by these universities: "Public institutions of higher learning within the Commonwealth should review existing academic freedom policies and procedures to ensure that a student-specific academic freedom policy, which ensures student rights and a detailed grievance procedure, are readily available."[20]

This draft failed to be ratified because when the two Republicans did not show up. The Democrats staged their coup days later, on the evening before the final deadline. The coup leaders did not bother to write a new report. So in the final document there was no summary of the proceedings that had gone on for nearly a year; only the politically motivated conclusions of the Democrats who had opposed the hearings from the start. Demoralized by their electoral defeat and

---

[18]I was the author of the original draft report which was then revised by the majority counsel.

[19]The text of the original report, before it was gutted and its recommendations rewritten by the Democrats and Republican legislator Lynn Herman, can be found here: David Horowitz, "Pennsylvania's Academic Freedom Reforms," *Students For Academic Freedom*, December 1, 2006, http://www.studentsforacademicfreedom.org/news/2324/pennsylvanias-academic-freedom-reforms; The official report—gutted and revised by the Democrats—can be found here: "Final Report of the Select Committee on Academic Freedom in Higher Education," *Students For Academic Freedom*, November 4, 2008, http://www.studentsforacademicfreedom.org/news/2656/final-report-of-the-select-committee-on-academic-freedom-in-higher-education

[20]Ibid.

facing a new majority on their committee, the remaining Republicans agreed to sign on to the revised and gutted report, which expressed the position the Democrats had maintained throughout the hearings—that there was no problem and the hearings were essentially a waste of time. It was a depressing display of government in action.

In producing the committee's final report, the aim of the new majority was to eliminate the key recommendation of the draft— that universities adopt *"student-specific* academic freedom policies." This would have been to admit a problem existed and to have taken a step to address it. In a new brief section called "Findings," the authors wrote: "Concerns regarding the effectiveness of academic freedom policies were raised during the four public hearings. However, at institutions with academic freedom policies in place, it appears the policies are effective at resolving disputes."[21] But there were no such policies in place at Pennsylvania's public institutions of higher learning, so the statement was meaningless and a dishonest defense of the *status quo.*

The "Findings" also reported: "The Committee received testimony from each sector of public higher education and determined that academic freedom violations are rare."[22] This was the testimony of university officials and teacher union representatives but not of the students, whose testimony was ignored. The existing academic-freedom regulations did not apply to students, as the gutted sections of the report made clear. Nor was there any grievance machinery in place at any Pennsylvania university for handling *student* academic- freedom complaints.[23] At Penn State, to

---

[21]Ibid.

[22]Ibid.

[23]The original draft, cited in footnote 19, documents the absence of student-specific academic freedom policies at all of Pennsylvania's public universities at the time of the hearings. For the section of the original draft that the Democrats eliminated, see the "Summary of Testimony" here: David Horowitz, "Pennsylvania's Academic Freedom Reforms," *Students For Academic Freedom,* December 1, 2006, http://www.studentsforaca demicfreedom.org/news/2324/pennsylvanias-academic-freedom-reforms

take one example, there was indeed an existing academic freedom policy—HR 64. But this policy could only be found in the university's *Employee Handbook* and obviously did not apply to students. Its grievance procedure specifically stated that it was only available to faculty members.

This defect in the Penn State regulations was recognized and then remedied in May 2005 by the passage of Faculty Senate Resolution 20.00. This resolution applied HR 64 to students and created a grievance machinery for them. The Faculty Senate Resolution was a direct response to the hearings and showed that creating "student-specific" rights was both necessary and also a non-partisan issue. The Penn State measure was followed by an action of the Temple University trustees to adopt a similar policy.[24] But this left approximately fifteen public universities in Pennsylvania without academic-freedom protections for their students. There were also problems with the new grievance machinery that would become immediately apparent.

In the fall of 2008, a Penn State student named Abigail Beardsley attempted to take advantage of the newly created grievance machinery. Beardsley had enrolled in a French class described in the college catalogue as a course in the French language—French vocabulary and syntax. During one of the classroom sessions, the professor showed a portion of Michael Moore's film *Sicko.* Like Moore's other "documentaries," *Sicko* is a political propaganda film, making a case for Cuban-style socialized medicine.

Abigail Beardsley regarded the showing as a violation of Penn State's new student academic-freedom policy. Here is an excerpt from her complaint: "According to the syllabus for French 112, the course objective is to develop students' skills in reading, writing and speaking the French language. The catalogue description defines the course goal as not only that the student should 'acquire new knowledge of the French language, but ... also build upon

---

[24]*Indoctrination U.*, op. cit., pp. 122–123

what you have already learned as a student of French. The focus of the course is on real-life language use, the integrations of language and culture, and the development of the four skills: listening, speaking, reading, and writing.'

"The clarity of these objectives is admirable. But during the spring semester of 2008, Nate Sebold, the instructor for Section 1 of French 112 took valuable class time to show the controversial Michael Moore propaganda film *Sicko*, which is an attack on the free market health care system in the United States and an endorsement of socialized medicine in England, Canada, France and Communist Cuba. The section of Moore's film praising France's socialized health care system was shown to the class on March 19th. No critical evaluations of the film or contrary views of socialized medicine were provided by the instructor, which would have allowed students to think for themselves on these controversial matters. Penn State Policy HR 64 explicitly requires instructors to 'provide [students] access to those materials which they need if they are to think intelligently.' It further instructs professors not to introduce controversial materials that are irrelevant to the class subject and outside their area of professional expertise. The showing of *Sicko* in French 112 was a clear violation of both these principles and of Policy HR 64 and is the gravamen of my complaint."[25]

When Abigail Beardsley filed her complaint with the chairman of the French Department, as the regulation required, the chairman rejected the appeal and supported the instructor's decision to show Moore's propaganda film in class. Without the prospect of support from other members of the Penn State faculty, Beardsley became discouraged and decided not to pursue her case. Another Penn State student, A. J. Fluehr, had filed a previous complaint under the new regulations, which was successful. But Fluehr was discouraged by the process, which dragged over 11 months and pitted him against

---

[25]A copy of the complaint was sent to me by Abigail Beardsley.

the department chair and faculty members, who clearly regarded his concerns as frivolous and himself as a nuisance. Fluehr was only able to obtain a positive resolution to his complaint after he submitted it to the college dean. The dean rejected a second Fluehr complaint and a third fell by the wayside.[26]

There are no visible conservatives on the faculty at Penn State and no significant support among liberal faculty for students such as Abigail Beardsley and A. J. Fluehr. The difficulty of filing student complaints in a hostile environment, with uncertain repercussions from faculty members, came up at the Pennsylvania committee hearings but could not be seriously addressed in the partisan atmosphere. For all intents and purposes, efforts to institute what ought to be a simple policy to protect students continues to be stymied.

Widespread classroom showings of Moore's films *Bowling for Columbine, Fahrenheit 9/11* and *Sicko*—without critical commentary—provide a useful index of the decline of intellectual standards documented in *Indoctrination U.* These showings are naked attempts to persuade students of the correctness of the instructors' personal views and could not occur without the similarly widespread acceptance of political agitation as an acceptable form of classroom instruction. They provide a benchmark of the success achieved by the entrenched opponents of academic freedom. As *Indoctrination U.* documents, and as books such as *Closed Minds* demonstrate, the denial that there is even a problem remains the prevailing attitude in the university community. In the bitterly contested atmosphere created by the opponents of reform, little progress is likely to be made, and the decline of academic standards will continue, which is unfortunate for liberal and conservative students alike.

---

[26]I advised A. J. Fluehr throughout the process. A record of his complaints is available at: "English 202A Academic Freedom Complaint Department Communications," http://www.discoverthenetworks.org/Articles/acadfreepsubuehler.html. An account of his experience is contained in Horowitz, *Reforming Our Universities: The Story of the Campaign for an Academic Bill of Rights*, pp. 185, 189, 192–193, 217, 272, 281

7

Campus Leftists Don't Believe in Free Speech

I arrived in Austin, Texas one evening recently to give a speech about academic freedom at the university there. Entering the hall where I was to offer my views, I was greeted—if that's the word—by a raucous protest organized by a professor and self-styled Bolshevik named Dana Cloud. Forty protesters hoisted placards high in the air and robotically chanted "Down With Horowitz," "Racist Go Home," and "No More Witch-hunts." This was familiar territory for me; when I spoke at the University of Texas two years ago, Ms. Cloud and her disciples had to be removed by the police in order for the talk to proceed.

This time, a spokesperson for the administration was present to threaten the disrupters with arrest if they continued on this course. The threat was administered very carefully, with three formal warnings before any action could be taken. This quieted the crowd enough that I could begin my talk, which proceeded without further serious incident.

Even so, there were occasional heckles and demonstrative cheers from the group when I mentioned the name of Sami Al-Arian, whose organization, Palestine Islamic Jihad, is responsible for the deaths of more than 100 innocent victims in the Middle East; when I referred to Black Panther Huey Newton, who was

---

Originally published April 18, 2009, as "Campus Leftists Don't Believe in Free Speech," http://www.wsj.com/news/articles/SB124000847769030489

convicted of killing an Oakland police officer in 1967 and was the
leader of a murderous gang; and when I uttered the word "communist, " which I did to remind the audience that communists killed
120 million people in the last century while trying to implement
Marx's ideas.

Among the organizations participating in these outbursts were
the International Socialist Organization, whose stated goal is the
establishment of a "dictatorship of the proletariat" in the United
States; Iranians for Peace and Justice, who are supporters of
Hezbollah and Hamas; and Campus Progress, the unofficial college arm of the Democratic Party.

One of the local members of the Democratic organization,
Campus Progress, had written a column in the campus newspaper
attacking me in advance of my talk, and defending the terrorist
Sami Al-Arian as a victim of political persecution. The conservative students who invited me told me that organizations such as
the Muslim Students Association routinely join with College
Democrats in protests against the state of Israel.

At the end of the evening, Professor Cloud stepped up to the
microphone to ask a question, which was actually a little speech.
Even though the protocol for such occasions restricts audience
participants from making their own speeches, I did her the courtesy she tried to deny me by letting her talk. She presented herself
as a devoted teacher and mother who was obviously harmless.
Then she accused me of being a McCarthyite menace. Disregarding the facts I had laid out in my talk—that I have publicly
defended the right of University of Colorado's radical professor
Ward Churchill to hold reprehensible views and not be fired for
them, and that I supported Erwin Chereminsky, the leftist dean of
the law school at UC Irvine, when his appointment was withdrawn for political reasons—she accused me of whipping up a
"witch-hunting hysteria" that made her and her faculty comrades
feel threatened.

When Dr. Cloud finished, I pointed out that organizing mobs to
scream   epithets   at   invited   speakers   fit   the   category   of

"McCarthyite" a lot more snugly than my support for a pluralism of views in university classrooms. I gestured toward the armed officers in the room—the university had assigned six or seven to keep the peace—and introduced my own bodyguard, who regularly accompanies me and other conservative speakers when they visit universities. I don't know of a single leftist speaker among the thousands who visit campuses every term who has been obstructed or attacked by conservative student groups, which are too decent and too tolerant to do that. The entire evening in Texas reminded me of the late Orianna Fallaci's observation that what we are facing in the post-9/11 world is not a "clash of civilizations" but a clash of civilization versus barbarism.

8

How Bad Is the Indoctrination
in Our Colleges?

I had occasion to see for myself the abysmal state of liberal arts education when I recently visited the University of Massachusetts, Amherst. While there I audited an hour-and-a-half lecture about the Warren Court's landmark decisions on civil liberties by a well-known and highly respected political scientist named Sheldon Goldman, a nationally recognized expert in the field.

There are no open conservatives on the faculty of the University of Massachusetts and none that the conservative students who were hosting me could identify. My student hosts were political science majors and the absence of conservative professors was a real problem for them, given the extreme and abusive nature of the UMass faculty. According to the students, one professor gave an exam that consisted of a speech by President Reagan and a single question: "Explain why Reagan is wrong." Another professor, a militant classroom leftist, required a paper on the Vietnam War. To avoid the political minefield which confronted him, the student who told me the story wrote a paper comparing military strategies for the war. The professor rejected the paper with the comment: "We shouldn't have been there in the first place."

When I entered Goldman's classroom I saw that half of my student hosts were taking his course—a relief, they told me later,

Originally published March 2, 2010, as "How Bad Is the Indoctrination in our Colleges?" http://www.frontpagemag.com/2010/david-horowitz/indoctrination-in-american-colleges/

from the harassment they experienced in other political science courses. Goldman was regarded by these conservative students as the "best" and "fairest" professor on the UMass faculty, someone who every now and then would vent a "liberal" sentiment or prejudice but whose lectures were relatively free from bias and whose classroom behavior was respectful towards them. Political Science departments in my experience are generally more academic and less politicized than other departments such as Anthropology, Sociology and the various interdisciplinary fields ("Peace Studies," "Cultural Studies") that tenured radicals have invented to establish their ideological claims. This was not the case at UMass Amherst.

Still, I was not prepared for what I encountered in Professor Goldman's classroom. I had previously suggested in my writings and lectures on universities that professors who use their classrooms as platforms for their political agendas represent a small but significant minority, which I have estimated to be about ten percent of a given faculty. After auditing Professor Goldman's course I will have to revise that judgment.

Let me begin by stating what I believe indoctrination to be and what it is not. Indoctrination is presenting opinion to students as though it were scientific fact—as though no rational, decent, and moral person could have any other view. It is the equivalent of presenting students with ready-made conclusions which they cannot realistically feel free to challenge.

Professor Goldman is not a radical and his presentation was of a much subtler order, but its import was no less disturbing. If Professor Goldman had presented the rulings of the Warren Court along with the conservative objections to those rulings and then said that personally—and based on his own years of study—he was of the opinion that the Warren rulings were wise or correct, I would have no problem with his presentation, particularly since the students were confident that he was fair-minded in his treatment of them. But Professor Goldman did not do this. Instead he presented a series of landmark Warren Court decisions as a salesman for the liberals, and without giving the conservatives' concerns a proper day in his court. To put it more bluntly, Professor Goldman suppressed or distorted the conservative arguments against the Warren Court rulings so that no one who was not already familiar with them would think that any modern person, or any rational or moral person for that matter, could fail to approve what the Warren Court did.

In discussing the Warren Court's prayer in the schools decision, for example, he made it seem as though the issue had been whether saying a prayer in school was a step in establishing religion and thus violating the First Amendment, or whether it was too inconsequential to trigger concern. But this was not the gravamen of the conservative argument. The conservative position was that the establishment clause refers to the establishment of a particular religion—not to a non-sectarian acknowledgment that a deity exists. After all, the Founders were descended from refugees who had fled to American as Christians persecuted by the Anglican Church, which as the established Church of England could therefore use government powers against rival denominations. Mentioning a non-denominational "God" in the classroom may or may not qualify as the kind of establishment the Founders had in mind; but obviously reasonable, moral, and modern people can disagree on this matter, something no student in Goldman's class would have understood from his lecture.

Goldman then turned to another important case, Griswold v. Connecticut, which as he pointed out provided the constitutional basis for Roe v. Wade. This, as he did not point out, was a decision that can be said to have transformed the politics of this country by virtually creating a "religious right" opposition, turning Supreme Court nominations into political battles and causing a polarization of the two major parties. The Griswold case involved a Connecticut law against contraceptives; it was resolved when the Warren majority invented a "right to privacy" which Goldman conceded cannot be found in the actual Constitution but then went on to argue in effect that it should have been there and to imply that we can be thankful it was put there by Justice Douglas under the mysterious doctrine of "penumbras." Goldman made the case for the ruling easy by making fun of the Connecticut law, acting out an imaginary knock at the door by the contraceptive police coming to look into citizens' bedrooms.

The effect was to insinuate that this was a stupid and dangerous law, and if we have to invent rights that aren't in the Constitution to get rid of it, well and good. Those rights should have been there and we as enlightened progressives are really obligated to supply them by whatever means necessary. At no point did Goldman point out to students that actually there was another way to get rid of a stupid and dangerous law, which was to repeal it through the legislative process. This would avoid having nine unelected judges, appointed for life, rewriting the Constitution and substituting themselves for the electorate. The closest Professor Goldman came to recognizing this conservative argument was a passing reference to Justice Stewart's dissent, in which he said that the majority decision was like having a constitutional convention every day.

At no point did Professor Goldman explain to students that the conservative opposition to the Warren Court decision revolved around this absolutely critical point; or, as noted liberal law professor Mark Tushnet acknowledges, "To conservatives, the Warren Court converted constitutional law into ordinary politics...." By circumventing (really subverting) legislatures and the democratic process instead of merely applying the Constitution as written, the Warren Court liberals made the selection of a Supreme Court justice a momentous political act—which is why Supreme Court nominations have since become such open political conflicts, while the Constitution as written by the Founders has been gravely weakened. That is the conservative argument absent from Professor Goldman's lecture.

All this would have been less problematic if the sole text Professor Goldman required his students to read for the course had not been a partisan liberal view of the Court written by Jeffrey Toobin.

It is not as though there aren't equally accessible conservative books about this very history. Robert Bork, a distinguished a law professor and jurist (whose name was mentioned derisively by Goldman) has written one himself, *The Tempting of America*. How difficult would it have been to assign students to read Bork's book alongside Toobin's, so that students could familiarize themselves with the arguments that Goldman left out of his presentation?

If Professor Goldman had exhibited the professional discipline to present the contending arguments over these controversial matters—to give his opinion and then let his students draw their own conclusions—I would have no problem with his lecture. But he didn't, and therefore I do. Implicit in his partisan presentation was the attitude that conservatives are stupid, immoral and reactionary. That would be a problem for the students in his class who did not subscribe to his political opinions, and were made to feel like aliens in his classroom, however fair his demeanor towards them. The larger problem is this: what happens to a democracy when its educational institutions are converted into training and recruitment programs for one political faction and its partisan worldview?

9

The Free Speech Movement
and Its Tragic Result

In 1964, a series of historic protests took place at the University of California Berkeley, with far-reaching consequences largely unappreciated at the time. The events were triggered when leftwing students defied a university rule, launching a mob protest that became the first major occupation of a university campus in American history. Thousands of students were eventually involved and eight hundred were arrested. The arrests led to further demonstrations, and eventually to the capitulation of the university's liberal administrators to the activists' demands.

The organizers called themselves, "The Free Speech Movement" and have been memorialized as such by an accommodating progressive culture, not least by the university itself. Today, the school's central plaza features a "Free Speech Monument" approved by university officials who also created a Free Speech Movement Digital Archive in the school library and a Free Speech Movement Café in the school complex. Reunions of the protesters have been held every ten years at which the leftwing activists gather to celebrate themselves for getting away with criminal behavior and for achieving, in their own eyes and the eyes of their academic admirers, a landmark victory for "civil liberties."

In fact, the Free Speech Movement was not about civil liberties. Nor was it about free speech; nor could it have been, since

Libertas magazine, Winter 2016 http://www.yaf.org

that is a right already guaranteed by the First Amendment and obviously honored by the liberal administrators at UC Berkeley and at all other public universities at the time. What the "Free Speech Movement" was about was the right to conduct specifically political activities on the university campus, including the recruitment of students to political causes.

Before the surrender to the Berkeley mob, such activities had been considered inappropriate for institutions dedicated to the "disinterested pursuit of knowledge." The Berkeley protest was about shattering this "ivory tower" concept of the university—the idea that institutions of higher learning should be places for the dispassionate, therefore non-partisan and non-political, examination of ideas.

The victory of the student mob was momentous. It led to a series of institutional developments that transformed American universities into partisan arenas hostile to America, to white people, to Christians, to males, and to views at odds with the agendas of the left.

These events proved to be the opening of a dark chapter not only for the academic world but for the nation at large. The politicization of academic institutions soon spread to schools throughout the country, affecting the training not only of English professors, historians and sociologists but also jurists, journalists, and the nation's future leaders. For the next five decades, a steady and poisonous strain of leftist ideologies poured into America's political and cultural mainstreams, with consequences that are now all too visible.

Barely five years after the Berkeley protest, black students carried loaded shotguns into the administration building at Cornell, demanding the creation of a Black Studies department whose curriculum they would design and whose faculty they would appoint. As at Berkeley, a liberal administration capitulated to the demands, which signaled the beginning of the end of a liberal arts curriculum governed by professional standards of discourse and scientific methods of inquiry.

Black Studies was not a scholarly profession but an ideological movement dedicated to the proposition that white people are oppressors and blacks mere victims—that America is a "white supremacist" nation. Cornell made clear that a university field could now be created through physical intimidation. This marked the beginning of the left's colonization of the academy and the transformation of liberal arts faculties into the debased indoctrination facilities we see today.

Black Studies led to other new fields like Chicano Studies and Gender Studies—a category familiarly referred to as Oppression Studies. These "interdisciplinary" fields liberated the tenured activists from standards of scholarship that had been established over the course of a hundred years, and had made American universities the wonders of the educational world.

To be part of these politicized departments, faculty and students had to be "politically correct"—that is, believers in and enforcers of the leftwing ideas and narratives that formed the new curriculum—a curriculum no longer dedicated to an inquiry into the truth but one that challenged so-called "oppressors" and advanced the cause of social justice.

These developments signaled the end of the classical liberal idea that students in a democracy should be taught how to think and not told what to think; that a college curriculum should inform students, not indoctrinate them; that scholarly inquiry should be dispassionate and non-partisan. In sum, the decades that followed the Berkeley and Cornell events saw the return of liberal arts schools to their 19th-century origins as doctrinal institutions designed to train students for the priesthood. In the new incarnation, it was the priesthood of leftwing ideologies and social myths the curriculum was designed to serve.

Because the new academic fields were fiefdoms of the intolerant left, insisting that all inquiry was and should be political, it was inevitable that conservatives, libertarians and other dissenters would become a vanishing faculty breed. Half a century after the Berkeley "Free Speech Movement," more than 90 percent of most liberal arts faculties are made up of political leftists. Most college students pass through four years of schooling without ever encountering a conservative adult.

It was equally inevitable that the "free speech" leftists would soon insist on restrictive "speech codes"—the precursors of "triggers" and "microaggressions" whose purpose has been to suppress dissenting ideas by declaring them "racist," "sexist" or simply indecent. Today, liberal arts colleges are the most regressive and least free institutions in America.

The so-called Free Speech Movement, which introduced political crusading into the halls of learning, has led to the destruction of a great institution, and a flourishing of ideological bigotry, viewpoint repression and intellectual fraud. The Universities of Missouri, Yale, Dartmouth and many other schools have recently witnessed eruptions by student mobs demanding the suppression of ideas that disturb them, and compensation for their alleged injuries in the form of politically mandated hiring of faculty and millions of ransom dollars, which they can use to make future mob protests even more compelling. Today, student leftists are demanding that universities provide them with a place "safe" from dangerous ideas—a bizarre but predictable result of the Free Speech Movement at Berkeley half a century before.

A Plan for
University Reform

The institutional mission and character of a university is defined by a series of contracts between members of the communities that support it and those who make use of it. The university makes representations to prospective students, to donors, and to state agencies that fund it regarding the nature of its purposes, the standards it sets for itself and its employees, and the quality of the products and services it provides.

Contracts with faculty who create its institutional product underwrite the university's promises to students, parents and the taxpaying public. Faculty receive extraordinary privileges—the prospect of lifetime tenure, a 9-to-12-hour work week, four months' paid vacation, generous medical and pension plans, wide latitude and little supervision over what they actually do in the workplace. Faculty are afforded these privileges because they are understood to be professionals who have devoted years of intensive study to developing expertise in an academic discipline and have conducted extensive research to acquire a professional credential. It is their specialized expertise which induces both students and the taxpaying public to pay extraordinary premiums for their services. In their teaching, faculty are understood to be following professional procedures in the classroom and to be transmitting to students the professional attitudes towards knowledge

Written in 2010, before the AAUP eviscerated Penn State's academic freedom policy.

in which they have become experts; specifically, respect for scientific methods of inquiry and discourse.

What if faculty fail to meet these standards or to follow professional guidelines in shaping their classroom curricula? What if they use their classes to indoctrinate students instead of educating them? What if they teach subjects that are outside their professional expertise and present opinions as though they were scientific facts? At present, under the doctrine of "shared governance," there is no university authority to hold them to account.

Fiduciary responsibility for maintaining university standards and the integrity of its contracts is vested in the university's board of trustees. Yet, at present, trustees are largely kept in the dark as to what actually goes on in university classrooms because of "shared governance," a wall of separation which has been erected over the years at the insistence of faculty.

Under the doctrine of shared governance, responsibilities for curricular matters are presumed to be the exclusive province of faculty, while trustee or administrative concern about these matters is regarded as unwelcome "interference." Unless there is a public scandal, such as transpired during the Ward Churchill affair at the University of Colorado, the same doctrine of shared governance also prevents university administrators from inquiring into curricular matters and holding faculty accountable to existing academic standards.

Thus there is presently no university authority to ensure that faculty will adhere to the professional standards in designing curricula and instructing students on which the contracts of the university with the taxpaying public and tuition-paying parents are based.

Under the present system, administrators and trustees are kept in virtual ignorance about the areas most vital to university performance—the academic curriculum and classroom instruction—and there are no lines of accountability regarding these matters over which trustees and administrators have any power of review. This makes it impossible for the governing boards of universities to oversee the contracts with the consumers of the university's product or with its financial supporters, in order to ensure that promises which underlie these contracts are met.

This break in the system of accountability can lead to tremendously damaging and costly consequences for universities. The University of Colorado, to take only the most obvious case, has lost tens of millions of dollars in student enrollments, and legal and other costs, as a result of the scandal involving Ward Churchill, which is still unresolved. At the time of the scandal, Churchill was a full professor and the chairman of the Ethnic Studies Department, in charge of hiring new faculty. He was earning $120,000 per year for three hours' classroom teaching per week.

After Churchill's article comparing the victims of 9/11 to "little Eichmanns" had become a national scandal, causing the governor of Colorado to demand that he be fired, the university convened a panel of faculty peers which found that Churchill was unqualified to have been hired as a professor in the first place, and that his academic career was marked by fraud, plagiarism, and unscholarly conduct. The panel concluded unanimously that Churchill had falsified and fabricated historical events, plagiarized research material from other scholars, and failed to attribute sources properly.[1]

The panel also identified a species of consumer fraud in that the "scholarly" books and articles he wrote (and presumably many of the classes he taught) under the university's imprimatur were not based on any professional expertise. "Although many of his writings, including nearly all those discussed in this report, address historical and/or legal issues, he does not have formal training at the graduate level in those fields. Professors writing on

---

[1] "Report of the Investigative Committee of the Standing Committee on Research Misconduct at the University of Colorado at Boulder Concerning Allegations of Academic Misconduct against Professor Ward Churchill," May 9, 2006 http://www.colorado.edu/news/reports/churchill/churchillreport051606.html

the topics he addresses would typically have a Ph.D. in history or a law degree; Professor Churchill's graduate degree is an M.A. in Communications Theory," the panel stated.[2]

The university eventually fired Churchill, who sued to be reinstated. A jury trial found that the university had fired him because of the article and the public scandal that ensued. In other words, if there had been no scandal, Churchill would still be chairman of the Ethnic Studies department. Every one of the department's faculty members, by the way, supported Churchill and his teachings. Churchill would thus still be in charge of new hires to the department. The university conducted no inquiry into the professional standards of the department members who had hired him, promoted him to tenure and elected him chairman.

If it had not been for the public scandal attending his article on the events of 9/11, Churchill's career as a tenured professor, showered with honors in his field, would have continued undisturbed. This was the conclusion of the jury trial and also of the panel of academic peers the university convened to review his case: "The Committee notes that this investigation was only commenced *after*, and perhaps in response to, the public attack on Professor Churchill for his controversial publications. Some of the allegations sent to the Committee related to events that apparently had been well known by scholars in the field, although perhaps not by responsible University personnel, for years before the University took any action whatsoever concerning them, and it did so only after the controversy over Professor Churchill's essays became national news."[3]

In other words, the Churchill affair indicated a corruption of academic standards that was not confined to the malfeasance of a single individual. It was system-wide—a direct result of the doctrine of shared governance and Colorado's failure to establish a

---

[2]Ibid., p. 21
[3]Ibid., p. 4

university authority to oversee the contracts it made with its professors.

The same problems attending Ward Churchill's career at the University of Colorado can be found in the curricula of other public universities, including Temple.

The Proposal: An Office of Academic Standards and Academic Freedom

To protect the university from similar scandals, to ensure that its contracts are upheld and its standards maintained, Temple trustees should establish an Office of Academic Standards and Academic Freedom which would inquire into the university curriculum and ensure that proper procedures are followed in curricular matters. The office should be part of the university's central administration and should include review committees made up of administrators, faculty, and students.

To make such an office effective, a grievance machinery that would allow students to file complaints about classroom misconduct without fear of faculty reprisal should also be created. Without a system of student rights and a grievance machinery to defend them, it will be impossible to know what goes on in the classroom. To assure students who file grievances that they will be protected from faculty retributions, a Student Advocate position should be created and filled by a university administrator. The faculty on review committees should be drawn from departments and schools in the university that are not part of the complaint; e.g., if the complaint is about a faculty member in the liberal arts college, the faculty committee member(s) should be drawn from schools and departments outside the liberal arts college.

The nature of the curricular standards and procedures on which the modern research university is based, and which the Office of Academic Standards and Academic Freedom would oversee, has been generally accepted for nearly 100 years. The universally accepted classic statement of these standards is the 1915

Declaration on the Principles of Academic Freedom and Tenure
published by the American Association of University Professors:

"Since there are no rights without corresponding duties, the considerations heretofore set down with respect to the freedom of the academic teacher entail certain correlative obligations. The claim to freedom of teaching is made in the interest of integrity and of the progress of scientific inquiry; it is, therefore, only those who carry on their work in the temper of the scientific inquirer who may justly assert this claim. The liberty of the scholar within the university to set forth his conclusions, be they what they may, is conditioned by their being conclusions gained by a scholar's method and held in a scholar's spirit; that is to say, they must be the fruits of competent and patient and sincere inquiry, and they should be set forth with dignity, courtesy, and temperateness of language. The university teacher, in giving instructions upon controversial matters, while he is under no obligation to hide his own opinion under a mountain of equivocal verbiage, should, if he is fit in dealing with such subjects, set forth justly, without suppression or innuendo, the divergent opinions of other investigators; he should cause his students to become familiar with the best published expressions of the great historic types of doctrine upon the questions at issue; and he should, above all, remember that his business is not to provide his students with ready-made conclusions, but to train them to think for themselves, and to provide them access to those materials which they need if they are to think intelligently."

This statement sets forth the terms of the contract with faculty—that its members will be scholarly and judicious, that they will follow scientific method and be professional in the classroom, that they will not indoctrinate students but teach them to think for themselves, that therefore they will provide them with materials reflecting contending perspectives on controversial questions, will present the major arguments in a fair and judicious manner, and will encourage students to draw their own conclusions. By holding faculty to these professional standards, and by reviewing the curriculum to see that it follows these guidelines, the proposed Office of Academic Standards and Academic Freedom would repair the present break in the system of accountability and would protect the university against the degradation of its product and the risk of damaging scandals.

(Penn State University already incorporates the above statement in its academic-freedom provision as regulation HR 64; Temple should adopt this language in its own academic freedom statement.)

Academic Freedom would be a concern of the proposed Office because of the integral relationship between academic freedom and the professional obligations of faculty. Academic freedom is not "free speech." If it were, professors of geography could teach that the earth is flat. If mere opinion qualified someone to be a professor, professors could be hired for much lower salaries than is presently the case. Opinion is freely available on talk radio and local street corners. Academic freedom is—and can only be—*freedom within a professional discipline.*

Robert Post, a liberal law professor at Yale, is one of the nation's leading experts on academic freedom issues and legal counsel to the American Association of University Professors. In a seminal article on "The Structure of Academic Freedom," Professor Post observed: "[A] key premise of the '1915 Declaration' is that faculty should be regarded as professional experts in the production of knowledge."[4] Professor Post explains this premise: "The mission of the university defended by the 'Declaration' depends on a particular theory of knowledge. The 'Declaration' presupposes not only that knowledge exists and can be articulated by scholars, but also that it is advanced through the free application of highly disciplined forms of inquiry, which correspond roughly to what [philosopher] Charles Pierce once called 'the method of science' as opposed to the 'method of authority.'"

---

[4]Doumani (ed.), *Academic Freedom After September 11*, Zone Books, 2006

Post continues: "The 'Declaration' claims that universities can advance the sum of human knowledge only if they employ persons who are experts in scholarly methods, and only if universities liberate these experts to pursue freely the inquiries dictated by their disciplinary training."[5] In other words: submission to a regime of prior (professional) restraint is the very *basis* of the academic-freedom privileges to which professors are entitled.

It is because their mission depends on the hiring of professionals that universities require an academic credential—the Ph.D.—which is a certification that hired faculty are professionals trained and disciplined in their fields, and that they have conducted extensive research which qualifies them as "experts" in their particular disciplines.[6] The implication (in the words of the 1915 Declaration) is this: "[The] liberty of the scholar within the university to set forth his conclusions, be they what they may, is conditioned by their being conclusions gained by a scholar's method and held in a scholar's spirit; that is to say, they must be the fruits of competent and patient and sincere inquiry...."[7] Or, as Post summarizes it: "The 'Declaration' thus conceives of freedom not as an individual right to be free from constraints but instead as the freedom to pursue the 'scholar's profession' according to the standards of that profession."[8]

In other words, academic freedom implies academic standards—restraint by disciplined, professional standards of inquiry and expression. The attempt to ignore or bypass this restraint threatens the integrity of the academic mission. It also threatens the university as an institution. When universities allow their faculties to enter the political fray by becoming opinionated partisans in the academic classroom, they expose themselves and their

---

[5]Ibid., p. 69
[6]Exceptions are (and can be) made to the Ph.D. requirement. But these are normally made in light of some comparable academic achievement.
[7]Ibid.
[8]Ibid. The term "scholar's profession" is in the 1915 Declaration.

institutions to the laws of the political arena and to its judgments and penalties as well.

Members of the public who find themselves on the other side of university faculties in political disputes will take a different attitude towards their classroom behavior than they would towards controversial positions that are professional and express an academic expertise based on research. The public will rightly defer to academic experts on such academic matters.

But when academics appear as political partisans in the university setting, members of the lay public will consider themselves equals. If they find the institution they are supporting is a political actor on the other side of a controversial issue, their enthusiasm for supporting that institution will correspondingly diminish. It may be regarded as a law of politics that one doesn't finance one's opponents.

These considerations have already become a significant problem—and not just for the University of Colorado, which lost tens of millions of dollars as a result of the adverse publicity generated by Ward Churchill. At an academic freedom conference in April 2006, Senator Lamar Alexander, a former Secretary of Education and major supporter of federal funding to higher education, was a featured speaker. He said: "The greatest threat to the American university today—to broad public support for the American university today—is political one-sidedness from the left, and that's a serious threat because if you look at the funding trends for higher education, federal funding is up, but state funding is flat, and tuition is up as a result of that. And constantly inferior funding by the states of higher education will produce substandard universities, and that will produce substandard incomes for the rest of us. So for the strength of the university, for the expression of free thought, your movement needs to succeed."[9]

By establishing an Office of Academic Standards and Academic Freedom which is part of the central administration and reports

---

[9]frontpagemag.com, April 18, 2006

directly to the Board of Trustees, the Board can establish quality control over the university product which will allow it to fulfill its fiduciary responsibilities to its donors and consumers. It will protect the university from adverse reactions to irresponsible statements and actions by its members. It will ensure a decent, professional education for its students.

Index